BOOKMARKED

BOOKMARKED

Reading My Way from Hollywood to Brooklyn

WENDY W. FAIREY

Arcade Publishing
New York

Arcade Publishing books may be purchased in bulk at special discounts for sales promotion, corporate gifts, fund-raising, or educational purposes. Special editions can also be created to specifications. For details, contact the Special Sales Department, Arcade Publishing, 307 West 36th Street, 11th Floor, New York, NY 10018 or arcade@skyhorsepublishing.com.

Arcade Publishing® is a registered trademark of Skyhorse Publishing, Inc.®, a Delaware corporation.

Visit our website at www.arcadepub.com.

10 9 8 7 6 5 4 3 2 1

Library of Congress Cataloging-in-Publication Data

Fairey, Wendy W.
  Bookmarked : reading my way from Hollywood to Brooklyn / Wendy W. Fairey.
    pages cm
  ISBN 978-1-62872-537-7 (hardback)
  1. English fiction--19th century--History and criticism. 2. English fiction—20th century—History and criticism. 3. Fairey, Wendy W. 4. Books and reading—Psychological aspects. 5. Fictitious characters—Psychological aspects. 6. Fellowship. 7. Inspiration. 8. Self-actualization (Psychology) 9. English teachers—United States—Biography. 10. College teachers—United States—Biography. I. Title.
  PR861.F24 2015
  823'.809--dc23
  2014041618

Jacket design by Lynne Yeamans
Cover photo: Thinkstock

Ebook ISBN: 978-1-62872-553-7

Printed in the United States of America

For Mary Edith

Contents

From Orphan to Immigrant   I

David Copperfield   24

Jane Eyre and Becky Sharp   56

Daniel Deronda   92

Isabel Archer and Tess of the d'Urbervilles   129

The Odd Women and *Howards End*   167

To the Lighthouse   200

A Passage to India and Beyond   233

Postscripts   272

Reading Group Questions and Topics for Discussion   276

Acknowledgments   278

From Orphan to Immigrant

Whenever I teach *The Great Gatsby*, as I have so many times in my forty years in the college classroom, I always wonder if I will tell the students my story. It's my mother's story, really. But it's mine, too, the story of a personal link to the book's author that tinges every professional comment I make about themes and narrative voice and structure and the other facets of fiction that English professors train their students to look for. I care about all these, to be sure, but I have an intensely private as well as professional understanding of the novel at hand. Or rather, the private and professional strands are so intertwined that I can't really say where one ends and the other begins. In class I present them as separate. I tell the personal story when I've proven to myself that I don't have to, when I feel we have satisfactorily "covered" the "material," as we call it, with professorial dispassion and dispatch. Perhaps the revelation comes in an impulsive moment of warmth for the group of young people before me—I want to be closer to them, to give them something they might find special. Or perhaps there's been a little sag in classroom energy and I turn to the story to reinvigorate us.

"Here's a personal connection that may interest you. My mother actually knew F. Scott Fitzgerald. It was in the last years of his life in Hollywood."

I see mild interest in their faces.

"She was involved with him," I say. A variant of this, if the group seems more sophisticated, perhaps a class of graduate students, might be: "She was his lover."

Interest at this point increases, usually mixed with a bit of understandable anxiety that an aging female professor, talking about her mother's lover, has become unpredictable.

"Yes, they were together for three-and-a-half years. He died in her living room—stood up and dropped dead of a heart attack. A few days before Christmas 1940."

Now I've made it vivid.

"But what interests me the most," I say, "is that he devised for her an education. The F. Scott Fitzgerald College of One. It was an entire college curriculum—with history and art and music, and even a little economics. But above all poetry and the novel. Dickens. Thackeray. Henry James. We had the books from the College of One in our library when I was a child. Those were the books I read growing up."

My private relation to F. Scott Fitzgerald is that he bought the books for my mother that I have loved all my life, the books, it's fair to say, that turned me into a professor of English literature. I loved the volumes in the College of One inside and out—their bindings, their pages, their print, their stories—and I lived in them more fully than I can remember living in the world around me. Thus, *my*

F. Scott Fitzgerald story is less that he was my mother's lover before I was born, dying dramatically in her living room, releasing her to go forth and be with other men and become my mother, than that he shaped my life's reading by having bought her those books. Long before I even knew of her connection to him, they lined the shelves along opposite walls of our den, there for me to take down and carry upstairs to my bedroom and immerse myself in stories that transported me to other times and places. The palm trees and eucalyptus of dusky Southern California gave way to the imagined bustle of Thackeray's London or the green landscape of David Copperfield's Suffolk downs. And as soon as I finished one book, perhaps *Tom Jones* or *Bleak House*, I would ask my mother to recommend another, thus building the shadow world that I would live in, have lived in all my life.

So reading and teaching *The Great Gatsby* entails for me, always, not only the themes of the great American novel with its tragic dreamer hero, believing in the wrong dreams, but also the subtext of my mother's relationship with Fitzgerald, my mother herself looming as a kind of female Gatsby, a woman who emerged from a Jewish orphanage and made herself up as Sheilah Graham, London chorus girl and Hollywood columnist, suppressing her Jewishness and her early poverty, believing anything was possible, and awesome in the energy of her self-creation, to which she proved faithful to the end. And I understand Gatsby as myself, someone who has wed her dreams to people, starting with my mother, whom I wanted to believe in as golden and magic. But I am Nick Carraway as well, awed by Gatsby but able to judge him; the level-headed spectator, who ultimately turns away from a gaudy world to seek something else, a more solid if more ordinary existence. And I link, too, with Fitzgerald in our shared love for my mother. And with him as a pedagogue devising his syllabi for the F. Scott Fitzgerald College of One, joining with me in our imagined shared love of Victorian novels. Everything is all mixed together.

I want to write of the private stories that lie behind our reading of books, taking my own trajectory through English literature as the history I know best but proposing a way of thinking about literature that I believe is every reader's process. We bring ourselves with all our aspirations and wounds, affinities and aversions, insights and confusions to the books we read, and our experience shapes our responses. I have begun by citing my relation to *The Great Gatsby*, but the story of reading *David Copperfield* or *Vanity Fair* or *To the Lighthouse* or any of the books discussed in this volume is just as dramatically personal. Young David has an evil stepfather, as did I, and I share in David's fear and loathing of this figure. The élan of Becky Sharp reminds me of my mother, and I can't help admiring Thackeray's witty, resourceful rogue. The yearning of Woolf's grief-suffused Lily Briscoe for the dead Mrs. Ramsay touches the chord of all the important losses of my life. Of course, reading is more complicated than this finding of biographical parallels. We also read, as one of my students has so well put it, "to escape the relentless monotony of being ourselves" as well as "to return from the experience with a slightly different mind than we had going in." All that is true, and much else besides, a subtle and magical interaction between the reader and the book that I hope to illuminate.

WHEN I first thought to write a book about reading and literary characters, I had a concept for a more strictly academic study that I called "from orphan to immigrant." Always attuned to patterns and structure, I saw a succession of figures in the English novel: the orphan of the Victorian period, the "new woman" and the artist of late nineteenth-, early twentieth-century modernism, and the immigrant of late twentieth-century postcolonialism that linked for me in a striking genealogy. Each in turn fits uneasily with his or her society, yet at the same time becomes representative of that society, the protagonist who speaks for a given age, expressing its energy, its fears and aspirations. I was struck, for example, by a passage in Hanif Kureshi's *The Buddha of Suburbia* in which a theatrical producer explains to the protagonist Karim that "the immigrant is the Everyman of the twentieth century." Karim has been asked to "play" an Indian—i.e. wear a loin cloth and cultivate an Indian accent—for a theater production of *The Jungle Book* in which he has landed the leading role of Mowgli. Yet Karim, born in London, sees himself as "an Englishman born and bred, almost." The Indian identity that goes unnamed creates the "almost." "Perhaps," he muses, poising himself on the brink of a modern day picaro's adventures, "it's the odd mixture of continents and blood, of here and there, of belonging and not, that makes me restless and easily bored." He declares himself "ready for anything," a prime condition for fiction.

As a professor of English literature I had developed courses with one or another of the figures I have named as a thematic focus: the orphan, the new woman, the artist, and the immigrant—these slim but hardy subjects about which the novel at different points in its history has seemed, to borrow a phrase from Henry James, to make "an ado." But I had always considered them separately—each a discrete literary and cultural phenomenon. In my rethinking, I saw ways that, whatever their differences from one another and their prominence in different periods, they align to serve the same function. Destabilized themselves and destabilizing others around them, moving in their fictional trajectories between margin and center, they are either outsiders seeking to come in or insiders seeking to go out in their quest for a realized personal and social identity. The reader asks what they will make of themselves, how they will change or be changed by the world. Their narratives dramatize the disruptions and reconfigurations of history, the thrills and dangers inherent in the assertion of individualism, the tensions and accommodations between selfhood and society. As we read, our stake in their fictional lives becomes our own lived experience of belonging and not belonging, their dramas our dramas of becoming ourselves in the world. It's not that readers ever were—or are—preponderantly orphans or immigrants, new women or artists, though some of us may be. But these figures absorb us. I felt that if I could understand their catalytic and galvanizing role in English fiction of the last two centuries, I would come closer to understanding something important about the complexities of culture, the shaping power of fiction, and the impressionable psyches of readers.

Such was the project that grew in my mind: the culmination of a life spent reading, teaching and thinking about English fiction and the major contribution that I hoped to make to my field. The project had all the more urgency for me because it represented a return to scholarship after years spent writing memoir and stories that drew from a personal realm. Parents more often than not are larger-than-life figures, but when the world conspires in giving them this status, it enmeshes the child in a particular way. I was the child of not just one but two well-known people—of course my mother, the Sheilah Graham of Fitzgerald romance and Hollywood-column fame, but additionally my father, the British philosopher Sir Alfred Ayer. Because of a web of lies and circumstance, these parents had unequal valence in my life. My mother had functioned as a powerful single parent as I was growing up in Beverly Hills, swimming in the pools of the movie stars and reading my Victorian novels. I met Freddie, as Ayer was called, only on my first trip to London when I was eleven. My mother introduced him to me as a family friend, a misrepresentation not corrected until after her death in November 1988. I got to see him once as his acknowledged daughter, and then he died, too, the following June. I was forty-six, bereaved and in possession of a story.

By the early years of this new century, though, at a point when my parents were some fifteen years dead and I, their daughter, had turned sixty, the story for me was a tired one. I had dissected it with friends and been asked to recount it at dinner parties. I had written about it, too, perhaps the most satisfying means of understanding. My 1992 memoir *One of the Family* had brought my separately renowned parents together, been critically well received, secured my promotion at Brooklyn College to the rank of Full Professor, and then failed to be the "sleeper" my publisher hoped for. In commercial terms it never quite awakened. Venturing into a different genre, I next published a collection of linked stories that centered on a group of middle-aged women playing poker. My mother still lurked in these, but I could explore her influence without the distraction of naming her. Writing the stories was exhilarating, but it also persuaded me I was basically a non-fiction writer, someone for whom the desire to capture in narrative what actually happens is the stimulus to imagination. The stories were, and more importantly *seemed*, too close to my own life. Even when I made things up, they did not really pass as fiction.

But now I was determined to turn away from autobiographical writing. Above all, I didn't want to be like my mother who kept rewriting her own life: three books on Fitzgerald, two on her childhood, one on her sex life (granted, in part embellished), and three on her years as a columnist added up to nine books devoted to the myth of her self-creation. To write as a scholar and critic, to plot my new book in terms of the language and conventions of my profession gave me a welcome sense of impersonality. Art must be impersonal, says T. S. Eliot. I wanted to become impersonal, to vanish from the pages of my text, to be in it only as "the reader" and as the architect of my construct.

So I mapped out my new book. Its starting point would be the Victorian orphan, that figure poised always just outside the circle of desired safety, identity and inclusion, mirroring both the vitality and the anxieties of mid-nineteenth-century England. Science and industrialism had disrupted place, faith, and home. The orphan is the uprooted self, experiencing loss and disorientation, on the one hand, and the excitement of uncharted opportunity, on the other. Ultimately to survive, the orphan must reattach to society.

Even if what readers remember, and thrill to, are the perils of endangered but resistant orphanhood, the happy ending of the orphan narrative is one in which life sustaining connections are affirmed (David Copperfield finding his aunt, his profession, his angel in the house). In its unhappy ending, connections fail; characters remain dismally orphaned and literally die of disconnection (poor Jo, the crossing sweeper in *Bleak House* who knows "nothink"; poor Jude, the unlucky stonemason in Hardy's *Jude the Obscure* cursing the day he was born).

The 1985 year of *Jude the Obscure*'s publication is a late date for an orphan hero. As interesting to me as the mid-nineteenth-century dominance of the orphan narrative was its end-of-the-century disappearance. Sue Bridehead in *Jude* is yet another orphan, but that's not how most readers remember her. Sue is a "new woman," that heroine of fiction of the 1890s who has a startling new agenda: perhaps not to marry. Her search for new freedoms reflects urgent issues of the day: the championing of causes such as women's higher education and married women property rights; the impassioned debates about everything from marriage and free love to women riding bicycles and wearing bloomers. I had long been fascinated by the way the English novel shifts in the late nineteenth century from reifying marriage as the heroine's end to probing its inadequacies as a way to resolve the heroine's selfhood. To continue her growth, the heroine must, if she can, move beyond its entrapments, and we see her first tentative steps to do so. She makes her attempts despairingly (Gwendolyn Harleth in *Daniel Deronda*, 1876), ambiguously (Isabel Archer in *A Portrait of a Lady*, 1881), confusedly (Sue Bridehead in *Jude the Obscure*, 1895). More boldly, in 1879, not in English fiction but on the Norwegian stage, a new narrative declared itself. Ibsen's Nora walks out of her "doll's house" to search for an alternative to confinement within the marriage plot. Her quest for a kind of freedom and personal integrity is in some ways comparable to Stephan Dedalus's, when a few decades later, at the end of Joyce's *A Portrait of the Artist as a Young Man*, he chooses "silence, exile, and cunning." Nora does not seek isolation, but to become herself she must go out the door into the world, unencumbered.

Stephan Dedalus is not an orphan. Nor is D. H. Lawrence's Paul Morel or Ursula Brangwen. By the early twentieth century the figure of the orphan had lost its focal place in English fiction. I saw the orphan fading as the "everyman" of fiction when the marriage plot failed for "everywoman." Modernist writers, disillusioned with bourgeois society, turn away from the plot that moves towards the protagonist's social integration. A new fictional icon emerges: the artist, actual or potential, who must free himself from the suffocations of family and the familiar to become whom he needs to be. The impetus of the story almost requires that he not be an orphan, in order that he may *choose* to become one. Most modernist artists in fiction are male; a few are female, though with generally quieter stories (remember Jason slays the Minotaur, Psyche sorts seeds). But men and women alike find themselves or begin to find themselves and their true callings in brave understanding of human aloneness. Their end is not to be settled but to be unsettled. Their end becomes a creative beginning.

The final representative figure in my reading, the late twentieth-century immigrant, plays with notions of the self and society, alienation and assimilation in recombined ways. Most obviously, the immigrant departs from his or her original home and traditions (like the new woman or the artist) and seeks to assimilate into a new society (like the orphan). The interplay of to and fro movement, however, is far more complex than this tidy formulation. In a world where, on the one hand, CNN is piped into Punjabi villages and, on the other, Londoner-born-and-bred Karim in *The Buddha of Suburbia* "plays" an Indian, what it means to be English or Indian, French or Algerian, American or Latino loses distinct edges, and the immigrant is caught in the trajectories of this confusion, someone living both in and *between* cultures, a transnational and hybrid figure. The immigrant narrative speaks for the age, for in this time of diaspora and globalization, especially now with all the instant connections of social media, hybridity becomes our cultural metaphor of choice.

BUT the book you read here is not, for better or worse, the study of English novels just described. It remains true to my original conception: I focus on my genealogy of fictional prime movers—the orphan, the new woman, the artist, and the immigrant—still interested in the ways these figures are both marginal and representative and create a historical line. But impersonality, it turned out, was not the best mode for me. As I went along, I found keeping to it hard—it seemed too dry, and perhaps I wasn't done yet with my own story. The personal seeped back into my project and transformed it to "an odd mixture."

My idea became to write a memoir of a life of reading. This would still be a study of literature, but it would document something intensely personal as well. It would be nonfiction about fiction, focusing on a key relationship—that between myself as reader and the object of my lifelong affection, novels—and honoring the remarkable *literary* characters, whom, ironically, I felt I knew and understood as well if not better than I had ever managed to know or understand those inevitably perplexing parents, lovers, children, and friends. Perhaps literary characters, intimately grasped in our reading, become transparent in ways that actual people, even our familiars, never can be. Also I could hope my story would be a means of communicating with other readers. I had been pleased when my books prompted people to speak or write to me about parallels in their own experience, confiding their stories of charismatic mothers or family secrets. Now as I put forward my fifty years experience of reading, studying, and teaching English literature, surely my account of a reading life would land me in good company—that of people who were not only readers but also readers in the same tradition—people for whom Shakespeare or Dickens were as contemporary as Roberto Bolaño or Jennifer Egan, for whom Becky Sharp was as engaging as Bridget Jones, for whom the fortunes of classical literary characters were as vivid as their own experience, indeed for whom such fortunes *constituted* part of their experience. In "The Decay of Lying" Oscar Wilde has his protagonist Vivian proclaim, as part of his extolling of Balzac, "One of the greatest tragedies of my life is the death of Lucien de Rubempré. It is a grief from which I have never been able completely to rid myself. It haunts me in my moments of pleasure. I remember it when I laugh."

I hoped in my memoir of reading to understand the way certain books manage to compel and haunt us in this way.

My seemingly opposing schemes—scholarship and memoir—began to converge when I realized they involved the same books. While the scholarly work would trace the trajectory in English novels from orphan to immigrant, the memoir of reading, if limited to fiction, would show a similar chronology. I, too, as a lifelong reader had progressed "from orphan to immigrant." The figures of the orphan, the artist, the new woman, the immigrant had each, in turn, absorbed me, marking a particular stage of my life and preoccupations. I had been a typical young girl reader of horse and dog books and then of the Landmark biographies that helped me to wonder if I could emulate Thomas Alva Edison or Clara Barton. Then my mother handed me a copy of *David Copperfield*. I was eleven, in sixth grade in 1950s California. From that entry point into Victorian fiction, the lives of David Copperfield and Pip and other orphan figures became my own life's adventures and my proxies. Reaching across a century and a continent, they fought my battles, joining with me to defy an unreasonable adult, seek a little popularity at school, make choices as to where and where not to belong.

Beginning my senior year of high school and continuing into college, which I entered in 1960, I discovered the modernists. Myself then aloof and awkward, I identified with the artist who seeks "silence, exile, and cunning," yet also, as with Thomas Mann's Tonio Kröger, looks longingly at the well-adjusted friends to whom he will always seem odd. I chose the modernists as my initial period of specialization in graduate school. They seemed to know everything there was to say about art and loneliness.

Up to this point in my reading, in keeping with the lack of awareness of the times, I hadn't yet thought about implications of gender. (The orphans and artists that engaged me seemed essentially unmarked by gender; I hardly noticed that more often than not they were male.) But in the 1970s, stimulated by the exciting new energy of feminist theory as well as my personal struggle to balance a tottering marriage with a developing career, I thrilled to Nora's walking out of the Doll's House and creating new literary options for woman other than marriage or death. By then a teacher of college students, I devised a course on "The Heroine's Progress," centered on the late nineteenth-, early twentieth-century figure of the "new woman."

That course, which included works by such authors as James, Chopin, Hardy, Gissing, and Virginia Woolf, would today be characterized as "Eurocentric." And I would be, too. I had never traveled beyond Western Europe. Or read beyond it. Then in the 1990s in connection with a life-changing trip to India with a friend, I started reading novels by Indian authors who wrote in English and worked up a course on Indian English fiction. My department, seeking at that juncture to be more global in its offerings, was pleased to have me teach it. I realized, though, after teaching the course a few times that most of the writers on my syllabus no longer lived on the Asian subcontinent. They had moved to London or New York or Toronto or Berkeley. This aware-ness led me to develop yet another course on transnational narratives and identities, focused on late twentieth-century immigrant and transnational experience. The line from the orphan to the immigrant has thus become the arc of my own personal and professional journey.

To write about this journey is to create a counter-narrative—counter to the more scholarly book this might well have been and counter as well to a more conventional memoir of a person's life and times. What does it mean to be immersed in fiction, especially when the works are ones of other eras and other places? Before she became a novelist, when she was still young, earnest, and devout, Marianne Evans wrote to a friend: "I shall carry to my grave the mental diseases with which they [novels] have contaminated me." Because the writer of this prudish letter became the great novelist, unbeliever—and moralist—George Eliot, readers can enjoy the irony of her fearing the immoral influence of fiction. Few novelists have done more than she to shape readers' explicitly moral sensibilities. Her great humanist moral vision became my own equivalent of a religion: the concern with how we might still aspire as secular people to rise to being our best selves and to touch and inspire one another. I try not to lose sight of this ideal. Yet I, too, shall carry to my grave the contamination, if you will, of reading fiction—serious fiction but fiction nonetheless, my stimulant and analgesic of choice. I have lived my life refracted through novels; they have shaped the terms of my existence. I think of their influence as positive, their place in my life a means of deepening understanding and compassion. But fiction is a realm into which I have escaped as well as one in which I have found myself.

When people ask me what it was like growing up in Beverly Hills, California, in the forties and fifties as the daughter of a nationally syndicated Hollywood columnist, I always feel my answer will disappoint them. Yes, Marilyn

Monroe came to parties at our house, and Hopalong Cassidy posed with my younger brother and me, all of us in black Hoppy outfits, six shooters drawn, under our Christmas tree. Our mother took us with her to movie premieres and famous restaurants and on trips abroad. Without doubt mine was an unusual and privileged childhood. But I have difficulty making vivid a world that always seemed to me at a remove. As soon as I could read to myself, I withdrew from it for long stretches every day. The adventures of the Five Little Peppers were far more engaging than the experience of attending Elizabeth Taylor's wedding to Nicky Hilton. With the little Peppers—Ben, Polly, Joel, Davie, and Phronsie—and their neighbor, the wonderfully named Jasper, I felt I belonged. There was a comfort in entering their lives that I was far from feeling, say, as a child sitting in Liz's dressing room before the ceremony while my mother interviewed the bride-to-be. At thirteen I passed up the chance to meet Elvis Presley to stay home and listen to my recording of *Madama Butterfly*. My heart could flow out to poor abandoned Cio-Cio San singing *un bel dei vedremo*, but it was never even faintly touched by the teen idol of my time. If I seem to be boasting, I'm not. It surely was a missed opportunity that I couldn't let myself be more present in my actual surroundings. But I couldn't. In many ways I still can't. Or don't as completely as I might. Living through all the interesting decades of my life from the forties to the turn of the twenty-first century, I have been, in an important sense, elsewhere. I wonder if because of my reading I have lived more fully or in some ways failed to live, at least in my own time and place.

I am helped in exploring this conundrum by the experience of other readers who have loved and lived in books—and not just any books but the same classic texts of English literature. On my desk lies a pile of literary studies and memoirs, testaments to others' "contamination." I quote from a few of them.

Rachel Brownstein in *Becoming a Heroine*, one of the first critical studies of texts to acknowledge the personal, writes of growing up in Queens:

> Reading the novels of Henry James at fifteen, I experienced a miracle. Behind the locked bathroom door, sitting on the terry-cloth-covered toilet seat, I was transformed into someone older, more beautiful and graceful. I moved subtly among people who understood delicate and complex webs of feeling, patterned perceptions altogether foreign to my crude "real" life.

Leila Ahmed in her memoir *A Border Passage* writes of growing up in Alexandria:

> Moving daily . . . under the blue skies of Egypt, we lived also in our heads and in the books we lost ourselves in, in a world peopled with children called Tom and Jane and Tim and Ann, and where there were moles and hedgehogs and grey skies and caves on the shore and tides that came in and out. And where houses had red roofs. Red roofs that seemed far better and more interesting and intriguing to me than roofs that were like, say, the terraced roof of our house in Alexandria.

Ahmed moved on, as I did, from children's books such as *The Wind in the Willows* to the novels of Dickens and Thackeray. She writes, "I don't know how I would have survived the loneliness of my teenage years without the companionship of such books." Thinking of my own lonely teenage years, I don't know either.

Francine Prose in *Reading Like a Writer* traces her development from being a child who was "drawn to the work of the great escapist writers . . . , [loving] novels in which children stepped through portals—a garden door, a wardrobe—into an alternative universe," to a preadolescent "with an interest in how far a book could take me from my own life and how long it could keep me there" to someone who became aware of language, marking up the pages of *King Lear* and *Oedipus* "with sweet embarrassing notes-to-self ('irony?' 'recognition of fate?') written in my rounded heartbreakingly neat schoolgirl print."

Prose's brief review of her reading life raises an interesting complication—the fact that we read differently at different stages of life. In her case she moves from being unaware of the power of language to "vaguely aware . . . but only dimly and only as it applied to whatever effect the book was having on [her]" to becoming the author of the text at hand, trained as she was in New Critical textual analysis, sophisticated and astute in her attentiveness to textual nuance—in short, able to read like a writer.

My own path of development is not unlike that of Prose. I learned to read ever more consciously, ever more critically, ever more aware of the components and strategies of literature. But doesn't this development then skew one's looking back? Trying, for example, to recover my eleven-year-old experience of *David Copperfield*, I must somehow uncover that first innocent reading through all the subsequent schooled and scholarly and writerly perspectives that overlie it. Ultimately reading *David Copperfield* at eleven is a memory, and memory, as we know, is highly unreliable. Nonetheless, I believe the warmth of that memory pervades my response to the book every time I teach it or make it the subject of a paper. And something of my original response to it persists in all rereadings. Something of the power books have in childhood remains at the heart of all our reading experience.

Instead of thinking of fiction as escape, Azar Nafisi in *Reading Lolita in Tehran* speaks of how she and her students "were, to borrow from Nabokov, to experience how the ordinary pebble of ordinary life could be transformed into a jewel through the magic eye of fiction." As I go back to Rachel Brownstein, I now see her reading of Henry James in Queens less as refuge from the quotidian than as the route to the quotidian's transformation as well as her own. The person who emerges from the sanctuary of the bathroom grows up to write about reading Henry James in her seemingly banal setting. She "connects," as E. M. Forster urges us to do in his famous epigram to *Howards End*, weaving together the different threads of her life. My book is at heart homage to the books that transform us, that shape our understanding of the world around us and lead us to make large and small connections. Through the books I have read you will know me. Without knowing these books, you cannot know me well.

If this volume is intended as an experiment in autobiography, both inner and outer, it's also envisioned as an exercise in a freer, more personal kind of literary criticism than I was schooled in. As was typical for members of my generation, the first thirty years of my excellent standard education were spent drumming the personal voice out of me. In grade school my classmates and I competed in spelling bees, strove to perfect our penmanship, and threw ourselves into the joys of diagramming sentences. In high school, we honed further the faculty of memory to retain the myriad rules and facts that defined the world. My subjugation to these was so complete that, arriving at college and given an opportunity in a freshman English course to write a free theme, I could think of nothing more imaginative than to compare the Middle Ages and the Renaissance. Fortunately, as I progressed, my topics became less stilted. But college and graduate school polish a mode of discourse in which the potentially unruly first-person pronoun is submerged. My writing was smooth. My points were clear. But who was writing? Who was reading? Someone called "One." Was that "one" I? I acknowledge its serviceability, but to what extent did that depersonalized figure convey an authentic reading experience?

A challenge to my academic writing came when my mother declared (with what, at the time, seemed a hurtful lack of tact) that the opening paragraph of my masters thesis on Virginia Woolf failed to hook the reader. She pronounced it dull and lifeless. On some level I knew I agreed with her, but it was also important to defend myself against her blunt judgment. She was a journalist who liked to proclaim that she "thought in headlines." Not only that. She had also spent thirty years writing her Hollywood gossip column, in which the string of short staccato items, separated from one another by ellipses, required pizzazz. Granted she was backed by the authority of her association with Fitzgerald and the College of One. He had even planned a graduation for her, complete with cap and gown, from the two-and a half-year program of study (though his death intervened to cancel the ceremony). But theirs had never been truly *academic* study. It was more playful, more slanted to appreciation, as teacher and pupil recited poems together and pretended to be characters of their favorite books—Grushenka and Alyosha from *The Brothers Karamozov*, shortened to "Grue" and "Yosh," Natasha and Pierre from *War and Peace* (my mother had rebelled against being cast as the worldly jaded Helene), Swann and Odette from Proust, Esther Summerson and Mr. Jarndyce or the Smallweeds slumped in their chairs from *Bleak House*, Becky Sharp and Rawdon Crawley from *Vanity Fair,* or, for a change, Scott would become fat Jos Sedley. Anecdotes of the education had brought my mother and Fitzgerald alive for me in their zest for one another and for literature. But despite an imagined Fitzgerald joining tacitly in her criticism, I managed, tenuously, to hold my ground. What did my mother, or even her attendant ghost, know of the expectations, indeed the requirements of serious scholarly work?

I followed the masters thesis on Woolf with a doctoral dissertation on George Eliot, a well-focused study with a cumbersome title. I didn't show any of it to my mother, who in any case seemed content to bask in the solidity of my achievement in completing my PhD and then becoming a professor. Often, though, in my early experience as a teacher, assigning the kinds of papers I myself had been assigned on themes and imagery and literary structure, I found my students' papers, dare I say, dull and lifeless. The better students made their points clearly, sometimes with grace, but seldom did their most vibrant energies seem engaged in the enterprise. As for weaker students, all too often I found them resorting to a desperate strategy of mimesis, imitating—badly—the kind of writing they thought was expected of them and failing to be either persuasive or genuine.

My dissatisfaction with academic discourse, long simmering, finally erupted in a plagiarism debacle. Halfway through a general education course that was part of our touted Core Curriculum at Brooklyn College, I assigned a paper on one of my favorite novels, Henry James's *The Portrait of a Lady*. Four students in the class plagiarized from the *Cliff Notes*, turning in almost identical papers about Isabel Archer's flaws and virtues as a heroine. The first paper I read seemed competent; by the third I had figured out the source and was forced to contemplate, among other things, my own failure to engage the students.

Shaken, I realized I must find better ways to help students care about the books and to develop and express their own voices. I started assigning ungraded weekly free response papers, in which students could write anything they liked as long as they wrote something connected to the reading. They could say they loved the book or hated it; they could bring in parallels to their own lives. I wanted to disrupt the categories that box us in and constrain both our imaginations and intellects, to help students to find their own point of connection to the literature and to build from there. As I increasingly sought to do in my own work, I wanted them to join academic rigor with freedom of self-expression. I hoped to teach them how freer rigor—if you will—could emerge from this fusion.

My study of English novels has become a kind of extended reader response. I always ask students to surprise me, and

I hope this book will surprise its readers as well. I have also asked it to surprise me, its writer. Though I approach each novel or pair of texts with a sense of initial direction, I have wanted to remain open to unanticipated detours and connections. Simply asking the question of what particular books have meant to me and to other readers, I follow the twists and turns of the emerging answers, seeking, too, to explore how the life of reading and other aspects of a life reflect one another. How does a figure in fiction come to "be" the reader? I am the orphan, I am the immigrant, though in literal fact I am neither. How can this be?

I turn to my life outside of reading to understand better the power of literature and to literature to understand better the shape and impulses of a life. It's my hope that by pulling them together, I can go deeper into both the books and the life and show, too, how they're really not separable. Reading and living, the academic and the personal, modes of critical discourse and of memoir: to deny ways they're enmeshed with one another is to tatter the fabric of experience. So if Sheilah and Freddie and Scott and other persistent ghosts have not been laid to rest, and perhaps never will be, I invite them to join with David and Becky and Tess and Isabel and Mrs. Ramsay, among others—and, of course, with me—to see where together we shall venture.

David Copperfield

I have always had a secret kinship with David Copperfield. He was the literary character with whom, early in my reading life, I felt the deepest bond of understanding and sympathy. Not only did I know and love him; I felt I *was* David Copperfield, so thoroughly did his sensibility and experience merge with mine. Reading on my bed in my pastel-wallpapered room, oblivious to the rustling eucalyptus trees outside my window, I was transported from my California Spanish-style house with its red tile roof and white stucco walls to a cottage built of stones on the green Suffolk downs. The green was a hue I could only imagine; it was not a color of the dusky Southern California landscape. But from the novel's beginning, I gave myself over to David and his world. My destiny became that of the posthumous protagonist—Davy to his pretty girlish mother and stout servant, Peggotty—a child alive with fears and aspirations, the pages of whose story unfold to answer a portentous question: will he turn out to be the hero of his own life?

Rereading now and recasting my life in terms of this link is a way of exploring the feelings as much as facts of my particular childhood—and perhaps every childhood's poignant mix of bliss and loss. I, too, like David, lacked but hardly seemed to miss a father. I, too, lived with my pretty mother and a beloved servant, Stella. No matter that David's mother was a silly, weak little thing and my mother a successful Hollywood gossip columnist. No matter that David's father lay buried in the village churchyard, and mine, or at least the man I thought was my father, lived far away in London, dispatched by divorce. Or that our home also included my younger brother, Robert. I knew the prelapsarian paradise, along with its edge of anxiety, of having a mother who seemed both doting and elusive, a figure I yearningly adored but never quite possessed. I knew the reassurance of Stella's calm Czechoslovakian presence and the pleasure of holidays spent at the homes, more modest yet cozier than mine, of her nieces Celia and Josephine and their respective sons, Leslie and Irvin. Towheaded, curly-locked Irvin was my first "boyfriend." We played together in his backyard, and at five I planned to marry him. You might say he was my "Little Em'ly," and his three-generation Czech immigrant family was my version of the Peggotty clan we are enchanted to meet in their wonderful beached boathouse when David goes with Peggotty to Yarmouth.

I also lived the disruption of the idyll. David's world is shattered when his mother marries Mr. Murdstone. Mine suffered the entry of a detested stepfather, whose nickname was Bow Wow. A hulking football coach in a Southern California prison, at thirty-six, twelve years my mother's junior, Stanley "Bow Wow" Wojtkeiwicz gained an introduction to her from the actor Glenn Ford. He sought her aid in raising money for his pet project, Bow's

Wow's Boys Town, arriving at our house with an impressive blueprint that he spread out on our living room coffee table. BOW WOW'S BOY'S TOWN read the words in bold caps at its top. There were dormitories and classroom buildings and a refectory and playing fields. I remember his telling us the nickname Bow Wow came from the frisky way he used to play college football, and we all—my brother and I as well as our mother—were charmed by him at first.

There never would be a Bow Wow's Boys Town, but after a six-week courtship Bow Wow and my mother married. As she later described the attraction, she had responded to his warmth and energy and to sex. Bow Wow moved into our house, as Mr. Murdstone moves into David's. My ten-year-old self watched while seemingly endless cardboard boxes of his shoes were carried up our curving staircase into my mother's bedroom. Later Robert and I would sit near the top of that staircase, listening to the raised angry voices audible behind the closed bedroom door. As Mr. Murdstone asserts his sway over David's mother, imposing his will on her, inhibiting her spontaneity, so Bow Wow sought to influence my mother. Giving up his job in the prison, he became her unofficial manager, trading the running of football plays for running interference in her influential name with the studios and publicists and stars, though often my mother had to curb his zeal. He never had the power of a Mr. Murdstone—my mother was too strong for that and perhaps Bow Wow too weak, notwithstanding all his bluster as he strode around in football jerseys covering his girth. But he and I quickly assumed our battle stations of open enmity, and his very presence in my mother's bedroom inhibited the unthinking access my brother and I had always had to her and to her room, the magnetic center of our universe before his arrival. In the mornings, especially on weekends, we had loved to climb into bed with her, one of us on each side, and make our plans. "What shall we do?" she would ask. "Shall we go to Ojai? To Palm Springs? Shall we go to Malibu and ride horses?"

I have always blamed Bow Wow for destroying our family happiness. It didn't right the balance that after three years my mother, as she said, "kicked him out," having discovered the diary in which he had written that I was a brat, Robert a sissy, and our mother a terrible bitch and, to her even more alarming, recorded the mortgage payments he was secretly making on our house with the aim of later claiming community property. Before they reached a settlement, he did everything he could to harm us, even calling up my school to say Sheilah Graham was a Communist and sending the ASPCA to our house to investigate a mistreated dog. "Is this a mistreated dog?" asked my mother, grandly indignant, as Tony, our Dalmatian, trotted to the door wagging his tail. It was one of her finest moments. But after Bow Wow, she was never the same. He didn't kill her the way Mr. Murdstone kills Clara Copperfield. But he killed an essential part of her spirit. She gained weight. Her nerves were bad. She shouted and wept at the strain of the divorce, sometimes going so far as to say it was all too much for her and she should just take him back. "No!" I would cry. "No! You can't do that!" In the end she got a tougher lawyer and they nailed Bow Wow on adultery. But getting rid of Bow Wow still came at a high cost—and money surely seemed the least of it. My world divided, like David's, into pre- and post-stepfather segments, the stark and abrupt transition defined by the intrusion of the hated rival.

There was other loss as well. Just as Peggotty leaves Davy to marry her persistent suitor, Mr. Barkis, so, too, our Stella went away to marry. One day, walking me the six blocks to my elementary school as she did every morning, she broke the news with a final hug that she would be gone when I got home that afternoon. Stella left us to marry Al, an alfalfa farmer in Thousand Oaks. I visited her for a weekend in her new home, a one-story concrete structure amid flat fields of alfalfa stretching over the desert landscape towards the distant blue mountains. As I lay there in a narrow bed at night, a lugubrious train whistle cut through the night air. When I got home and was sullen, my mother got mad at me and said I should have stayed with Stella.

My battle against Bow Wow stands as one of my life's defining experiences. Its imprint doesn't fade, and as a reader and rereader of Victorian fiction, in which so many children do battle with adult tyrants, I continue to find its traces. I take note, for example, when Jane Eyre, the retrospective narrator, reflects about her young self's defiance of her unkind aunt, Mrs. Reed: "A child cannot quarrel with its elders, as I had done—cannot give its furious feelings uncontrolled play, as I had given mine—without experiencing afterwards the pang of remorse and the chill of reaction." And I think about the cost of my own defiance. I opposed Bow Wow, just as Jane Eyre does the Reeds, stripping away their false faces, naming them as bad people. I ought to claim kinship with passionate, outspoken Jane Eyre more than with passive David Copperfield. It's odd that I don't; I was certainly as reckless as she. When Bow Wow kicked our dog Tony, when he caught him chewing one of his shoes—*he*, Bow Wow, was the only person in our house ever to mistreat a dog—I openly challenged the tyrant. "You can't kick Tony," I said, placing myself between my angry stepfather and the cowering animal. My mother, who was watching, later said she'd been afraid in that moment that Bow Wow would kick me. But he didn't. It was one of the unspoken rules of the house that he mustn't lay a hand on me or my brother, though once when he found me reading in bed after I was supposed to have the light out, he did come in and cuff me on the head. I wonder on which of my cherished nineteenth-century novels I was shining my flashlight under the covers. *David Copperfield? Bleak House? Vanity Fair? Jane Eyre? Wuthering Heights?* By the end of sixth grade, I had devoured all of these. By eighth grade I was on to the Russians. *War and Peace. Crime and Punishment. The Idiot.*

The price of being Bow Wow's enemy was that I cut off the possibility of being his friend. There is a passage in *David Copperfield* that I find particularly poignant. David reflects on how easy it would have been for Mr. Murdstone to win his allegiance:

> God help me, I might have been improved for my whole life, I might have been made another creature, perhaps, for life, by a kind word at that season. A word of encouragement or explanation, of pity for my childhood ignorance, of welcome home, of reassurance to me that it was home, might have made me dutiful to him in my heart henceforth . . . and might have made me respect instead of hate him.

The one day I can remember Bow Wow's being nice to me, I melted instantly. My younger brother, Robert, occupied the position of Bow Wow's favorite, but that day, because of some small transgression, Robert had offended him.

My mother and Bow Wow used to drive separate cars from Malibu Beach, where we rented a beach house, to our regular home in Beverly Hills. Normally Robert would have gone with Bow Wow and I with our mother, but for once Bow Wow asked *me* to accompany him. I was flattered, even thrilled, to be preferred. Bow Wow could be charming, and he exercised the full weight of that charm, joking with me and drawing me out, as the metallic blue Chrysler station wagon—the car my mother had received as a gift because Chrysler was the sponsor of *The Sheilah Graham Show*—wound along the Pacific Coast Highway. By the time we turned off Sunset Boulevard onto our street, North Maple Drive, I was his. But only for a day. I quickly resumed my role as his enemy. It was a role, however, that left me feeling unlovely, even unlovable.

Many years later, in Paris where my grown son, Sean, had settled, I went with him, a young zestful father, and his two-year-old daughter, Louise, to a little neighborhood playground that had a slide. Sean made feints at scampering up the slide while Louise swept down it. "Papa! Papa!" she cried in glee, as she stood at the top of the slide preparing to reenact the ritual. That's what I had missed, I thought to myself. Being a father's daughter. My mother might have married anyone, and she married Bow Wow, an uncouth, uneducated man who hated me and whom I hated. Bow Wow, of course, did not read nineteenth-century novels, though he did teach me to recite in chronological order the list of presidents of the United States—something I can do to this day.

Just as David Copperfield is sent away to school at Salem House, I was sent to Rosemary Hall in Greenwich, Connecticut. The idea of my going to boarding school had formed when Bow Wow was still with us. It was a way for my mother to get me out of harm's way at home and also to see me advance in the world. By the time I was fourteen, Bow Wow was gone, but the boarding school plan had gained momentum. Of course, to equate prestigious Rosemary Hall with miserable Salem House, our austere but fair-minded headmistress, Miss McBee, with Salem House's sadistic headmaster, Mr. Creakle, is patently a stretch and a distortion. Boarding school was meant to be my opportunity. The educational trajectory my mother conceived for me was modeled on that of Scott Fitzgerald's daughter, Scottie, who had gone to Ethel Walker, an elite girl's school in Schenectady, and then on to Vassar. This was the route to being an insider and an Easterner. Mine would be the education my mother hadn't had.

My mother's schooling in the Jews Hospital and Orphan Asylum in the Norwood section of London's East End, where the girl then named Lily Shiel lived from 1910, aged six, until she "graduated" at fourteen, was the real parallel to Davy's Salem House. On her admission to the orphanage Lily had her golden hair shaved to the scalp as a precaution against lice. Students who failed to live up to the codes of conduct had their punishments recorded in the "Sulking and Punishment Book." This was an experience one could— and my mother in hindsight did—call "Dickensian." But no slightest hint of the grim conditions of Salem House troubled either of our minds as she whisked me to New York's Saks Fifth Avenue to buy me jodhpurs and riding boots because riding at a nearby stable was one of Rosemary Hall's many extra-curricular activities. She didn't want me to miss out on any pleasure or privilege.

Yet I remember the boarding school as desolate much of the time. We called it the "pink prison" because of our confinement within its faded rose-colored stucco facade. I moved through cold, ill-lit corridors, off which, through doors left ajar, you could glimpse the dorm rooms, small and austere, no matter how girls tried to brighten these with a poster or a rug. We ate our meals in the dining refectory, a large high-ceilinged room modeled on the dining hall of an English college. The teachers sat at a raised high table and we students in rows of rectangular tables beneath them. The food was institutional—overcooked and bland. Often as I lingered, captive in my seat, a fast eater waiting to be allowed to rise and go back to studying, I would stare at the dulled gold-lettered plaques on the walls, bearing the names of girls who had won prizes for Latin or English, or who were former captains of the field hockey or tennis team. Who were these girls? They seemed alluring and remote.

In the chapel, plaques hung as well, these with the names of the Optima girls, the students, one each year, deemed simply the best. We attended the chapel every weekday morning and again, for a full service, on Sunday afternoons, as Rosemary Hall was nominally Episcopal and chapel in that era still an unquestioned staple at most Eastern boarding schools. I welcomed any distraction from the oppression of enforced religion, silently parsing the gold-lettered names on the plaques as the congregation intoned the mellifluous yet automatic words of the Nicene Creed: "I believe in God the Father Almighty, Maker of Heaven and Earth, and in Jesus Christ, His only Son our Lord . . ." Although I had willingly joined the choir, I had also decided I was an atheist with a personal rule that I would sing but wouldn't pray. While my schoolmates knelt in prayer, I would look all about me, scanning the rows of bent heads from my conspicuous place in the second-soprano section of the choir stalls. Many didn't like this scrutiny and told me so. I wasn't popular. As David learns, a world has its rules and culture. If you fail to conform, you will at the very least be teased—your bed short-sheeted, as mine was. I was a studious girl, often with ink on my fingers, three thousand miles from home.

But somehow I managed. Like David, who worships the charismatic but deeply flawed James Steerforth and takes decent Tommy Traddles for granted, I made a few friends, who seemed sufficiently ordinary for me to relax with, and I fixed on an object of veneration in the class above me.

My best friends were Pam Wilkinson, a wry scholarship girl from Pittsfield, Massachusetts, who used to stick pins in a little doll effigy of her mother—my own mother was alarmed to learn about this—and Sue Stein, dark-haired and overweight, one of the very few girls in the school who was Jewish. At that point, I didn't know about my mother's Jewish background. By the time I learned of it, at age sixteen, my friend Sue had already left to finish high school back with her family in Brooklyn. One year at Rosemary Hall had been enough for her. I remember confiding in Pam that I was half Jewish and being counseled that it wasn't necessary to broadcast this inconvenient alteration to my identity.

My idol was Judy Wilson, a tall big-boned blonde with a pixie haircut. Judy was not just a rider but one of the best riders in the school. Those of us who had signed up for this expensive activity rode at a nearby stable run by a florid-faced man named Teddy. Despite the correctness of my Saks Fifth Avenue riding togs, I never quite got the hang of East Coast equestrian style; I was used to Western saddles and trail rides in the hills above Malibu. Without a saddle horn, the Eastern saddle seemed alarmingly bare; its stirrups were too high, and you weren't supposed to neck-rein the horses. Judy Wilson, in contrast, had a wall in her room lined with blue ribbons from jumping competitions, and her popularity was such that she was elected head boarder marshal her senior year. She moved through the corridors of Rosemary Hall, often in her riding boots, with a calm assurance I considered the epitome of grace. My attention quickened as she approached; I cherished every stray word and smile she granted me.

I'm still sometimes asked how I liked my boarding school, and the question always stirs a little regret in me. When two years after I started at Rosemary Hall, my brother began at the Putney School in Brattleboro, Vermont, a coed progressive school where the students excelled in the arts, worked on a collective farm, and called teachers by their first names, it seemed to me he'd gotten a much better deal. We hadn't known about Putney when I was deciding on Rosemary Hall. Or perhaps just hadn't looked for it. My mother had been fixed for me on the model provided by Scottie.

Dickens's near contemporary Matthew Arnold considered the portrait of Salem House and its cane-wielding Mr. Creakle in *David Copperfield* a brilliant depiction of the sort of puritanical English miseducation that, as he writes in *Irish Essays*, serves to form the "hard, stern, and narrow" nature of a Mr. Murdstone. David Copperfield's nature, though, is the opposite of hard, stern, and narrow, and despite its severities, Salem House, oddly, does not hurt him. In part he is saved by the threadbare master Mr. Mell, who sees David's worth and seeks to protect him. Also David takes a first step towards becoming a novelist through his role as Scheherazade—regaling Steerforth with the plots of *Perigrine Pickle* and other eighteenth-century novels. Later, forced into degrading work at the London warehouse of Murdstone and Grinby, he looks back to Salem House as a time of opportunity; Steerforth and Traddles are achingly remembered as the associates of his "happier childhood"; the time at the school represents his crushed "hopes of growing up to be a learned and distinguished man."

Rosemary Hall was narrow as well. It wasn't a cruel place, but it was unimaginative in its conventional snobbery and anti-Semitism. The education it offered was decent, but its limiting and limited assumption was that its graduates would go on to lead genteel upper middle-class lives. Yet I, too, like David Copperfield, found boarding school a setting in which to begin coming into my own. I had a few excellent teachers—perhaps that's all one really needs—who saw my potential and encouraged me. I won prizes (when my daughter enrolled in the coeducational and more diverse Choate-Rosemary Hall thirty years later, my name was among those she read on the plaques). I loved learning and was a great reader. By then, though, I had left Dickens behind me, at least for a stretch of years. I plunged more fully into the Russians, especially Dostoevsky, who showed me new possibilities of passion and also of humility. In a notebook of my "reflections," I exhorted myself to follow the example of Father Z. in *The Brothers Karamazov* to "condemn no man." Then I discovered Thomas Mann and saw myself in his figure of the outsider artist in "Tonio Kröger," who idealizes unthinking, healthy normal beauty just as I had idealized Judy Wilson.

If I had been asked as a high school senior to name my favorite novel, I might have said *David Copperfield*, but I can't be sure of that. What I know for a certainty is that I cherished the character of David—Davy, still to me—planning to give a son this name, though that ended up not happening in the real world. Yet his figure lived potently inside me. I didn't need to reread the book; I never wrote a paper about it nor talked to anyone about my special sense of it. I never, in my French class, proclaimed, "David Copperfield, *c'est moi*." But the sense of loving and *being* David Copperfield persisted—and has persisted to this present moment in which I write, early in a new century, nearing the end of a long teaching career, knowing I am in many ways ordinary yet still striving to count myself heroic.

ii

DICKENS DECLARED *DAVID COPPERFIELD* his "favorite child," and much has been written about the novel's striking autobiographical components: the parallel between David's enforced sojourn at Murdstone and Grinby's, whose trade is in wine and spirits bottles, and the author's own terrible time at Warren's Blacking in the Strand, the shoe polish factory where the young Dickens, visible to passersby through the shop window, felt searing shame at having to work in public view fixing labels to bottles of blacking; the reversal of initials through which his own C.D. becomes D.C.; the links between the improvident Mr. Micawber and Dickens's father, who was also incarcerated in debtor's prison; Dickens's admission in his letters to Maria Beadnell Winter that his memories of being infatuated with her had animated his depiction of David's courtship of Dora Spenlow; and, more generally, the fact that *David Copperfield* is ultimately a bildungsroman, the story of the novelist as a young man. It sets out to show how a sensitive child with the faculty of keen observation grows up to be a successful author.

David Copperfield is, I've learned, many readers' "favorite child." Since the early days of my reading life in which I adopted the novel as my own, I have discovered how many people, spanning generations and genders, classes and continents, have loved and embraced it.

First for me is my mother, the person who took the book from our den's library shelves to hand to a child asking for something new to read. Even before Scott Fitzgerald discovered her struggling to get through the first volume of Proust and set out to complete her education, my mother had read Dickens in her orphanage and been quick to understand that "Norwood," as it familiarly was called, was a Dickensian institution. As she recounts in her memoir *College of One,* looking back to her earlier reading:

> Books were the breath of my existence. *David Copperfield* was my favorite—the first part. His childhood was worse than mine. My Mr. Murdstone was the headmaster, but he was a remote dragon, except for the terrifying time when I happened to pass him and he would for no apparent reason give me a whack across the back to speed me on my way.

I am tempted to argue with my mother, or at least with her ghost, that the headmaster in her orphanage was more aptly her Mr. Creakle than her Mr. Murdstone. But to do so would be a cavil, for Mr. Murdstone is the one truly terrifying villain in the novel, the figure who enters the sanctity of David's childhood home and destroys it, the villain who in no way can be called or seen as comic. The other "bad" characters all have some comic tic—the vicious Creakle splutters and applies his "Tickler"; fulsome Uriah Heep is "umble" and wrings his hands; even Miss Murdstone snaps shut her steel-clasped reticule and proclaims against boys. Mr. Murdstone has no such verbal or physical idiosyncrasy. He is simply a killer of joy, a purveyor of misery.

My mother's childhood "home," for better or worse, was the orphanage, its frightening headmaster her Mr. Murdstone just as my intruding stepfather seemed mine. I see the irony that young Lily Shiel, reading the novel in her orphanage, consoled herself at seeming better off than David, whereas I in my comfortable Beverly Hills home lived his hardships in my imagination as if they were my own. Perhaps David's childhood seemed worse to my mother than her own because from her earliest memories she had—and needed to have—a bedrock sense of self-reliance. She couldn't afford to feel as vulnerable as David Copperfield. I could.

A few years after my mother was reading Dickens in the Norwood orphanage, the man I would later learn was my father, the British logical positivist A. J. Ayer, was reading him, also at a young age, in his own far more privileged upper-middle-class family home in London and then as a public school boy at Eton. Freddie Ayer would continue to read Dickens to the end of his life. As Ayer's biographer Ben Rogers speculates:

Ayer never wrote about Dickens in any detail, but he returned to him again and again, and the novels are often a source of incidental reference in his philosophical writings. Dickens's stories abound with vulnerable, receptive and enterprising orphans—children "of excellent abilities with strong powers of observation, quick, eager, delicate, and soon hurt bodily or mentally," more or less obliged to make their way in an unfeeling world. There was certainly much to which Ayer might have related in these creations. He was physically small, perceptive, and determined; at once bookish and resourceful, sad and enthusiastic, gifted but emotionally perhaps a bit neglected.

Rogers's quotation, it so happens, is from *David Copperfield*. The description begins the chapter in which David is sent to London to Murdstone and Grinby's. David as narrator expresses his surprise, "even now," that a child of such abilities could have been "thrown away" at such a young age. I wonder how many of us have memories of a similar childhood self: gifted, delicate, sensitive, forced to go forth into a world that so often fails to value us as we value ourselves, yet persisting despite our delicacy. I do, for one. As for Freddie, he seemed without self-pity and was not drawn to *David Copperfield* in particular. He once told me his favorites were the later, darker Dickens novels—*Bleak House*, *Little Dorrit*, *Our Mutual Friend*. Yet it makes sense to me that his biographer sees him as David—observant, delicate, and tough—and I know he was bullied at Eton.

Because David Copperfield so often casts himself as passive—an observer of others, someone acted upon—it's all the more striking when he isn't, when he lashes out against a tormentor and shows he can defend himself. For one friend and colleague, among those whom I started questioning about the novel, seeking to fathom its captivating power, this was her point of attachment. She told me of her early fascination with Mr. Murdstone's hand, the hand David bites as Mr. Murdstone thrashes him.

"Mr. Murdstone's hand?" I echoed. Of course, I remembered David's biting Mr. Murdstone, but I'd never given much thought to the tooth-marked hand.

"It obsessed me," my friend confided, as we sat at our table at Arte Café, our favorite Upper West Side Italian restaurant, two gray-haired ladies savoring our early-bird special. "I could feel the hand throbbing."

When I returned home from dinner, I looked up the passage. David fails in the recitation of his lesson, and Mr. Murdstone coldly determines to flog him:

> He walked me up to my room slowly and gravely—I am certain he had a delight in that formal parade of executing justice–and when we got there, suddenly twisted my head under his arm.
>
> "Mr. Murdstone, Sir," I cried to him. "Don't! Pray don't beat me. I have tried to learn sir, but I can't while you and Miss Murdstone are by. I can't indeed!"
>
> "Can't you indeed, David?" He said. "We'll try that."
>
> He had my head as in a vice, but I twined round him somehow, entreating him not to beat me. It was only for a moment that I stopped him, for he cut me heavily an instant afterwards, and in the same instant I caught the hand with which he held me in my mouth, between my teeth, and bit through it. It sets my teeth on edge to think of it.

Mr. Murdstone proceeds to beat David after this "as if he would have beaten him to death." David is locked in his room, feels wicked, and crawls up to the mirror to look at his red and swollen face. After a five-day incarceration, he is packed off to Salem House where he must initially wear the placard, "Take care of him—he bites." He doesn't again encounter Mr. Murdstone until his half-year holidays. When they meet, David apologizes. The hand Mr. Murdstone extends to him, David recounts, "is the hand I had bitten. I could not restrain my eye for resting for an instant on a red spot upon it; but it was not so red, as I turned when I met that sinister expression in his face."

As a child, I remember being thrilled but frightened at David's biting Mr. Murdstone's hand. Thrilled to see him fight back. Frightened because I could anticipate the consequences of this instinctual act of self-defense. I thought of it as self-defense, not aggression, just as my fantasy that if Bow Wow ever returned, I would thrust a knife into his protruding stomach was my imagined defense of our home, not an act of premeditated murder.

For years, well into adulthood, I harbored my fantasy. The stabbing would occur on the sidewalk of our quiet tree-lined Beverly Hills street. A sentinel but always a child, I would be outside on our manicured front lawn, alert to the immanence of harm. Bow Wow would come walking up the sidewalk, heading towards our house, slowly but inexorably—an odd aspect of the daydream since almost no one walks in Beverly Hills. Pedestrians are stopped by the police, suspect simply by virtue of not being in a car. Somehow I would have a kitchen knife in my hand. Concealing it as I calmly approached him, I would stare at him hard, raise my hand in one swift motion, and before he could detect my purpose, plunge the knife into his beefy middle.

After our mother died, when my brother and I were both in our forties, I confessed my evil thoughts to him. "And what do *you* think you would do if you ever saw Bow Wow again?" I asked him.

"Oh, I don't know," said Robert, "I guess I'd invite him out for a beer and ask him what he'd been doing all these years."

Robert's answer startled me. I found it hard to think of Bow Wow as someone one could talk to, yet my brother's pacific inclinations put into stark relief the violence of my metonymies.

Mr. Murdstone's hand is echoed in the novel in the long, skinny, grasping hands of Uriah Heep. Later David uses his own hand to strike Uriah on the cheek, Uriah who wants only what David wants and gets: to be a gentleman and claim Agnes Wickfield as his own angel in the house. Although I hadn't until recently focused on Mr. Murdstone's bitten hand, I have long been fascinated by imagery of hands—hands as touching, hands as grasping, hands as greedy. "Keep your hands to yourself," my grandson, who tends to get into trouble, was warned over and over in his elementary school. At least unlike his younger cousin, who lives in France, he didn't bite other children in his class. Another friend I teach with—and another devotee of *David Copperfield*—confessed to a persistent dream that she's biting everyone in sight and then hurling them over a banister. This particular friend happens to be the best-loved professor in our department, renowned for her kindness to her students. Neither she nor I has lost touch with the passions or the wounds of our childhoods. But we feel we're making progress, doing our best to contain our bitings and our stabbings to our nightmares, waking and sleeping. I no longer even see myself stabbing Bow Wow. I don't know, though, that I could go so far as to ask him out for a beer.

iii

I BELIEVE I'M MOVING towards a better understanding of the role of *David Copperfield* in my life as well as in the lives of so many other readers, the cohort of people who loved the novel as children and continue to love it into adulthood. I've spoken of myself, my mother and father, my colleague fixated on the bitten hand, and the one throwing her enemies over the banister. To add just one further testimonial, I recently mentioned my link with the character of David to yet another of my colleagues, a specialist in Shakespeare. She's my age and we, in fact, attended the same college though we hardly knew one another back then. She has always seemed very tactful and self-controlled. "I *was* David Copperfield," I told her. "So was I!" she said. "At a very young age. I just loved that book, especially the early part."

A tantalizing synchronicity emerges: one girl reading in Park Slope, Brooklyn, another in Beverly Hills, each lost in the same book. Suddenly we seemed like sisters. My colleague went on to say that, although the nineteenth century wasn't her period, she had taught the book recently and been deeply moved by it. Now living in another Brooklyn neighborhood, she would come down from the upper floor of her brownstone, her eyes all swollen.

"Oh you've been reading *David Copperfield* again," her husband and daughters would say almost accusingly. "There's such an emotional richness to it," said my friend.

That's it, of course—the emotional richness. I've begun thinking about that, about the ways *David Copperfield* manages to touch us and also invite such identification. For one thing, why become David rather than Pip or Oliver or Little Nell or any of Dickens's many other orphan children? Perhaps a clue lies in David's mix of qualities. He's not unbelievably pure like Oliver or Little Nell—surely neither of them would have bitten Mr. Murdstone. Nor is he unrelievedly miserable like Pip, suffering from earliest memory as either wronged or in the wrong. David is between these extremes—a bright, promising child who feels hurt and embarrassment but who also shows himself to be resilient.

He's also at once flexible and constant. Other characters in the novel keep renaming him. His aunt Betsy, whom he reaches in Dover after many misadventures of the road on his flight from London, gives him a bath and renames him Trotwood. To Steerforth he is always Daisy. His young "child wife" as she's called, Dora, calls him Doady. He bears the names others give him but remains himself, moving ever further from any threat of nullity and failure—at its most alarming when he is at the mercy of Mr. Murdstone—to become at last, securely, the hero of his own life. The novel has an aspect of the picaresque; as readers we are excited to follow David on his adventures. We ask what will happen to him next, how he will manage. The odds might seem against this small frail boy. But he comes out on the safe side of harm.

This is the pattern of fairy tale, in which you don't need to start out heroic to survive heroically and triumph, and it's reassuring. As a young reader of *David Copperfield*, I, too, felt vulnerable but persistent, sorrowful but optimistic, variable in the ways I was perceived by others—classmates, teachers, family friends, my brother, my mother—but nonetheless constant to myself. In my case that self was female, in David's male. But this was not a difference that concerned me. The way that each of us is and was a child "of excellent abilities and with strong powers of observation, quick, eager, delicate, and soon hurt bodily or mentally" seemed a state of being in which gender played very little part.

Another aspect of David's story, also akin to the fairy tale pattern, is that he has friends who shelter and help him, friends, to borrow Mrs. Micawber's phrase, who will never desert him ("I will never desert Mr. Micawber!" this wonderful character can be counted on to proclaim every time she enters the novel) and who assist in keeping evil at bay. So Betsy Trotwood, the aunt who in Chapter One "walked out and never came back," *is* back—there at the end of David's walk to Dover, never to leave him again and to rout the Murdstones. And Mr. Micawber, whose abiding hope is that something will turn up, keeps turning up himself—in Canterbury, in London where amiable Tommy Traddles, moreover, reappears as his lodger, and then once more in Canterbury, for his heroic unmasking of Uriah Heep.

Of course, it's not just David's protectors who keep reappearing. This is a book so centered in the protagonist's early years that just about all the *dramatis personae* assemble in its first third—the part readers almost always remember and love best—and then keep coming back as their roles in David's life and psyche play out. Steerforth is reencountered—"My God, he exclaims, "It's little Copperfield!"—when David is seventeen. The Murdstones reenter as, respectively, Dora Spenlow's "confidential friend" and Mr. Spenlow's client. Even Mr. Chillip, the doctor from the novel's first chapter, looking "just as he might have looked when he sat in our parlour waiting for me to be born" comes in to give a last report of Mr. Murdstone inflicting misery on a new young wife, while Mr. Creakle pops up as the warden of a model prison in which Uriah Heep, still wringing his hands, and Steerforth's former valet, the hypocritical Littimer, are incarcerated. Finally, Mr. Peggotty, back in England on a visit from Australia, catches us up on Little Em'ly, Mrs. Gummidge, and the Micawbers—the émigrés we know are there—and tells of a prospering Mr. Mell. No one, nothing from childhood is forgotten. The original cast of characters is always being reassembled and rearranged as the psyche struggles to repair itself.

I realize this may not be entirely reassuring. That the Murdstones are still constraining others' lives and Uriah and Littimer still at their wiles shows that evil persists and childhood demons never completely leave us. But if we're lucky, these forces weaken; they get pushed to the outskirts of our stories. David, at long last married to Agnes and surrounded by old friends, is heartening proof that ties to others can be sustained and be sustaining and that experience can feel whole.

It may be my inclination to be positive—so wanting things to turn out right that I've often been accused of not giving proper weight to hurt and difficulty, but I can't help seeing *David Copperfield*, for all its terrors, as in many ways a gentle book. It tells a painful story but then finds ways to cushion the pain—through humor and the charm and vividness of characters, and also, very importantly, through its setting, a southern English landscape from which mid-nineteenth-century capitalism and urban grittiness have been largely banished. These may be hinted at in David's London sojourn at Murdstone and Grinby's or in Betsy Trotwood's reversals in the stock market. But the young reader of *David Copperfield*, whether in Beverly Hills, Brooklyn, or a London orphanage, is carried out of herself into one of Dickens's greenest, most pastoral worlds.

Just look at the opening chapter in which David, from inside his parlor "warm and bright with fire and candle," feels "indefinable compassion" for his father's white grave-stone "lying out alone in the dark night," against which the doors of the house are bolted. Then even that outside darkness lifts in the ensuing reflection. "There is nothing half so green that I know anywhere," the narrator muses, "as the green of that churchyard; nothing half so shady as its trees; nothing half so quiet as its tombstones. The sheep are feeding there, when I kneel up, early in the morning, in my little bed in a closet within my mother's room, to look out at it."

David will soon be expelled from this womb with a view—cast out from his room, house, and green countryside. Thus the pastoral is qualified; it is never untinged by loss. Rooks, after all, even at the outset, have deserted the Rookery, and the pigeon house and dog's kennel are empty. Snakes come into the garden: Mr. Murdstone, Uriah—that's part of the book's fascination—but even when the sea rises in storm to punish Steerforth for seducing and abandoning Little Em'ly and claim as well the good Ham Peggotty, the reader is drawn into a world that can only be called enchanting.

I was happy to be transported to Sussex, to Yarmouth, to Canterbury. I was delighted to travel by coach with Barkis, to enter Mr. Peggotty's boat of a house and meet its colorful inhabitants, or even, at the nadir of young David's fortunes in London, to encounter the wonderful Micawbers and to lose myself in their phrases and fantasies. *David Copperfield*, more than any other novel in my early reading, laid the foundations in my mind and heart of an ideal of England, an ideal I have continued to cherish and believe in despite all the dystopic novels of Doris Lessing or Martin Amis I have read since, despite my own first-hand knowledge of a post-WWII to twenty-first-century country in decline. I could understand all Steerforth's faults, but I was also seduced by his immense charm. Steerforth was England. Peggotty and her brother were England. Little Em'ly was England. David was England. Even 'umble, treacherous Uriah Heep helped to round out the picture as the snake in England's garden. . . . And I gave my heart to them all.

Thus, through David I entered a completely absorbing, "knowable community"—the critic Raymond Williams's wonderful phrase for a world of imaged coherence—to which the narrator himself is attached by bonds of memory and love. When, like my colleague, I returned to the book as an adult, I was struck by how strongly the force of memory colors the telling of the story. Despite the question hanging over the book of whether David will turn out to be the hero of his own life, *David Copperfield* is, above all, one of those books that look back on the past with at once aching and lyrical nostalgia for the felt experience of childhood. The past is remembered with compassion; pain is recast as reverie. Even the pain of the time at Murdstone and Grinby's softens in retrospect. Thinking how he made up stories about the debtors in Kings Prison, David reflects: "When my thoughts go back now to that slow agony of my youth . . . when I tread the old ground, I do not wonder that I seem to see before me, an innocent romantic boy making his imaginative world out of such strange experiences and sordid things."

Memory, which itself is a form of imagination, is David's gentle and compassionate friend, recovering dear past moments that then exist for him almost out of time—Worthsworth called these "spots of time." David's "spots of time" include memories of the beach at Yarmouth with Little Em'ly; of his first evening home on holiday from Salem House with the Murdstones thankfully absent from the house; of Salem House itself, when he stops on his flight to Dover to sleep in a haystack behind a wall at the back of the school and remembers, not smarting under Mr. Creakle's ruler or feeling shame at his placard, but "lying on my old school-bed, talking to the boys in my room." Here experience is filtered through a double layer of memory with David the narrator's nostalgically remembering the ten-year-old boy, who is already nostalgically transforming his school days. The tyrannies of Salem Hall fade into bedtime stories evoked in a pastoral haystack.

The power of memory in *David Copperfield* is linked to the faculty of love. Steerforth, fearing his own fallen nature and the changes it might work, pleads to his friend, transformed into a flower: "Daisy, if anything should ever separate us, you must think of me at my best, old boy." But David's answer goes one better, removing Steerforth from all vicissitudes of best and worst: "'You have no best to me,

Steerforth,' said I. 'And no worst. You are always equally loved and cherished in my heart.'"

Loving remembrance of his mother, of Steerforth, of Dora restores them to David Copperfield. Loving, compassionate remembrance of the past reconstitutes it whole, with no best and no worst. At one point when David is coming out of the theater after seeing *Julius Caesar*, he is filled with "the mingled reality and mystery of the whole show." The play becomes "like a shining transparency" through which he sees his "earlier life moving along." This passage seems to me the achievement of the novel. To revisit the past is not to deny its hardships but to deny "any severing of our love." The past then looms through the creative force of remembrance like "a shining transparency."

My past is my experience of Beverly Hills, of my mother and brother, of Rosemary Hall and Pam Wilkinson, Sue Stein and Judy Wilson. My past is also my life of reading, which I began young. The early reading of *David Copperfield* is as much a part of my personal history as anything "real" that happened to me. *David Copperfield* happened to me. It is one of my spots of time. The book has become like a shining transparency through which I see my earlier life moving along.

iv

THE ONE PART OF David's past that never softens for him is the history with his stepfather, Mr. Murdstone. When Miss Murdstone reenters the novel as Dora's companion, David has the opportunity to say to her, "Miss Murdstone, . . .

I think you and Mr. Murdstone used me very cruelly, and treated my mother with great unkindness. I shall always think so as long as I live." This is an important utterance. It remains within the bounds of civil discourse but manages, nonetheless, to convey unvarnished truth. I find it interesting that when, a few chapters later, David reencounters Mr. Murdstone—the character who, after all, is the primary villain—his language, though still truthful, is more constrained. Mr. Murdstone reenters the text for just a few pages as a client for whom David's father-in-law, Mr. Spenlow, is helping to obtain a marriage license (the reader shudders to anticipate Mr. Murdstone's next victim). The meeting occurs in Mr. Spenlow's office. Peggotty, for whom David is transacting some legal business, is present as well. Mr. Spenlow unwittingly suggests that David knows "this gentleman," and the two old antagonists exchange cool greetings. Then Mr. Murdstone addresses himself to Peggotty:

"And you," he said, "I am sorry to observe that you have lost your husband."

"It's not the first loss I have had in my life, Mr. Murdstone," replied Peggotty, trembling from head to foot. "I am glad to hope there is nobody to blame for this one,—nobody to answer for it."

"Ha!" Said he; "that's a comfortable reflection. You have done your duty?"

"I have not worn anybody's life away," said Peggotty. "I am thankful to think! No Mr. Murdstone, I have not worried and frightened any sweet creetur to an early grave!"

He eyed her gloomily—remorsefully I thought—for an instant; and said, turning his head towards me but looking at my feet instead of my face:

"We are not likely to encounter soon again;—a source of satisfaction to us both, no doubt, for such meetings can never be agreeable. I do not expect that you, who always rebelled against my just authority, exerted for your benefit and reformation, should owe me any good will now. There is an antipathy between us—"

"An old one, I believe?" I said interrupting him.

The scene ends with Mr. Murdstone continuing to impugn David's character. Both, however, are mindful of their obligation to behave as gentlemen, and David wonders what constraints he might have shed if he had not felt anxious about what Peggotty, less class-bound than he, might have gone on to say. But in a sense David gets to have it both ways. *He* behaves as a gentleman, yet between his own cool comments and Peggotty's more biting sarcasm enough truth gets spoken: Mr. Murdstone is called to account.

In my own life, I never had the chance to reencounter Bow Wow. I was never able to tell him how he had scarred me and afflicted my family. I never experienced the catharsis of showing him I knew the harm he had done us, naming it with accuracy and without fear. So Bow Wow remained the bogeyman of my imagination, a shadow in my psyche. Then one day, a good six or eight years after the death of my mother, I learned that Bow Wow, too, had died. An old California family friend had read a short obituary in the *Los Angeles Times*. Perhaps it was Bow Wow's link with my mother that earned him this notice. Or the fact that in his later years, he had become a hanger on—almost a kind of mascot—of the Los Angeles Rams. I calculated he must have died in his seventies and had trouble thinking of him as an old man.

To learn of Bow Wow's death was a relief. The death meant he could never pop into our lives again to harm or embarrass us, never again send me a card, as he had last done when I married at twenty-six, thirteen years after his exit from our home, addressed to "Princess Wendy Westbrook" and offering the perverse gift of a hundred Hail Marys to be said for me at Beverly Hills All Saints Catholic Church. He could never boast again to the football players he hung out with of his years with Sheilah Graham; never again write to Matthew Bruccoli, the Fitzgerald scholar, about his alleged cache of Scott Fitzgerald papers. Perhaps I could now move a step further away from my still simmering rage. But I was left strangely disquieted at old business left unfinished.

My mother had resolved her history with Bow Wow by cutting him literally out of the story. In our family archives we have a picture from the reception celebrating her wedding to Bow Wow of my mother with Marilyn Monroe, but not a single one of her and Bow Wow, though that means some of the pictures were torn in half. His name was stricken, too. She would refer to him either as "the monster" or as "my unfortunate third husband." But at the same time she stored him up as material for fiction. Though she never did more than compile a few notes for it, she talked about writing a short story called "Athlete's Foot," in which the protagonist dreams of being a great athlete but is thwarted by his small feet (Bow Wow hadn't been the college football star he had claimed to be—that was just one of his lies.). At the end of the story, my mother planned for this character to redeem himself by dying to save a girl from drowning in the ocean. *She* thus managed to turn Bow Wow into, if not a hero, at least a *comic* villain, you might even say something out of Dickens, a blowhard wobbling on small feet, easily toppled. As for me, though I linger with my Dickensian trauma, an experience akin to that of the young boy working in the blacking warehouse, the reversal and shame to which he returns again and again, I have hopes as well of more release from it.

My relationship to *David Copperfield* has a less ambiguous coda. For a few years in the late 1990s, I taught one course each semester at New York University. One day I saw a notice on a bulletin board in the NYU English department announcing a conference in Sydney, Australia, on *The Victorians and Childhood*. I thought of my Brooklyn College friend Roni Natov, who is a preeminent scholar in Children's Studies and also a specialist in the Victorian Novel, my field as well. I detached the poster from the wall and took it to Roni.

"You've got to try to do this," I urged her.

"Yes," she said, "But you've got to come, too."

The deadline for paper submissions had passed, but we got permission to send in a proposal if we could dispatch it the next day. Overnight we concocted a topic and an abstract. Our paper, "Dickens's David and Carroll's Alice: Representations of Victorian Liminality," would examine reverie in *David Copperfield* and nightmare in *Alice in Wonderland*, the two expressions of self we identified as liminal. We posited that the reverie is always seeking to repair the psyche's sense of loss and the nightmare allows for that loss to be expressed without acknowledging any real wounds to the psyche. The books joined for us in their use of the child and his or her wondrous journey to penetrate the margins of Victorian experience. Roni would do the Alice portion, and I the David. Our proposal was accepted, and I wrote my part of the paper with astonishing ease.

My first afternoon in Australia, fresh, or not so fresh, off the plane, I set out on a walk from our motel. I meant only to get a little exercise after the nineteen-hour confinement of the flight from New York to Sydney. With no set destination in mind, I found myself heading towards the ocean, not stopping until, three miles farther, I descended a hill to the expanse of water. The coast was reminiscent of California's arid cliffs swooping down towards crescent beaches. I walked onto the sand and stood gazing out to sea, on the opposite side of the ocean I had known and loved as a child. Australia seemed a lot like Southern California before it got so built up and crowded.

When I was a child, *David Copperfield* had figuratively transported me across a continent and an ocean to the green pastoral landscape of England. Now I had literally traveled across a continent and an ocean to read a paper about that green landscape in a contrasting one of dry hills, rustling eucalyptus trees, and sheer cliffs sweeping down to the Pacific. Dickens himself never traveled to Australia, though a number of his characters do, including the cluster in *David Copperfield*. Now I had come to the country and continent that had been a remote land of real exile for the British government and for Dickens a place to send characters he didn't want to kill off but needed to get out of the way, a convenient land of last resort. Yet Australia is also where poor Mr. Mell and improvident Mr. Micawber get to thrive. I felt I was thriving, too. A few years short of sixty and happy in many aspects of my life, I seemed, like David Copperfield, to have come out on the safe side of harm. It was nice to linger a moment with that sparkling seascape before turning from it to move on.

Jane Eyre and Becky Sharp

Reliably popular with students and, to borrow a phrase from Roland Barthes, "moist with meaning," *Jane Eyre* is a convenient book to teach. First at the University of Hawaii in the early seventies, and then as I have moved in my life and career to England, Maine, New York, Virginia, and New York a second time, I have turned to it again and again, finding students of all ages, mostly women but men, too, ready to suffer and exult with Brontë's small, plain heroine, hating those she hates, forgiving those she loves, keeping company with her in her evolution from unloved orphan to charity student, governess, fiancée, schoolteacher, and finally wife. They have applauded her in her defiance of Mrs. Reed, rooted for her in gaining the love of Mr. Rochester, and supported her in her decision to leave him, a would-be bigamist. They have understood why she cannot marry the icy St. John Rivers and then rejoiced at her return to her chastened and symbolically castrated true love. "Reader, I married him" must rank as one of the most deeply satisfying sentences in English literature. I teach the book because it is an important canonical, feminist, and even colonial text, serving to raise questions of narrative, the status of women, realism versus romance, the loneliness and hardiness of the individual, and sexual and cultural politics, to name just some of the inviting topics of discussion; I teach it because I can count on my students' engagement with it, whether they are English majors or accountants, graduate students or freshmen. Yet *Jane Eyre* is a novel that has never moved me. It left me cold when I first read it at age ten or eleven, and my interest in it up to this present day has never risen above the academic. It's a great book for the classroom, but I have never loved it—not it and not its heroine.

The text I counterpose to *Jane Erye* is Thackeray's *Vanity Fair*. "Panoramic," according to the critic Percy Lubbock, a "large, loose baggy monster" for Henry James, it includes in its extensive cast of characters the other most renowned female orphan-turned-governess in English literature, the pointedly named Becky Sharp. *Vanity Fair* is a much less serviceable book to slip into syllabi than *Jane Eyre*. Too lengthy for any general education course, too ironic for a course in women's studies—Thackeray's wry, ambiguous humor seems not especially compatible with feminist approaches—the novel might be a good choice for a course in postcolonialism, a vehicle to consider the reaches of Empire since the East India Company more than hovers in the background of the text. But in the final analysis this book works best for students of the nineteenth-century novel. And even with these, whatever their presumed tolerance for the genre, experience has prepared me to brace for the complaints.

"Too many words," said one bold older woman, a former nurse and returning student, referring perhaps less to the length of *Vanity Fair* than to its pace and chattiness. The intrusive—and elusive—narrator bothers some. Others are troubled by the characters' flawed nature in this novel, as its subtitle announces, "without a hero." George Osborne is a cad, who but for dying on the battlefield at Waterloo would have deserted his young wife; that innocent wife, Amelia, is a simpering nitwit, grieving all those years over the dead George and failing to see what's real around her; William Dobbin is a fool—a "spooney," as Thackeray calls him— for his thankless loyalty to Amelia; and Becky Sharp, from beginning to end of the ploys that we follow over nearly two decades, is a conniving, some would say heartless, social climber.

I'm grateful for those students who do appreciate *Vanity Fair*, for I am a committed enthusiast. My love of this novel goes back to that *annus mirabilis* of my reading life, sixth grade—the year I also devoured *David Copperfield* and *Bleak House*, learning to savor the pleasures of seemingly endless immersion in such intricate fictional worlds. Thackeray won me from the opening sentence of Chapter I when "two fat horses in blazing harness, driven by a fat coachman in a three-cornered hat and wig," arrive at the gate of Miss Pinkerton's Academy for young ladies. Within a few pages I had met snobbish, hypocritical Miss Pinkerton and her silly, well-meaning sister, Jemima, sentimental Amelia, and her knowing "best friend," Becky Sharp. And under Thackeray's authorial tutelage, I had grasped their social and moral standing. I also understood that Becky, and Becky alone, is endowed with the wit to penetrate the vanities and weaknesses of those around her. And even before her awesome revolutionary gesture of throwing Dr. Johnson's

Dictionary out the window of the carriage speeding her away from the school she despises, this character had me in thrall. Thackeray calls her his "famous little Becky puppet," an acknowledgment of her power to fascinate as well as an assertion of *his* power as her maker. She has remained one of my favorite characters in English fiction, unwaveringly through the more than half century of my reading life.

My colleague, who also teaches the nineteenth-century novel course, argues that we are allowed to love Becky because the balance tilts towards the good in her morally complex nature—after all, she helps Amelia in the end to give up her illusions about George and marry Dobbin. I'm not so sure of my colleague's judgment; I'm not sure the good in Becky Sharp prevails over her amorality, some would say over her wickedness. Doesn't Thackeray stack the deck against her by making her an uncaring mother? It may be amusing that "whenever Mrs Rawdon wished to be particularly humble and virtuous," she hems the little shirt "for her dear little boy" that "had got to be too small for Rawdon long before it was finished." But when she boxes his ears after she catches the boy listening rapt on the staircase as she sings to her aristocratic "benefactor," Lord Steyne, and Thackeray tells us that "after this incident the mother's dislike turned to hatred," it's hard as a reader not to shudder and condemn her. But despite my maternal scruples, I don't let this damning incident tip the scales. Becky has already won me. Perhaps I side with her all the more readily because she's not aspiring to be good. She's a rogue who plays the game of life, uncomplaining when she loses a hand, just anteing up again. I love her zest and resilience, her wit and irreverence. Even in the face of my better judgment, I forgive her everything.

As I look back on myself as a girl reader of these novels, I see someone who was herself more a Jane Eyre but who admired and wanted to be like Becky Sharp.

To begin with appearance, Jane is small and plain. Mrs. Gaskell, Brontë's first biographer, tells us that "Jane Eyre was naturally and universally thought to be Charlotte herself, but she always denied it, calmly, cheerfully, with the obvious sincerity which characterized all she said," asserting "the basis was no more than thus: she determined to take in defiance of convention a heroine as small and plain as herself who should nonetheless be interesting."

I was small and, in ways I shall explain, plain as well. After sizing up my seventeen-and-a-half-inch length and head of dark hair at birth, my mother decided I wasn't a Penelope, the name she had reserved for an imagined long-legged blond. Maybe my mother would have named baby Blanche Ingram Penelope, even though Blanche, Jane's seeming rival, is a brunette. Growing up in Southern California, I was surrounded by Blanche Ingram types, at least in terms of their stature—long-legged California girls, who always stood in the rows behind me in class photographs. At one point, I remember worrying if I was going to be a midget, a concern I'm happy to report that proved unfounded— by fifteen, I had reached my adult 5'3 3/4" height. Still, I remained permanently shorter than most of my friends and classmates, and shorter, too, than my mother who was 5'5". Long-legged as well, she loved to show she could still do the high kicks she had performed in the twenties as a chorus girl on the London stage.

I wasn't an unattractive child, but I felt myself to be plain. Not ugly, just plain. And plain is also what I sought to be. From age six or seven, for a stretch of years, I insisted on a daily uniform of jeans, a checked flannel shirt over a T-shirt, and brown oxfords—with cowboy boots reserved for special occasions. These clothes couldn't be worn to school–skirts were required there—but my skirts were always as plain as possible. When I was in sixth grade, my mother tried to upgrade my wardrobe by taking me off to the Saks on Wiltshire Boulevard and helping me choose two outfits—one red and one yellow. The red outfit had a flared skirt to be worn with a crinoline; the skirt of the yellow outfit was straight with a pleat in the back. Both had color-coordinated cotton print blouses and cardigans. When I wore the red outfit to school, classmates asked me if I was dressed for something special. Their assumption mortified me. I was only trying to be more like them. But anything at all fancy seemed a betrayal of my true self.

Jane Eyre, as I did, feels violated in being adorned. In the period of their engagement, Rochester tries to shower her with jewels and dress her in satin and lace. "And then you won't know me, sir," retorts Jane. "And I shall not be your Jane Eyre any longer but an ape in a harlequin's jacket—a jay in borrowed plumes." I don't know if I paused over this exchange as a child reader, but, thinking now about both Jane and myself, I find it telling. Jane feels as if fancy clothes and jewels will diminish, not enhance her. Her plainness is a point of pride. She is Rochester's "plain Quakerish governess," and that should be sufficient. In my own life, I think, plainness was also a means of holding onto myself in a milieu that thrived on artifice. "You want to be plain!" accused my mother in exasperation over my hair when I was twenty-five. By then I had long softened towards nice clothes, but to this day I wear little makeup and do not dye my hair. The one time I put in blond highlights, I felt like Jane Eyre's jay in borrowed plumes.

It would be easy to build a contrast between me and my glamorous Hollywood-columnist mother. Just imagine a typical scene: me on a couch in the corner of the beauty salon at Max Factor, idly thumbing through movie magazines, while my mother's hair is lightened to platinum, then teased, and, finally, heavy makeup is applied to her face for a television appearance. Yet my mother underwent such transformations only for her work. At home she never wore makeup, and she didn't drink or smoke. She got up early and worked hard. In a sense, she was plain, too. "Just a plain girl at home," is how our old Swiss housekeeper remembered her when I sought this woman out for her recollections thirty years after she had left my mother's employ. Perhaps in the artificial milieu of Hollywood, to be plain becomes the only possible expression of authenticity.

Jane Eyre's plain external appearance, which the novel is very insistent in keeping before us, at once hides her inner self and reflects a Wordsworthian insistence on her "soul's immensity." The soul is camouflaged by that plainness; yet it also shines through it in a way that it could never shine through artifice. Thus, to look at and *see* plain Jane Eyre, as Rochester manages to do, is to penetrate to her authentic self. Meanwhile, the reader also comes to know Jane Eyre's soul from the inside out, drawn in by means of the character's intense first-person narrative to her desires and resentments, her dreams and her principles, her strategies for coping in inimical surroundings, her passions, and her self-restraint. I resembled Jane in my subjectivity as well as in my appearance. I resembled her in my own intensity, ferocity, and bluntness, in my reserve and discipline, and in my sense of deprivation I also resembled her in the solace I sought in reading.

Whereas Becky Sharp throws Dr. Johnson's Dictionary out the carriage window, Jane Eyre is introduced reading Bewick's *History of Birds*, though that very book is shortly thrown at her head by the nasty John Reed. Jane has taken refuge in the window seat of the breakfast room, drawing the red moreen curtain to ensure her seclusion as well as underscore her exclusion from the family hearth, while the clear panes of glass on her other side protect without separating her from the "drear November day." The bird book paradoxically warms her by allowing her to escape in imagination into an Arctic realm—of frost and snow and a ghastly moon. She likes stories, having listened to the housemaid Bessie's fairy tales and "passages of love and adventure," drawn, she later understands, from the pages of *Pamela* and *Henry Earl of Norland*. Goldsmith's *History of Rome* has taught her about Roman tyrants, thus giving her the frame of reference that allows her to denounce John Reed as unjust.

I was never excluded from my family hearth. Indeed, one of my fondest early memories is of sitting on a beautiful quilted sofa in the warmth of the gas jets of our artificial fire while my mother read to me from the pages of *Black Beauty*, a book I then completed on my own, the first full-length book I ever read independently. When I think of reading, both being read to and reading myself, I have an image of a river, of myself flowing into stories, empathic and unbounded. In my everyday life, though, I was stern and bounded. I was also quick to decry injustice. I defended the dog against Bow Wow. I defended my mother when with her I met Errol Flynn. He was rude to her over something she'd written in her column. Placing myself protectively in front of her, I glared at him with my serious dark-brown eyes. Errol Flynn threw back his double chin and laughed. "The cub defending its dam," he said. I was then eleven.

My mother often took me along with her when she went to interview the stars. Some—including Ingrid Bergman and Marilyn Monroe—were nice. Mostly they didn't notice me. It was my role to sit in the corner of, say, the Beverly Hills Brown Derby and to eat my filet mignon. How terrible is that, you might ask? Well, it's terrible, even as a child, or maybe particularly as one, to seem invisible. Once we went in a limousine to a premiere at Graumann's Chinese. The car drove up to the entrance. Fans strained behind the ropes to see who'd be arriving. "Who's in there, who's in there?" they pressed as I stepped in my Mary Janes and bobby socks onto the red carpet. Well, I'd been in there. But that didn't count.

So I understand how Jane Eyre feels at Gateshead or at Thornfield when Rochester has all his fashionable guests, who hardly know if she's in the room. I understand her loneliness and her rage. I understand her terrible, frightening sense of deprivation—and her indomitable sense of self-worth in the face of all the neglect she experiences. When she makes her passionate declaration of love to Mr. Rochester, it is driven by her conviction of radical equality. "I am not talking to you now," she declares to the man she believes has spurned her, "through the medium of custom, conventionalities, nor even of mortal flesh; it is my spirit that addresses your spirit; just as if both had passed through the grave, and we stood at God's feet, equal as we are."

Growing up in Hollywood, I refused to be judged by its standards. The milieu, as my mother encouraged me to assess it, though she was part of it herself, was phony. My time would come, she told me, just as we know Jane Eyre's time will come. I clung to that expectation. I clung to unadornment, to plainness if you will, as a synonym for self. I was a self, a not very popular self at school, an invisible self in Hollywood, but a self that I sensed would some day be acknowledged.

Yet isn't this all rather tiresome? Virginia Woolf says it well in her essay on the Brontës in *The Common Reader*: "When Charlotte wrote, she said with eloquence and spendour and passion, 'I love,' 'I hate,' 'I suffer.'" But Woolf's implication is that Charlotte's focus is narrow, that to be so consumed in intense first-person emotions is both limiting and exhausting. Suggesting broader ways to engage with the world, Woolf cites the perceptual and intellectual range of characters in Austen and Tolstoy. She does not speak of Thackeray. His characters, after all, are "puppets"; he never lets go their strings. Yet Thackeray, too, offers an alternative, perhaps more than one, to "I love, I hate, I suffer."

The alternative, I'd hazard, of *Vanity Fair*'s intrusive narrator is: "We love, we hate, we suffer." *Vanitas vanitarum*. And Becky Sharp's alternative—she does hate Miss Pinkerton but soon learns to be more dispassionate—is: "You love, you hate, you suffer, not I—and I will take advantage of your folly."

My mother as a Hollywood gossip columnist can be seen as a combination of Thackeray and Becky. She chronicled the vanities of a superficial world: the loves, feuds, and risings and fallings of the stars. The stars were in a sense her puppets. "My paragraphs," she called them. They were fodder for her column; she didn't take them too seriously because she knew all were playing a game. Like Becky, she saw through the world she was scrutinizing while at the same time aspiring to be part of it. And also like Becky, she was an interloper. To anyone who knows anything of the story of Sheilah Graham, the parallels between her life and Becky Sharp's must be obvious. Before she came to America, my mother gained entry to the highest circles of British society. Like Becky she concealed her background, in her case early poverty and Jewishness. Her entry card, like Becky's, was her mix of beauty and brains—and a certain unscrupulousness about the means of getting ahead. Neither my mother nor Becky can be imagined as ever stopping to worry about being true to oneself, the pursuit of sincerity that Lionel Trilling sees as an essential value of Western culture from the Renaissance onward. For both Becky and my mother such scruples would have seemed a luxury. Respectability has its importance but only as appearance, not as moral essence. I think of both of them as driven, not as Jane Eyre is by the outsider's loneliness, but by the outsider's pragmatism. The pinnacle of Becky's achievement is attending Lord Steyne's party at Gaunt House. The pinnacle of my mother's "English society period" was being presented at the court of George V and Queen Mary. We have the pictures to prove it. When everything collapses for Becky, she removes herself to the continent. My mother also changed continents—running from entanglements of one sort or another, she came to America. People in America, she said, judge you by what you can do, not by who you are.

My mother acknowledges the parallel between herself and Thackeray's character in her book *College of One*. Scott Fitzgerald chose *Vanity Fair* as the first novel my mother should read in the College of One curriculum (was he thinking she reminded him of Becky Sharp?), and my mother comments:

> It seems incredible that before Scott's College of One I had not read *Vanity Fair*, the first of the novels in the curriculum. It was easy to read in the good edition Scott bought me in three volumes with good paper and strong print. . . . I did not consider the "how" of Becky Sharp. I found her interesting and she was somewhat like me. I much preferred her to the meek Amelia, who was put upon repeatedly without protesting. Becky fought for what she wanted, as I did. Her ambitions had been somewhat different from mine; she had wanted money and position, I had wanted acceptance. Perhaps they are related.

Ironically, my mother achieved money and position—*and* acceptance in her chosen milieu, whereas Becky ultimately holds onto none of these. My mother set herself the goal of earning $5,000 a week, an income she achieved in 1954 when she had her daily television show, though, granted, the $5,000 was her gross budget for the show. Becky, as she drives away from Queen's Crawley, the estate that got away from her, muses that she "could have been a good woman on 5,000 pounds a year." We never get to know if this might have been true because Becky never reaches her level of imagined financial stability. Still, it's not the ultimate success or failure, or even the particular details of the ascent or descent that seem to me the main point of the comparison.

What I responded to at age eleven in Becky Sharp and recognized in my own family experience—not knowing then that Sheilah Graham was really Lily Shiel who had spent six years in a Jewish orphanage, not knowing that the paired, framed pencil drawings of my mother as a small girl, daffodil in hand, in a sweet blue dress and her "dead brother David" in a sailor suit were fakes, reworked to create an impression of genteel ancestry from childhood photographs of herself and her first husband Johnny—were Becky's qualities of wit and zest and resourcefulness and a bizarre underlying honesty. It is the honesty of the rogue who may fool others but ultimately does not fool herself. I could sense these qualities in my mother—and also, buried beneath my serious Jane Eyre side, lurking somewhere in myself.

Part of our "honesty" as a family is that we acknowledged the gamesmanship of our taking advantage of Hollywood. Becky and her husband Rawdon, in the famously titled chapter, show us "how to live well on nothing a year." In our family's case there were no bill collectors pounding at the door, but we were no less engaged in a scam. "We weren't millionaires," said my mother, looking back on it all, "but we lived like millionaires." Lunches and dinners at the Beverly Brown Derby, at Trader Vic's, and Chasen's, and then when we started traveling, in all the best restaurants of New York, Paris, London, and Rome were always free. By the time I was in college and our family had moved to New York, the game was winding down. Still, we could count on dinner every Sunday at Luchow's—a staple of sauerbraten and red cabbage or maybe wiener schnitzel –and at the beginning of every new season—fall, winter, summer, spring—a meal for the three of us along with maybe a couple of awed, grateful friends at The Four Seasons. The maitre d' would glide obsequiously to my mother's table— always a good table or she would get it changed. "Tell me who's been here lately," she would ask. "Ah, last week Marlene Dietrich . . ." he would begin as my mother, keeping pace with him, would scribble in her little spiral notebook. At the end came the anticipated reckoning. "The check, please" my mother would propose, her voice at once firm and uncertain. "Oh no, Miss Graham, please, it's on the house." We enjoyed this little ritual immensely.

While we were still in California, there were also the getaway weekends. In Palms Springs, Ojai, and Santa Barbara, a range of hotels—which if not the best at least had swimming pools—offered us either low rates or free accommodations. Also, beginning in the mid '50s, as more movies were made on location abroad, there were the free plane trips and hotel stays in Europe, or in New York, all the way through the '60s, a pair of free tickets to every Broadway opening. When my mother wasn't in town, I would take a friend. I attended hits and busts, the 1958 opening of *Camelot* and long-forgotten plays that closed almost the night they opened. It was a scam, a game, a performance, perhaps all the more zestfully fraudulent for me since I derived its benefits without even putting in my mother's labor.

My mother showed me the zest of calculated performance in an imperfect world, the same lesson taught by Becky Sharp, and it's hard for me not to conflate the two of them. Being equal to the moment at hand. Knowing what to say when threatened. Becky knows how to humiliate Miss Pinkerton by speaking to her in French or to rebuke the prying Mrs. Bute by her "honest" admission that she was never a Montmorency. When my mother, in the late '30s, encountered Constance Bennet on a studio set and Bennet accosted her—"At last I get to meet the biggest bitch in Hollywood!"—my mother was equal to the occasion and retorted with barely a pause, "Not the biggest bitch, Connie, the second biggest bitch!" We also loved her guile and gusto, when threatened with a lawsuit by Jane Wyman, in making a radio show "retraction" that managed to repeat the offending item. "It is *not* true that Jane Wyman wears long sleeves and high collars to cover up hives." Poor Jane Wyman! But such were the family stories we thrilled to as children. How could I not adore Thackeray's witty, embattled character?

And also make her my own model. Despite my avowed dislike for masks and disguises, I find that much that I have done and sought to do has been conceived in terms of performance. In seventh grade I had to give an oral book report on a Dorothy Parker short story. Standing before the class and talking from my index cards, I managed to keep everyone laughing throughout the presentation. That was the beginning of my aspiration to panache.

In college and a bit afterwards, I acted in plays—largely Shakespeare, a bit of Shaw and Christopher Fry—and thought I might like to be an actress. My mother asked if I were willing to starve. I said no. Choosing, instead, to teach, I entered a sober profession but also one that is theatrical. Even participating in department meetings can seem so. Making the right comment at the right moment. Entering the play, assuming a role, as much caught up in the zest of the occasion as concerned with its purpose or content. And always a bit detached. When I was a college dean, another job people take seriously, I think I kept signaling that I held myself at an ironic distance from the role. That may be why, ultimately, I was fired. But no matter. The performer looks to new roles, new opportunities. Losing my job as dean meant a twenty-five-thousand-dollar salary decrease. Within months I had a book contract to write a family memoir. The book advance I received offset the drop in salary. My mother had recently died, but I imagined she would have been proud of my resourcefulness. It was in the mode of Becky Sharp: scrambling to stay on top of things yet viewing any set of circumstances as a drama which could ultimately run to its end; engaged in events but also impervious to them; feeling oneself inextinguishable because there is no essence of self to extinguish—only one role after another, and one's abiding energy to keep playing them.

But having said all this, I must pause to remember my mother's remark. Becky Sharp is "somewhat like me," she wrote. The qualifying "somewhat" is important, and all the more so if I think of Becky as myself. Even more markedly than my mother, I have never sought wealth or social status and certainly never sought them through men. Also I do not forget that Becky Sharp is an imposter, an interloper, someone quite disreputable, a gambler, a character without a loving heart, a venal conniver, and, to top it all, a bad mother. Were I to meet her, I probably wouldn't trust her, just as I'd have to be wary of Moll Flanders or of Arabella in *Jude the Obscure*. These are women who'd sell you out as soon as look at you. Women who use men. Who know only how to take care of themselves and survive. Why make such a character as Becky one's heroine when Thackeray expressly says she isn't heroic? Why prefer her to plain Jane?

I have two answers.

One: Becky Sharp has a sense of humor, and Jane Eyre doesn't. Imagine having tea with one or the other. "No woman was ever nearer to her mate than I am: ever more absolutely bone of his bone and flesh of his flesh," Jane would confide, proudly straightening her posture as she raises her teacup to her lips. What could one say? "I'm very happy for you after all you've gone through." But I'd feel ill at ease, as if I were intruding on something too private. I think I'd also feel a bit bored.

Becky, on the other hand, could be counted on to amuse me with gossip and practical good sense. Leaning forward confidentially, she'd call a cad we both knew "that self-ish humbug, that low bred cockney dandy, that padded booby. . . ." and I'd delight in her description. Perhaps she'd relate her woes, dramatizing herself as a "poor castaway scorned for being miserable." I'd sympathize while at the same time seeing through her schemes and her poses. I'd have fun with Becky, even if I couldn't trust her. It would be hard to have fun with Jane.

Two: more than finding Becky a lot more fun than Jane, I also judge her as ultimately the less self-referential, the less selfish of the two characters. To put this differently, Jane's finest moments are ones of self-assertion—"I love, I hate, I suffer." I claim my due; Becky's, on the other hand, are ones of surprising disinterestedness.

In the scene in which Rawdon, released from prison through the kind intervention of his sister-in-law, Lady Jane, returns home to shock a glittering, bejeweled Becky dining *à deux* with Lord Steyne, Becky gives a "faint scream," musters a "horrid smile," and protests her innocence, all to no avail.

Steyne accuses Rawdon of complicity with Becky, then moves to make his exit. At that point Rawdon rips the brilliant from her breast, twice strikes the peer with his open hand, and flings him bleeding to the ground. "It was all done," writes Thackeray, "before Rebecca could interpose. She admired her husband, strong, brave, and victorious." Steyne slinks out. Rawdon makes Becky open her little desk and discovers how much she's been hiding and hoarding. "You might have spared me a hundred pounds, Becky, out of all this—I have always shared with you," he reproaches her. "I am innocent," Becky repeats weakly as Rawdon leaves her without a word.

Everything in this enjoyably dramatic, even melodramatic scene strikes me as predictable *except* Becky's admiration for Rawdon's moral and physical bravery in the very moment of her own downfall. That feeling goes completely against her self-interest. It is an instance of aesthetic appreciation, the recognition of a supreme performance: Rawdon acting his best self in the exchange with the corrupt Lord Steyne. But it is also her acknowledgment of Rawdon's moral superiority to Steyne and perhaps even to herself. I think this moment prepares the reader for the climactic exchange between Becky and Amelia at Pumpernickel (the two meet again by chance in the wonderfully named German ducal town), which brings the relations of the pair we have followed since their departure from Miss Pinkerton's Academy to their final reckoning.

Not just spontaneously but with premeditated resolution Becky determines to rescue Amelia from the Pumpernickel riffraff. "She shall marry the bamboo cane [Dobbin]. I'll settle it this very night," she "reasons to herself." Acting on her good intentions, she produces the letter George Osborne gave her seventeen years before, on the night of the Duke of

Richmond's ball in Brussels, the night before his death on the Waterloo battlefield, in which he asks her to run away with him. And she produces it, Thackeray tells us, "with provoking good humor." One might argue that getting Amelia out of the way will allow Becky freer room at long last to ensnare Amelia's brother, Jos Sedley. The cynical reader can make that connection, but Thackeray doesn't. Without regard in that instance for herself, Becky urges Amelia to write Dobbin. "She treated Emmy like a child and patted her head," this woman who hasn't managed to love her own child. This is the closest Thackeray comes, not to redeeming Becky Sharp, for she certainly doesn't stay redeemed, but to giving her a moment of transcendence. Then learning that Amelia has already written to Dobbin, Becky, ever the actress, ends the scene "screaming and singing." "'*Un biglietto*' she sang out with Rosina. '*Eccolo qua.*'" In Rossini's *Il Barbiero di Seviglia* when Figoro proposes Rosina should write a letter to Count Almaviva, she produces after some hesitation the letter she has already written. Uppermost in Becky's response to Amelia's admission is the understanding not that her self-exposure was unnecessary but that she finds herself in a recognizable *opera buffa*. "The whole house," writes Thackeray, "echoed with her shrill singing." Presumably Mrs. Crawley's voice is not now what it was of yore. But her zestful sense of the game is undiminished.

ii

I ADMIT TO ZEST of my own in championing Becky Sharp over Jane Eyre, in taking sides with the witty rogue against her poor plain foil. A friend expressed her reservations. "I don't think you've resolved this yet," she cautioned me. Probably she's right. I know I'm not at peace with my inner Jane Eyre, that serious dark-eyed girl (Jane Eyre actually has hazel eyes; Becky's are green) with her penetrating stare, a person who can be so demanding and willful. I'd like to laugh away her somberness, her sense of being hard done by, her inability to be teased. Alas, she won't go away. She abides in my psyche, sometimes even in my adult behavior. For the moment, though, as Thackeray might say, let's draw the curtain on her and leave her to her private sorrows. I'd like to change tack. For all that I've done to contrast them, I have another way of thinking about Jane and Becky—in terms of the themes and patterns of the mid-nineteenth-century English novel—that actually shows them to have a lot in common. Both are orphans. Both become governesses. Both marry the master, though in Becky's case it's the master's son. Both prove themselves to be indomitable survivors and tamers of men. Both are exceedingly smart. Both are cultural brokers, agents of change. Were I to teach *Jane Eyre* and *Vanity Fair* together in a course, I would take pleasure in developing these parallels,

If we think of the Victorian-era orphan as male, he is Oliver in Fagin's den of thieves or Pip shivering in a graveyard, or ten-year-old David being told on his tenth birthday that his mother is dead.

"There was no real need to tell me so," writes David the narrator. "I had already broken out into a desolate cry and felt an orphan in the wide world."

But what if the orphan is female? Jane Eyre comes at once to mind, and Dickens's Little Nell. I wouldn't think immediately of Becky Sharp—we don't get much of her childhood in the novel, and Thackeray also tells us she never really was a child, by which comment he surely means that she has always been sharp and savvy, adept in the ways of the world. Still, Becky is first encountered as an orphan, living on sufferance at Miss Pinkerton's Academy, not so different from the way the orphaned Jane lives with the Reeds.

Probably my mother's story of incredible survival colors my thinking, but I would argue that the female orphans of Victorian fiction are generally tougher than their male counterparts. While Pip shivers, both Becky and Jane get on with what they need to do. Becky, as we've seen, is awesome in her resourcefulness and resilience. As for Jane, small and plain though she may be, it's still the case that at every crisis in the novel from her first encounter with John Reed to her resistance to St. John Rivers' proposal that she become a missionary's wife, we feel her drawing strength from the one thing she can count on—herself. "Who in the world cares for *you*? Or who will be injured by what you do?" her own "Feeling" urges, when Rochester, revealed as a would-be bigamist, pressures her to stay on as his mistress. "Still indomitable was the reply, 'I care for myself. The more solitary, the more friendless, the more unsustained I am, the more I will respect myself." In truth, it's a stretch to see Jane as friendless. She has Bessie at Gateshead, Miss Temple and Helen Burns at Lowood, Rochester at Thornfield, the Rivers sisters at Moor House. But when these die or fail her or circumstances change, that bedrock self abides. And how different is this, really, from Becky Sharp? Becky—brilliant player of roles—might seem more to exemplify panache and wiliness and Jane sincerity, but *both*, as I perceive them, have the constancy of self-reliance. They move along, propelled by circumstances, not quite daring in Jane's words to ask for liberty but seeking at least new servitude.

Jane and Becky both become governesses, perhaps the one respectable employment available in the 1840s to genteel women in distress. In fiction the governess like the orphan finds herself in an unresolved position. She has worth but needs it to be recognized. She's vulnerable to possible mistreatment but also well placed to overcome her disadvantages. Jane Fairfax in *Emma* refers to the life of a governess as "the slave trade," but for Becky and Jane it's a "career open to talent," to borrow that revolutionary phrase. Becky's good French, her singing and her wit, Jane's drawings, which express her almost vatic power as do her bold retorts to Rochester, help gain them their one possible prize. Both exemplify how the narrative of the nineteenth-century *female* orphan invariably merges—unless like Little Nell she dies in childhood—with the narrative of the heroine who must marry. The list expands from Becky and Jane to Esther Summerson, Dorothea Brooke, Isabel Archer, Clara Middleton, Laura Fairlie, Eustasia Vye, and Sue Bridehead— all orphans though not all introduced as children. But their orphaned (read unprotected) condition is relevant to the key task before them. "I must be my own Mama," says Becky. She is speaking not in current self-help parlance of her need to "mother herself," but of that to find her own husband.

But then aren't heroines always more or less on their own when it comes to this task, even if they have living parents? Think, for example, of Austen's Elizabeth Bennet or Anne Elliot. In the story of the young woman about whom Henry James says the novel makes that "ado," parents, if not dead, are usually absent, tyrannical or foolish. Or if both parents aren't dead, then one is, so that the heroine without a father lacks standing and protection and the heroine without a mother lacks guidance. Able to count only on herself, our young woman must muddle through, and the qualities she shows in choosing and winning a husband define for us who she is.

The whole of *Jane Eyre* builds to Jane's marrying Rochester. Becky Sharp, on the other hand, has her series of campaigns, failing first with fat foolish Jos Sedley, then missing the chance to marry the master, Sir Pitt Crawley, because she has already married the master's son. Thackeray mocks both Becky and the expectations of novel readers in the way he depicts this supposedly climactic event. Far more dramatic than Becky's marrying Rawdon is the "tableau," as Thackeray calls it, in which she must refuse Sir Pitt.

> Rebecca started back, a picture of consternation. In the course of this history we have never seen her lose her presence of mind, but she did now and wept some of the most genuine tears that ever fell from her eyes.
>
> "Oh, Sir Pitt!" she said. "Oh, Sir—I am married already."

A chapter intervenes before we learn about the marriage to Rawdon.

> How they were married is not of the slightest consequence to anyone. What is to hinder a Captain who is a major, and a young woman who is of age, from purchasing a license and uniting themselves at any church in this town? Who needs to be told, that if a woman has a will, she will assuredly find a way. My belief is, that one day, when Miss Sharp had gone to pass the forenoon with her

dear friend, Miss Amelia Sedley in Russell Square, a lady very like her might have been seen entering a church in the city, in company with a gentleman with dyed mustachios. . . .

And so the passage continues. I find quoting it irresistible, forcing myself to break off with ellipses that at least might suggest its continuing build-up and gusto. The prose conveys Thackeray's irony, his techniques of distancing, his clever coyness that is a way of telling us everything while seeming to withhold information, his tendency to resist the climactic, a contrast, of course, to Brontë, who builds to her earnest exclamation of "Reader, I married him."

Perhaps a cynicism I have come by almost as an inheritance inoculates me against the charms of the unironic marriage plot. "I do hope Wendy will be happy in her marriages," my mother once proclaimed to a friend. We laughed at her telling slip. Into my sixties I'd had only one marriage, yet I feel my choice as a young woman of a husband, as good a person as he was, seemed on some level arbitrary. In the early years of that marriage, I kept having a dream in which I knew I had married someone but couldn't remember who this was. Various candidates flashed before me as my anxiety mounted. I knew it wasn't x and I knew it wasn't y. When I woke up, I was vastly relieved to remember I had married Donald Fairey. The marriage lasted quite a while though not forever.

Thackeray understands the arbitrariness of the heroine's choice. If Becky can't marry Jos, she'll try for a Crawley. She settles for the son, but she could have had the old baronet. In social terms that would have been preferable. What's love got to do with it? Amelia loves; her choice seems sacred. Yet the reader knows George Osborne is not bone of her bone and flesh of her flesh. Even the marriage to Dobbin, which the least tender-hearted reader is hard pressed not to cheer, has no merging of bones and flesh. "Farewell, dear Amelia," writes Thackeray sentimentally—and cynically. "Grow green again, tender little parasite, round the rugged old oak to which you cling."

But if Thackeray is cynical about love and marriage and Brontë is not, on another key point they come back together: the curtailing of licentious male energy. In an essay I have always found very suggestive and useful, "The Brontës or Myth Domesticated," Richard Chase argues that in Heathcliff and Rochester, Emily and Charlotte have created passionate, sexual, lawless Byronic heroes who mesmerize the heroines but at the same time must be tamed to achieve a socially and morally acceptable outcome for Victorian England. Hence, the story of *Wuthering Heights* replays in a second generation that is ultimately gentler and more malleable than the first (at the end of the book the second Cathy is teaching the unlettered Hareton to read). In *Jane Eyre* it's Rochester himself who gets tamed. The man who enters the novel bearing down on Jane on his horse (and is unhorsed in prefiguring of change to come) ends up maimed and blind. Even regaining enough sight literally to recognize his son, he is a reformed, domesticated, some would say emasculated husband.

Extending Chase's paradigm to *Vanity Fair*, I see a parallel domestication of the unruly male in Rawdon Crawley's change from dashing gambling captain of the Guards to underemployed father trotting his son around on a pony in Regents Park. But if I can appreciate the need to curb the sexual license of a Rochester, I have to wonder about Thackeray's good-hearted booby. Does the Captain really need this marital castration?

Nina Auerbach says yes in her chapter on "Incarnations of the Orphan" in *Romantic Imprisonment*. For Auerbach, the mythic force in these mid-century works is not the Romantic male but the female orphan/governess—an "angel/demon," using her powers not just to reform and domesticate men but also to effect a revolutionary change in society. Here is Auerbach on Jane:

> Throughout the novel she [Jane] talks oddly about her "powers." She conquers every environment she enters, but her powers are most dramatically evident at Thornfield, one of the great bleak houses of English fiction, bastion of feudal authority and of nineteenth-century English fiction. . . . When Rochester's opulent estate is reduced to rubble and his opulent body to a charred shell, Jane can return to him as little wife, rather than little witch, tending the ruins of the house she has passed through, cleaned up, and helped bring down.

Becky, too, for Auerbach has extraordinary *salutary* powers. Reviewing how Becky's marriage to Rawdon loses him his inheritance which passes to his brother who uses it to renovate their ancestral estate King's Crawley, and how she accomplishes a similar destruction and renovation in the house of Sedley, weaning Amelia away from the dandified George and encouraging her union with the good Captain Dobbin and then finishing off Jos Sedley for good measure, Auerbach concludes:

> Becky's selfhood is less absolute than Jane's, but her powers are the same: she transforms every great house

she enters, and by the end of the novel has become an inadvertent catalyst of social revolution. . . . By the end of the novel Becky has directly or indirectly killed off all the dominant Regency bucks who obstructed the coming of the new Victorian era. . . The orphan with all her dangerous magic, has functioned as the agent of benevolent change.

I quote from Auerbach because I find her theories persuasive and also hope to show the rhetorical power of good criticism, the ways it can expand a work's range of meanings. Over the forty years I have been professionally involved with *Jane Eyre* and *Vanity Fair*, part of the pleasure of rereading these novels has been the changing critical lenses through which they've been viewed. Especially in the case of *Jane Eyre* the successive approaches of modernist/new critical, second-wave feminist and third-wave feminist/postcolonial critics have radically altered readers' understanding of this novel.

In the 1960s, the years of my undergraduate and graduate school education, *Jane Eyre*'s "stock," as one of my grad school professors startled me by calling it, was way down, and it was accorded far less literary value than was *Wuthering Heights*. Neither work is included in F. R. Leavis's "great tradition" of morally serious English fiction (his influential critiques appeared in book form in 1948), but the latter at least gets a nod for its idiosyncratic brilliance. Asserting in a one-paragraph "note on the Brontës," that "it is tempting to retort that there is only one Brontë," Leavis famously dubs *Wuthering Heights* "a kind of sport"—a work of quirky genius beyond the pale of tradition—while begrudging only "a permanent interest of a minor kind to Charlotte."

Leavis himself was not afraid to be quirky, but be this as it may, his preference for Emily over Charlotte is echoed in most of the critics, writing from the twenties into the fifties, I was assigned to read. Kathleen Tillotson grants *Jane Eyre* a chapter in *Novels of the 1840s*, but Dorothy Van Ghent chooses *Wutherings Heights* as the Brontë novel to discuss in *The English Novel: Form and Function*, as does Arnold Kettle in *Introduction to the Novel*. Edwin Muir uses *Wuthering Heights* as his model of exemplary dramatic structure in *The Structure of the Novel*, deeming it "more impressive" than *Jane Eyre* because the balance in it "of freedom and necessity is held more tautly," whatever that means! And then, of course, there is the influential judgment of Virginia Woolf in *The Common Reader*, from which I now quote at greater length:

> *Wuthering Heights* is a more difficult book to understand than *Jane Eyre*, because Emily was a greater poet than Charlotte. When Charlotte wrote she said with eloquence and splendour and passion, "I love," "I hate," "I suffer." Her experience, though more intense, is on a level with our own. But there is no "I" in *Wuthering Heights*. There are no governesses. There are no employers. There is love, but it is not the love of men and women. Emily was inspired by some more general concept. The impulse which urged her to create was not her own suffering or her own injuries. She looked out on a world cleft into gigantic disorder and felt within her the power to unite it into a book.

The verdict seemed decisive: *Jane Eyre* is earthbound, *Wuthering Heights* transcendent; *Jane Eyre* is a work of power but also self-indulgent fantasy and emotion; the "impersonal" emotion of *Wuthering* Heights (remember T. S. Eliot's authoritative pronouncement that art must be impersonal) achieves a higher level of truth. *Wuthering Heights* is also deemed superior because its passion is contained within the novel's exquisite narrative double frame: the stranger Lockwood narrating the tale he has heard from the family servant Nelly, through whom we hear the aroused voices of Heathcliff, the Earnshaws, and the Lintons, loving and hating with their unbridled intensity. It was studying *Wuthering Heights* as well as the novels of Henry James and Ford Madox Ford that I understood the concept of the unreliable narrator. *Wuthering Heights* brilliantly confounds as a puzzle of enigmatic boxes within boxes, of rival subjectivities, thereby morphing into a modernist text, while *Jane Eyre*, its stock down on the modernist/new critical exchange, grows ever more awkwardly Victorian.

Then, on or about October 1973, all this changed. It was Adrienne Rich who flung down the gauntlet. In "Jane Eyre: The Temptations of a Motherless Woman," she sets forth a totally different heroine from Virginia Woolf's creature of self-delimiting passions. To Woolf's ironic, arguably catty pronouncement—"always to be a governess, always to be in love is a serious limitation in a world which is full, after all, of people who are neither one nor the other"—Rich offers an indignant corrective: "Always a governess and always in love? Had Virginia Woolf really read this novel?" Not only is Rich's Jane a complex alternative to Woolf's pining impassionata; Rich also challenges Woolf on the basic grounds of what the self, especially the female self, should be and do. Jane Eyre is an exemplary heroine for Adrienne Rich precisely because she asserts a forceful self she is repeatedly tempted to sacrifice but chooses at every turn, in the face of every temptation, to be true to and to strengthen. "I would suggest," writes Rich, "that Charlotte Brontë is writing a life story of a woman who is incapable of saying 'I am Heathcliff' because she feels so unalterably herself." In fealty to this self, Rich's Jane resists temptations besetting the traditional female heroine: of victimization and hysteria at Gateshead, self-hatred and self-immolation at Lowood, romantic love and surrender at Thornfield, passive suicide in her wanderings, and at Moor House marriage without love to St. John. The character we accompany on this journey, "a person determined to live, and to choose her life with dignity, integrity and pride," endows Brontë's novel, Rich goes so far as to claim, with "a special force and survival value"—i.e., it helps its female *reader* to survive. The feminist apotheosis of *Jane Eyre* and its heroine had begun.

It was completed, I would say, in the 1979 work of Sandra Gilbert and Susan Gubar, whose *Madwoman in the Attic* secured Jane Eyre's position, in one critic's words, as "a cult text of feminism." If Adrienne Rich's Jane is heroically stalwart, the Jane of Gilbert and Gubar is heroically enraged. The co-authors, whose very collaboration stands as an alternate to singular patriarchal authorship, explore what happens to women whose voices are repressed. They focus on the incarcerated, incendiary figure of Rochester's wife in the attic, Bertha Mason, and find in her an emblem of justified female madness and rage. This is the rage that consumes Jane, Charlotte, and all women whose lives have been circumscribed and voices silenced. It is the self-same rage Virginia Woolf had seen as a defect and Adrienne Rich had countered with her delineation of the heroine's constructive quest. For Gilbert and Gubar rage is the truth that will out and the route to liberation. Powerful in its influence, *Madwoman in the Attic* established *Jane Eyre* as the voice of feminist anger, exploding to protest women's oppression. Burn down the house, burn your bra, burn in righteous anger. Women, as Jane says, want action, too. *Jane Eyre* thus became the Brontë text white middle-class second-wave Feminists of the 1970s and '80s had to read and teach and write about. As a committed white middle-class feminist myself, I was happy to put it on my syllabi, my enthusiasm to teach its themes overriding my personal failed connection to the novel. I have probably taught it more times than any other work of English fiction.

In the twenty-first century *Jane Eyre* is still prominent on my syllabi, but yet another paradigm shift has occurred. In recent postcolonial and global (third-wave) feminist readings, Jane has been reassessed as both racist and insufficiently feminist. She has been cast as colonial oppressor, a white woman marginalizing the Creole Bertha as she herself has been marginalized by a patriarchal culture; she has been castigated for her ultimate failure to break out of the bourgeois domestic sphere. One of my graduate students for whom the old feminist Jane Eyre clearly has Rich's "special force and survival value" was so indignant that she wrote her masters thesis using the new historicist approach that seeks to ground a text in its times to rescue the heroine from these latter-day revisions. Jane, the student posited, is as much of a rebel as she can be and should be honored for her proto-feminist achievement.

Postcolonial critical approaches make *Jane Eyre* more controversial, but still, they keep it at the top of reading lists. The novel, as I have said, is a serviceable text. Just as its feminist strains could be mined, it lends itself to postcolonial readings in the abundance of its colonial material. Critics can engage in what Edward Said in *Culture and Imperialism* calls "contrapuntal reading"—"reading a text with an understanding of what is involved when an author shows, for instance, that a colonial sugar plantation is seen as important to the process of maintaining a particular style of life in England." Contrapuntal reading of *Jane Eyre* highlights that Rochester has enriched himself through marriage to a West Indian Creole, that Jane's inheritance, securing her financial independence, derives from an uncle's fortune made in Madeira, and that St. John Rivers joins the missionary arm of empire.

Postcolonial approaches also find textual metaphors that we had somehow overlooked before. It took Gayatri Spivak in her influential article "Three Women's Texts and a Critique of Imperialism" to show that Bertha Mason's death could be read as an act of suttee: the third-world wife sets herself on fire, acting out of hate but serving the cause of love and empire. Bertha, Spivak argues, must "play out her role, act out the transformation of her 'self' into that fictive 'Other,' set fire to the house and kill herself so that Jane Eyre can become the feminist individualist heroine of British fiction." Another critic, Deirdre David in *Rule Britannia*, gives us a chastened Rochester, now a true widower cleansed of his sultanic excesses, reunited through the purgation of Bertha with the British heroine who has redeemed him for the colonizer's mission. These readings set Jane and Bertha in opposition, Jane thriving at Bertha's expense. But there's also a postcolonial-era Jane who herself faces dangers of suttee and the seraglio, at least metaphorically. She will not join Rochester's harem. She will not marry Rivers because that, she says, would kill her (though she is willing to go to India where she feels she would certainly die).

I myself—it's part of my essential uneasiness with *Jane Eyre*—have always been disturbed by how much Jane Eyre seems to relish her metaphors of subjugation. "Do you think I can bear to have my morsel of bread snatched from my lips and my drop of living water dashed from my cup?" she asks. The dashing and the snatching have always seemed as vivid to me as Jane's resistance to these violent acts. A way to engage this aspect of the novel, different from the postcolonial, is to filter it through psychonanalysis, a useful lens through which to explore Jane's seeming masochism. One of my masters students, in an approach I would call socio-psychological with an overlay of feminism, argued in her thesis that Jane's "social masochism" serves as an effective weapon for someone powerless "to take possession of her own maginalization and use it as a narrative and social technique to ally readers with her plight."

And so it builds: the list of competing and compounding interpretations in the ongoing reimagining of *Jane Eyre*. Modernist, new critical, feminist, Marxist, new historicist, psychoanalytic, psycho-social, psycho-biographical—the approaches proliferate, the bibliographies lengthen. Then, too, the text has generated postcolonial rewritings of itself: Jean Rhys's *Wide Sargasso Sea,* in which Jamaica-born Antoinette, the novel's central character, gets sadistically renamed Bertha by her unnamed fortune-hunting new husband, the man we know to be Rochester, and her triumph is the burning of his English house; or Bharati Mukherji's *Jasmine,* one of whose Hindu incarnations is as "Jane," married to a crippled Iowa banker. One can only guess what's to come. Surely tomorrow or next month or next year, the critical ground will shift and a new Jane Eyre, multiple new Jane Eyres will emerge. . . .

I realize that while my interest in *Jane Eyre* is in large part how it has been interpreted, *Vanity Fair*, though subject, of course, as well to shifting critical trends, seems somehow more constant, and I find myself drawn back into the sheer pleasure of rereading it. Adrienne Rich calls *Jane Eyre* a "tale"—something "between realism and poetry." A tale can exist in its outline. It can be summarized and can signify. *Vanity Fair* compels my attention in a different way. While absorbing the good work critics have done on it—Lubbock, Tillotson, Said, Auerbach, and others, I want to immerse myself in its words—never too many for me—and see their writerly construction. I want to savor Thackeray's wit. I want to think about particular moments in the text: Becky throwing the dictionary out the window, Dobbin defending Georgie at school, Rawdon and Becky getting married, Becky selling her horses in Brussels in the aftermath of the Battle of Waterloo. Such moments proliferate to endow the novel for me with the "special force and survival value" Rich speaks of in connection with *Jane Eyre*. I can understand why one of my colleagues, a professor of religion, chooses to reread *Vanity Fair* every time she moves. It's a book that gives me, too, the courage to launch myself anew upon the world, the courage, if you will, to go on

And Becky Sharp goes on, even beyond the text. Thackeray himself plays cruelly with her future in a May 1848 letter to the Duke of Devonshire. Having espied her, he reports, "kicking up her petticoat in Kensington," he dwells with some relish on her visible decline:

> She has lost what little good looks she once possessed and wears fake hair and teeth (the latter give her a rather ghastly look when she smiles). . . .

P.S. The India mail just arrived announcing the utter ruin of the Union Bank of Calcutta, in which all Mrs. C's money was. Will Fate never cease to persecute that suffering saint?

No, I say. That's not in the book. You can't do that to her. If one must take liberties, I prefer those of Mira Nair's 2004 film version of *Vanity Fair*, in which Becky, now Reese Witherspoon, is last seen in India, essentially untouched by time, seated in an elephant howdah with Jos Sedley at her side. This ending, or new beginning, both honors and mocks the novel's enmeshment with Empire. And what fun to set Becky loose in India. I am sure she will soon snag a maharaja.

One of the most astute assessments of Becky Sharp I have come upon is that of Thackeray's contemporary George Henry Lewes, in his August 1848 review of *Vanity Fair* in the *Athenium*. "The character of Becky," he writes, "is among the finest creations of modern fiction. She is perfectly unlike any heartless clever woman yet drawn . . . Profound immorality is made to seem consistent with unfailing good humor."

What Lewes presents in this assessment might be seen as a formula for resilience—that quality in Becky Sharp that I have supremely prized. Becky is endowed with resilience, as was my mother. Resilience means picking yourself up no matter what difficulties or inconveniences befall you and proceeding undaunted with the business of your life. The undaunted part of this is important. Undaunted implies being undefeated. It also suggests being impervious to change. You may be older and you may have lost your singing voice. But your ebullient spirit remains intact. Perhaps your survival depends on your being a little heartless. Life hasn't really touched you. You haven't allowed that to happen. You are unchanged though ever adapting to changing circumstances.

Jane Eyre has another, more painful way of surviving. She holds onto her sense of herself, no matter what happens, no matter what blows she receives. She feels these blows acutely; she feels the morsel of bread snatched from her lips and the drop of living water dashed from her cup. But she is tenacious. She holds on.

When I was a child, I needed to believe that my mother was resilient, because she was all I had and she wanted her children to believe in her invulnerability. Surely, though, she must have suffered. When she was in that awful orphanage, when Scott Fitzgerald dropped dead in her living room, when Bow Wow tried to ruin her, when she aged and lost some of her great beauty, she, too, must have suffered and just held on. Probably she was *both* resilient and tenacious. And I am both of these things as well. I'm still plain Jane, however this disquiets me, doggedly caring for a tough little self. But I'm Becky, too. With zest for the game, whatever its vagaries. So Becky Sharp and Jane Eyre come together. Perhaps they both deserve our compassion.

Daniel Deronda

I am moved by the letter the widowed Gwendolyn Grand-court writes to Daniel Deronda after the two have met for the last time. From the opening of the novel he has served as the moral compass for George Eliot's fallible, engaging heroine: the young woman who believed she could "manage" Hen-leigh Grandcourt—one of English fiction's most chilling husbands—who married to save her family from financial ruin, though knowing of Grandcourt's illegitimate children, and has paid for her rash gamble with harrowing suffering that even her husband's death does not assuage. Gwendolyn has turned eagerly, desperately to Deronda to help her to be "better." But if all their encounters are taut with urgency, this last is uniquely so because Daniel, an orphan figure who neither reintegrates into English society like David Cop-perfield nor acts as a catalyst to change it like Jane Eyre or Becky Sharp, must tell Gwendolyn of new directions in his life she cannot share in. He comes to her to reveal his discov-ered Jewish identity and to communicate his plans both to depart from England and to marry. The reader who still har-bored hopes Gwendolyn and Daniel might come together is out of luck. That's not George Eliot's plan for them in this last, and perhaps strangest, of her great novels.

Failing at first to understand—how could Gwendolyn have imagined a life for Deronda so distant from her own needs and sphere of reference?—the character is jarred into a sense of her insignificance, "dislodged," George Eliot tells us, "from her supremacy in her own world." Hers is "a shock which went deeper than personal jealousy—something spiritual and vaguely tremendous that thrust her away, and yet quelled all anger into self-humiliation." Yet however "spiritual" this scourging of ego, Gwendolyn feels lost. The reality of Daniel's marrying Mirah, who to Gwendolyn has been only an insignificant little Jewish singer, causes her to cry out that she is forsaken. Daniel grasps her hand in agonized sympathy. They part. She sobs and collapses, then in hysterical outbursts to her mother keeps asserting, enigmatically and emphatically, she will live.

The letter Gwendolyn writes to Daniel in the wake of this shock is the last time her voice is heard in the novel. She tries to reassure the man she has relied on as a lay confessor:

> Do not think of me sorrowfully on your wedding day. I have remembered your words—that I may live to be one of the best of women, who make others glad they were born. I do not yet see how that can be, but you know better than I. If it ever comes true, it will be because you helped me. I only thought of myself, and I made you grieve. It hurts me now to think of your grief. You must not grieve any more for me. It is better—it shall be better with me because I have known you.

I think of Gwendolyn sorrowfully—but also admiringly. Her pain is palpable. She fixes on "grief," reiterating her worry about *Daniel's* grief, but it is Gwendolyn's grief I share here. Daniel, in departing, has laid out for her an ideal of altruism that he links to Victorian womanhood. To be "the best of women" is not to be a doer of great deeds or a famous actress and singer, like his own mother, but to "make others glad they were born." It's almost as if he's suggesting Gwendolyn become a kind of Dorothea Ladislaw "the effect of [whose] being on those around her," we are told at the end of *Middlemarch* in an apology for her not succeeding in an uninspired era to accomplish greater things, "was incalculably diffusive." Or that she emulate him in his exquisite sympathy for others, though in that he is a *man*, its very diffusiveness, that word used so affirmatively at the end of *Middlemarch*, makes it almost a disease of action-inhibiting awareness, at least until he assumes the "social captaincy" of his serving his new-found people. I love the simple honesty of Gwendolyn's self-doubt. "I do not see yet how that can be," she avers. And the precision of her final shift of verb tense: "it is better—it shall be better with me because I have known you," which underscores her hope, her despair, and her integrity in refusing to express false certainty.

Daniel Deronda for me is George Eliot's most fascinating novel, and it is also among the books of my reading life that I have found most affecting. The struggles of its complicated heroine say so much about the author's values and her fears—and about my own: a perceived need to rise above egotism, however ebullient, and to find—George Eliot's phrase—a "wider life," some purpose larger than the advancement of self, however challenging that quest may prove. It's also of relevance to me that the wider life her hero

Daniel Deronda finds is as a Jew. I share this heritage and also an original ignorance of it, although, unlike Daniel's, my own discovery of being Jewish has never seemed to offer me either an identity or a direction.

I confess it seems a bit pat to me how the Jewishness for Daniel settles everything. Not to be, as he had assumed, the illegitimate son of the worldly Sir Higo Mallinger, but rather, as he discovers from the mother who sought to deprive him of his heritage, the grandson of a renowned Talmudic scholar—it's all so providential, allowing our hero full entry to the culture he has already been drawn to. If Gwendolyn, by the novel's end, can hope only for a yet vaguely defined "better" future, Daniel has found his future in his reclaimed past. He has received his grandfather's trunk of Jewish documents and is further guided by the inspired union with Mordecai/Ezra, the vatic figure teaching him Hebrew, who serendipitously turns out to be Mirah's brother.

It is thus not Gwendolyn, and hardly even Mirah, but rather the spirit of Mordecai who metaphorically gets to go off into the sunset with Daniel Deronda. Eliot's final focus is on the departure plans for the East of Daniel, Mirah, and Ezra. The Mallingers have thoughtfully supplied as a wedding gift "a complete equipment for Eastern travel," though we are left to wonder what that might consist of—I see flowing head gear. Ezra, as fate would have it, expires before the trip; the novel concludes with an account of his peaceful, measured death, illuminated by the setting sun. His parting words assert his inextricable union with Daniel Deronda. "Where thou goest, Daniel, I shall go. Is it not begun? Have I not breathed my soul into you? We shall live together."

Much has been written about the two halves of *Daniel Deronda*. George Eliot insisted that she meant "everything in the novel to be related to everything else there," but, from the moment of its publication, readers and critics have responded to its bifurcation. In the "English" part of the novel, the part focused on the fashionable society of Gwendolyn, Grandcourt, and the Mallingers, we get a brilliantly rendered world of cold, shallow, or lost characters, incorporated into no unifying community, guided by no uplifting passions or vision. In the opposing warm Jewish world, on the other hand, characters care for one another and have identity and values, but, as Henry James observes in his amusing "Daniel Deronda: A Conversation," this half of the novel is "at bottom cold." A small cadre of readers has admired and praised Eliot's championing of Jews and of Judaism, but the majority has considered the Jewish half of *Daniel Deronda* a colossal failure. F. R Leavis proposes the radical cure of excising it from a novel that would then be renamed *Gwendolyn Harleth*.

My response to *Daniel Deronda* has been less to marvel that the novel could be at once so brilliant and so problematic as to try to understand the tensions in George Eliot's vision for it that might have led to the work's thematic and aesthetic dividedness. This was a key focus in my doctoral dissertation. But before I revisit some aspects of that study, I want to turn back and remember how I became interested in George Eliot in the first place and how I chose her as an author whom I would "work on" for four years of my life, an interest sufficiently consuming that my husband Donald could use it as ammunition in a marital spat. "All you know about is George Eliot!" he accused in one of our more embattled moments. "That's not true," I said. But later I thought that to know about George Eliot was to know a great deal.

Eliot is not one of the Victorian authors I loved in childhood. Does any child, I wonder, love George Eliot? Dickens, yes. The Brontës. But George Eliot?

Virginia Woolf describes *Middlemarch* as "one of the few English novels written for grown-up people." The converse of this statement is that it is not written for children. And are any of Eliot's works? Most children dislike *Silas Marner*, once standard seventh-grade reading. I don't remember liking or disliking it, though I have looked again at the ponderous opening, which distances the setting from the author's own time. "In the days when the spinning wheels hummed busily in the farmhouses . . ." begins the long dense opening paragraph, a description of the outcast social standing of itinerant linen weavers at the beginning of the nineteenth century. George Eliot's early novels are set in country towns of the 1830s or turn-of-the-century rural Midlands (the eras when, respectively, Eliot and her parents were young), but her country villages did not draw me in the way *David Copperfield* transported me to Suffolk. I was with David, I *was* David in the Rookery. In the works of George Eliot, the reader is always aligned with the author, looking back into the past through the film of her tolerant nostalgia and through the medium of her meditations. I must also have read *The Mill on the Floss* as a child since I have among my books an Illustrated Classics edition. But again, the author approaches the story through the distancing mechanism of nostalgia, and Eliot's Dodsons and Tullivers are no match for Dickens's Peggottys and "Barkis is willing." Also it may simply be too perilous to identify with Maggie, a heroine who ends up drowning because there's no place for her in her provincial world.

The drowning notwithstanding—how plausible is it to be done in by a piece of machinery in a flooded river? Maybe more so in light of Hurricanes Katrina and Sandy and the Japanese tsunami, but still . . . George Eliot is perhaps too much of a realist to appeal to children. A realist *and* a moralist, who would see as blindness the sense of potency such heroines as Jane Eyre and Becky Sharp express and rely on. Eliot's heroines who believe in their own potency are called egotists. Like Gwendolyn, or even Dorothea, they have to be chastened.

As I think of George Eliot's world view and I think of my mother's, with its emphatic faith in the individual, I'm not surprised my mother never handed me a volume of George Eliot when I asked for another book to read from her library's shelves. It's perhaps more surprising that there were no George Eliot novels on those shelves, that Eliot, in fact, is missing from the F. Scott Fitzgerald College of One curriculum. Fitzgerald was a zealous student of the nineteenth-century novel, so either he didn't think much of Eliot or he didn't think my mother would be drawn to her. I try to imagine them in their role-playing games taking on, say, Dorothea and Mr. Casaubon:

> Dorothea: "Can I help you, dear, with your great life's work, your key to all mythologies?
>
> Casaubon (blinking): I don't think so, my dear. We're not ready for that yet.

At Gwendolyn and Daniel I stop short. Henry James complains that all Daniel Deronda actually *does* is pull repeatedly at his shirt collar. Somehow the thought of enacting

George Eliot's characters doesn't seem much fun. Is it that they are too serious? Perhaps there's a way they are not dramatic. A reimagining of their scenes doesn't leave much room for improvisation. It's not that the characters lack free will; they make moral choices of great import, but they're enmeshed in webs—that image Eliot is so drawn to—webs of circumstance that are always closing in on them. Eliot is merciless towards their romantic illusions, which the circumstances of their lives crush out of them. Their salvation, if it comes, lies in disillusionment. To be stripped of illusions is the basis for more humble and accurate knowledge. It is a beginning, not an end. Henry James appreciated this theme in Eliot, and Fitzgerald appreciated it in James. By then, though, the dream had become the American dream. Fitzgerald is less hard on his dreamers than Eliot is on hers. His dreamers are the "sad young men," dreaming of golden women. The dream has its own glory for Fitzgerald.

So for one reason or another—George Eliot's exclusion from the College of One, her not being taught in high school, the fact that in college I elected the year-long course in Romantic poetry instead of the course on the novel—I had not encountered even *Middlemarch* until I got to graduate school, by which time I was more or less a grown up and, Virginia Woolf would argue, ready for this great work and for its author.

ii

MIDDLEMARCH AND I CONVERGED in Professor Alice Fredman's seminar on the nineteenth-century novel.

Alice, who later became my dissertation advisor, was one of three tenured women at that time, the late '60s, in the Columbia English department. The other two were Carolyn Heilbrun, who seemed every bit as intimidating as Alice, and Elizabeth Donno, a Renaissance scholar who I think wasn't intimidating at all, but I never took a course from her or heard much about her.

But for Alice Fredman I might never have finished graduate school. She was tough-talking and known for smoking thin cigars, but she was someone who fought for the students she took under her wing. She had been a brilliant undergraduate at Swarthmore, and at Columbia she wrote a prize-winning dissertation on Diderot and Sterne under the tutelage of Marjorie Hope Nicholson, the first woman chairperson of the Columbia English Department. Alice's dissertation became her first book, a second small book followed on Trollope for the Columbia Modern Writers series, but here the list ends. Her long-awaited magnum opus, a critical biography of Mary Shelley, remained always a work in progress. I think Alice's teaching combined with her family life to absorb her. At the end of the nineteenth-century-novel seminar, she invited our whole class to a picnic at her house in Kings Point, Long Island, where we met Irwin "Freddy" Fredman her husband, who had retired from a modest career in advertising to write arcane books on Long Island history, her two pleasant teenaged daughters, and Alice's widowed mother who lived with the family. Going to that picnic was like discovering the clerk Wemmick's domestic nest in *Great Expectations*, complete with an "Aged P," after encountering him in the harsh public world of Mr. Jaggers's law office. I think George Eliot would have rendered

Alice sympathetically if she had been a character in one of the novels—perhaps as someone who strove for greatness but settled in many ways for "the common yearning of womanhood." At least, though, Alice got to be a wonderful professor. When she died in 1993 of a heart attack at, alas, only sixty-eight, her *New York Times* obituary stressed how "she became a mentor to many Columbia students and was known for her generosity to them and to her colleagues." I also learned that "twice offered teaching awards, she refused them, saying they would be more helpful and encouraging to younger colleagues." Of this egoless, self-subsuming gesture George Eliot would certainly have approved.

In the nineteenth-century-novel seminar Alice drove us hard, expecting us to read two major novels each week. This was, of course, completely unrealistic. How can one, for example, read *Dombey and Son* and *Bleak House* in one week? I can't remember now what I actually managed to read, but I did tackle *Middlemarch*, falling completely under the spell of its breadth and intricacy, its melancholy and its moments of great tenderness, the author's wise and vast understanding of human nature, and her sardonic wit, as uncompromising as her sympathies are broad.

Daniel Deronda followed, even more mesmerizing in its wise, cynical understanding of society and human nature. I remember being struck by the way Grandcourt's entry into the novel echoes the famous opening of *Pride and Prejudice*: "It is a truth universally acknowledged that a single man in possession of a good fortune must be in need of a wife." Austen's irony is unsurpassed. Yet Bingley, the man in possession of the fortune at hand, proves the socially *and* morally appropriate husband for Jane Bennet, and his even richer and more aristocratic friend Darcy the supremely right husband for Elizabeth. In Grandcourt, the social and the moral part company. Coming on the scene at the archery meet at Arrowwood, Sir Hugo's heir to the baronetcy is described as "good looking, of sound constitution, virtuous, or at least reformed," an irony then extended as the perspective of Gwendolyn's worldly cleric uncle, the Reverend Gascoigne:

> He held it futile, even if it had been becoming, to show any curiosity as to the past of a young man whose birth, wealth, and consequent leisure made many habits venial which under other circumstances would have been inexcusable. Whatever Grandcourt had done, he had not ruined himself; and it is well known that in gambling, for example, whether of the business or holiday sort, a man who has the strength of character to leave off when he has only ruined others, is a reformed character.

The effect on me of reading such a passage was to feel the strengthening of my own moral anchor and sound judgment. George Eliot led me to understand the intricate social maneuvers of her provincial world, and somehow that put me on the author's plane of perspicacity. Characters in the novel may be willfully or naively obtuse about Grandcourt, but George Eliot is wise to him, and so am I, her reader. I join the author in penetrating the ways of the world and also share, through my discernment, in the linguistic tools at her command—her irony, her apt metaphors, her well-controlled sentences. If Eliot fails to find interesting gestures for Daniel, who can pull only at his shirt collar, she creates wonderful ones for Gwendolyn and Grandcourt: Gwendolyn beating the rhododendron bushes and dropping her riding whip to ward off Grandcourt's proposal; Grandcourt teasing his dog to arouse its jealousy.

When it came time to enlist a faculty member to direct my dissertation, I turned to Alice Fredman. She was not Columbia's foremost nineteenth-century novel scholar—that was Steven Marcus, the disciple of Lionel Trilling, who had recently published a well-received book on early Dickens, *From Pickwick to Dombey*, which combined close textual analysis with Freudian insights, and who would later write on Victorian pornography in *The Other Victorians*. But my awe of him was too great to imagine myself as his student. I had sat through two years of his lectures on Victorian literature, which after one week in a regular classroom had been shifted to an amphitheatre in the Law School to accommodate his following. At the end of the first year we were only halfway through the syllabus, so Marcus said he would assume the privilege of European lecturers and continue the course the next year. I still have his notes and use them in my teaching. But despite my sense of receiving, almost like Leda from the swan, his brilliant insights and interpretations, Steven Marcus still seemed a god and I a lowly mortal. Gender as well as rank entered into my sense of the gap between us, for Columbia in those years right before second-wave feminism was not an encouraging environment for women. When female students applied to be preceptors—graduate students who taught freshman English—it was rumored that we were chosen on the basis of our legs. I'm not sure that's true, but the culture was one of male luminaries and their male acolytes. Of the four young women in our first-year proseminar in the modernist period—my major period through my PhD orals—I was the only one who finished

the degree. Two dropped out at the end of the first year—
one choosing the alternative of a career in music and the
other drifting to London where she got a low-paying job in
publishing. Today the musician is a well-known conductor
and the woman who went to London a successful poet,
courted by academic institutions. Probably they made
good decisions. The fourth woman, whom I've lost track of,
completed the M.A., then married her boyfriend and took a
teaching job in a private day school in New Jersey.

I alone persisted, as much from doggedness and lack of
interest in other possibilities as from any sense of talent or
calling. To myself I was the opposite of a George Eliot heroine. Rather than needing my ego to be scourged, I saw it as
needing to be bolstered. As I write, I can hear my friends
and children laughing at this notion. Perhaps I was already
more strong-willed and strong-minded than the person I
remember being. It's hard to reconstruct the reality of one's
earlier self. Nonetheless, I wonder how I would have fared
without Alice Fredman, the tough-talking, cigar-smoking
New Yorker with her family tucked away on Long Island,
whom I knew I could turn to and count on. She sagely
steered me through Columbia politics, guided the dissertation, and later wrote generous references to help me get a
job. Or perhaps it was the most help of all that I knew she
liked me. She and Freddy even came to my wedding. I have
a wedding-album photo of her dressed in a no-nonsense
checked spring suit and smoking, as best I can make out,
not a thin cigar but a cigarette that is held out in one hand.
Freddy is in the background of the photo, standing a bit
diffidently behind her.

iii

THE FOUR YEARS I spent researching and writing about George Eliot coincided for me with the early years of marriage. In a sense this is a random link, but given everything that happened, it's one that became filled with meaning.

In the fall of 1970, I was twenty-eight years old. I had been married for a year and a half to Donald Fairey, given birth to my first child, Emily, passed my PhD oral examinations, as it turned out, with distinction, and, despite short legs inherited from my father, been now teaching for two years as a Columbia preceptor. It was a time of great turmoil for the university and the nation, as we protested the Vietnam War, grieved the assassinations of Robert Kennedy and Martin Luther King, and supported the SDS university strikes and shut downs. And yet it was a settled and harmonious time for me personally. Donald and I were tenants on the top floor of a brownstone in Brooklyn Heights, owned by one of my Bryn Mawr classmates, who had married an architect. My classmate and her husband lived on the first two floors, and another couple rented the garden apartment. Susan Suzman, the garden-level neighbor, and I gave birth to our daughters within weeks of one another. That meant all three families were raising small children, and we fell into easy semi-communal living. Susan and I traded off babysitting with her taking care of Emily the two mornings a week I went to teach. One day, up at school, having scheduled an appointment with Alice Fredman to discuss a thesis topic, I decided, only as I walked across the campus to her office, that I would propose working on

George Eliot. I didn't yet have a specific focus other than a general interest in Eliot's heroines. I didn't know then, because feminist criticism was not yet a formulated literary approach, that feminist critics would be angry with George Eliot for not giving these heroines their author's own options and that other feminists would defend her for her compassionate sense of fellowship, not just with all women, "even those still in 'bondage,'" but "with men as well" (See Zelda Austen—surely a renaming—"Why Feminist Critics Are Angry with George Eliot," 1976.) Eliot simply seemed an author whose novels gave me the satisfactions I've described and about whom I thought I might be able to write a few hundred pages. It wasn't yet apparent—because I had not yet had to suffer in ways that make you doubt your own choices—she had anything acutely personal to say to me.

I look back on this period, our two years in the Brooklyn Heights brownstone, with a great swell of nostalgia for a happy time. Two decades later I heard the critic John Bayley discuss a passage in *Anna Karenina* in which Vronsky sees a street sign and knows he will go home and describe it to Anna. "And that," said Bayley, "is ordinary happiness." Yes, I thought. I recognized what he was talking about. We had had it in Brooklyn—ordinary happiness—something I think I valued all the more because I hadn't really known it growing up in Hollywood. Donald and I shopped together for groceries and cooked meals out of Craig Claiborne and Julia Child. Having a baby enriched our life together, and living in the building provided community. I remember everyone, especially the Suzmans and us, as always laughing. I liked going to work, and I liked coming home.

Yet a more soberly nuanced narrative also asserts itself, one less tinged by nostalgia or that gathers pace and clarity as nostalgia subsides. I need only imagine how George Eliot would have probed and even pitied us as characters in her fiction. Poor Wendy, poor Donald, she would have begun her paragraph of sympathetic but relentless analysis, piercing into the shadows and the secrets of our idyll. I say that I was happy to be married, but it's also true that I married impulsively, not sure what I was fleeing or seeking, though eager for some ill-defined transfiguration. A brief romantic entanglement with a woman classmate in Alice Fredman's seminar, sexual though not quite consummated, had frightened me. Donald was one of several men I was going out with at the time of this involvement. He was amiable, kind, and emotionally undemanding. I appreciated that he didn't pressure me, for similar to Gwendolyn, I recoiled from "being made love to" and was often on the run from male ardor and insistence. Donald fell in gracefully with my friends, my mother liked him though he wasn't rich or on much of a career path in his job as assistant foreign student advisor at Columbia, and I sort of slipped into loving him. At Bryn Mawr, we had quoted our founder, M. Carey Thomas, "Only our failures *marry*." What she really had said, I learned only years later, was that "our failures *only* marry." This may seem a consequential corrective, but in a practical sense it hardly mattered. Whatever her words, most of my classmates got married—the pull of conventional aspirations trumping a spinster's aphorism. Soon Donald and I were engaged—I think that was my idea (so much for my vaunted immunity to the charms of the marriage-plot in fiction). Then it all seemed to work out well—a nice wedding, the brownstone, the baby, the circles of colleagues and friends. In many ways we suited one another, though sometimes, especially if Donald were late coming home, I'd have a flash of fear that I hardly knew him.

What followed was harder. In February 1971, almost as a joke to imagine escaping winter, I signed up for an interview with a recruiter from the University of Hawaii's main Manoa, Oahu campus. The University of Hawaii was seeking ABD—all but dissertation—instructors to teach for a three-year stint. To my surprise I was offered a position, and without much worry or even much thought, we opted for adventure. Donald quit his job; we sold our furniture, most of which came from my mother, shipped our books and wedding china with the dubiously reputable Seven Santini Brothers, and flew off with one-year-old Emily to the middle of the Pacific Ocean. I remember looking down from the plane at a small island, my new home, dwarfed in the vast expanse of glittering blue water, and wondering if I hadn't made a terrible mistake.

In the three ensuing years in Hawaii, I gave birth to our son, Sean; my husband left me for another woman four months after the baby was born and three months later came back; my mother visited at least twice a year, expressing her wonderment each time she stepped off the plane that anyone could work in such a tropical paradise. And no matter what else was happening, I taught my three courses a term, listened a lot to Toscanini's recordings of Brahms symphonies, and, sitting at a table on the screened porch, or lanai, of my rented suburban house and looking out onto a garden of plumeria blossoms and banana trees, I wrote my dissertation on George Eliot. It was one of the hardest times of my life but also, oddly, one of the most productive.

The thesis I developed, which today would probably fall under the rubric of cultural studies, was to trace a recurrent plot in Eliot's fiction in the context of the author's outlook and values. Always attuned to narrative patterns and structure, I saw the novels repeatedly telling the story of a woman caught in personal distress and isolated from the community around her. Her success or failure to find release from her crisis in a reunification with the surrounding world seemed to me to form the central dramatic action in books ranging from George Eliot's first published work of fiction, *Scenes of Clerical Life,* to her last, *Daniel Deronda.* When the heroine succeeds, it is with the help of a sympathetic man, often a religious leader, to whom she confesses her distress and who in turn has connections with the community. In the later novels the notion of community becomes more problematic; still, the plot is never resolved as a personal love story. The relationship of heroine and confessor may be erotically charged, but it does not lead to marriage. Usually the heroine is unhappily married already. Though George Eliot obligingly kills off a number of inconvenient husbands, from Dempster in the early "Janet's Repentance" to Tito in *Romola* to Casaubon and Grandcourt in the later works, this is not to free the heroines for further romance so much as it is to allow them some greater scope for egoless altruistic activity. Granted Dorothea marries Will Ladislaw and Gwendolyn's nice cousin Rex Gasgoigne is still hovering in the background at the end of *Daniel Deronda.* But if George Eliot advised her friend Barbara Bodichon to be "greatly dissatisfied with the ending of *Middlemarch,*"

I presume this is because marrying Will is seen by George Eliot as Dorothea's lot when greatness eludes her. As for Gwendolyn, whose fate is crueler still—she sees her insignificance but doesn't yet know how she may change this—her only deep bond at the end of *Daniel Deronda* is to her mother, though in this I believe George Eliot wants us to see the seed of her redemption. Scourged by suffering, the heroine is ready to lead that "wider" less self-absorbed life. George Eliot confided her intention to have her be "saved," "but as if by fire."

During the crisis in my marriage, it did not escape me that my dissertation's focus on isolated unhappy wives had become rather gruesomely autobiographical. In Hawaii, where I, far more than Donald, felt far from our sustaining New York community, the marriage grew strained. We lived in Kailua, Oahu, on the windward side—the opposite side from Honolulu—of the steep-cliffed volcanic Na Pali range. Those were the cliffs from which the legendary King Kamehameha used to hurl his enemies. I would think about that sometimes on the drive home from work when, emerging in my little blue Toyota from the high tunnel that cut through the mountain, I took in the bright stretch of ocean below. Hawaii was interesting in so many ways—in its geography, geology, history, social culture, racial mix, arts, and politics. I lived there in the final years of the Vietnam War, when soldiers returned to Hawaii for R and R and dignitaries were always passing through. I wasn't blind to all this, but in ways I now regret, I resisted fully being there. Sometimes I would look up at the mountains, so green and always cloud-covered—the same ones I had to drive through—and mutter to myself,

"These mountains are *igneous*." I took a childish relief in the harsh sound of the geologically correct word. On the more positive side, I made a few new friends, mostly other haoles (white people from the mainland), whom I liked spending time with, and I played a lot of tennis at the Kailua Racket Club, an informal and friendly club near my house. But Hawaii always remained *unheimlich*—not my landscape, not my true home. Perhaps it was too far from the world of English novels. Though it embarrasses me now to confess it, I couldn't stretch.

Donald, meanwhile, was blending in far better than I. He had been hired by the American Federation of Teachers, engaged then in an intensive campaign to be the bargaining agent for the University of Hawaii faculty. This meant his working long hours, often until nine or ten or even later at night, while I stayed home with the children, but even on the evenings he was with us, he and I hardly interacted. He drank a lot, in a quiet way, then would stagger off to bed, leaving me to my own unhappiness. (George Eliot would here give his point of view as well as mine—why always "poor Wendy," why not also "poor Donald?" Surely he felt unhappy, too.) Then came his affair with the administrative assistant from his office, his leaving me, a terrible blow, to move in with her (I'm afraid we're back to "poor Wendy"), and after what for me were three most difficult months, his desire to return. The short version of this story is that I let him come back—I didn't have the fortitude not to. Emily and Sean needed a father, I told myself, and I guess I still clung to hope of something from him, too, for myself. The marriage lasted another thirteen years, but I never felt again, as I had before, happy whenever he walked through the door. I realize, though, in saying this, I don't know how *he* felt in that doorway. George Eliot speaks in *Middlemarch* of our being "well wadded with stupidity," her metaphor for our obtuseness to others' subjectivity.

I don't, though, want to make too much of the dreary confluence of the themes of my dissertation and my life circumstances. That might suggest writing the thesis was depressing, and it wasn't at all. George Eliot is not an especially cheerful author. But reading the novels and six volumes of her letters that, among other things, seem to detail every headache and toothache and other ache she and George Henry Lewes ever had, reading as well the biographies, literary criticism, and books about Victorian England, I had a steady and steadying activity that became a kind of anchor. To build my argument, day by day, chapter by chapter, to strive to understand Eliot's novelistic universe and feel such understanding was possible, I had this to turn to, no matter what else was happening in my life. I'm not claiming the outcome was in any way extraordinary. The dissertation had an uninspired title, *The Relationship of Heroine, Confessor and Community in the Novels of George Eliot*. If I were to be the judge of it now, I would call it good but hardly great. Still, it represents my life's most focused and sustained attempt to make sense of another's sensibility. I was committed to figuring something out, a puzzle, a paradox, as I set out to analyze what the recurrent heroine-confessor-community plot in Eliot's novels reflects of the author's lifelong struggle to balance a determined idealism about the possibilities of human interaction and community with an unsparing penetration of human folly and weakness.

GEORGE Eliot wanted to improve the society around her with an earnestness it's easy to pigeonhole as Victorian—as if we had no earnestness ourselves. She had lost her faith in God at twenty-two, a crisis of belief that developed through her reading and her friendships. An attendant crisis ensued with her father when she refused to go to church with him. Ultimately she gave in, willing to accompany him on Sundays despite her freethinking, and in time she softened about religion to the extent that she came to see it as a force for moral and social good. In her mature years she loved to sit in churches because she felt they engendered "emotions of fellowship" as people came together to aspire to a higher plane. To promote such emotions was her aim as a writer. As she confessed to an admirer of her books at the time of the publication of *Middlemarch*:

> The inspiring principle which alone gives me courage to write, is that of so presenting our human life as to help my readers in getting a clearer conception and a more active admiration of those vital elements which bind men together and give a higher worthiness to their existence.

George Eliot especially believed people could touch one another individually, as, for example, when Dorothea's goodness moves egotistical Rosamond Vincy to one unselfish moment or when Daniel acts as a benevolent influence on Gwendolyn. The selfish or narcissistic characters are susceptible in these encounters to expanding their moral sympathies. They glimpse "those vital elements which bind men together" and take their first steps beyond private egotism and suffering. Eliot believed one can overcome the insistency of a desire by considering whether its fulfillment means a deprivation for another person, or grasp from others' suffering that one's own share of trouble is "not excessive." Thus, to understand one's links to others becomes a guide for proper conduct. "Community of interest is the root of justice; community of suffering, the root of pity; community of joy, the root of love," she writes in "Leaves for a Notebook."

But the ideal of altruistic self-restrained participation in community is only half the vision. George Eliot's intention to affirm the best influence of religion and society in elevating human nature persists throughout her fiction. But such idealism is increasingly in conflict with a more pessimistic view of her own day and age. Mid-Victorian society appalls George Eliot because of its essential immorality, and numerous of her letters from the 1860s and '70s express her dismay. Instead of the old "plain living and high thinking," there flourishes a prosperity that strikes her as vulgar, impersonal, and frantic. People lose proper values in "more and more eager scrambling after wealth and show." England is a restless society "of 'eels in a jar,' where each is trying to get his head above the other." The results of material progress strain her faith in moral progress. How can one believe in progress when the world is so clearly getting worse?

Daniel Deronda represented the climax of my thesis, for I saw it as the novel in which George Eliot's idealism and pessimism finally splinter. *Middlemarch*'s integration of her melancholy perception of a modern world with her hopes for human nature and a better future meant the severe constriction of idealism. Such muted optimism then worried her—again I quote from her letters—"lest the impression which [the novel] should make ...for the good of those who read should turn to naught." She was particularly disturbed when *The Spectator* labeled her a "melancholy" author. In *Daniel Deronda*, motivated in part by the intention to show human life as its most inspiring, George Eliot develops the idealized milieu of Judaism, in which man's "higher plane of thought and feeling"—a phrase from the letters—flourishes unchecked by any realistic negative circumstances, with elements of myth, fantasy, and the occult, as critics have noted, coming in to further the hero's quest. But at the same time that Deronda finds his providential identity, Gwendolyn, in her part of the story, is granted less relief from the oppressive conditions of environment (it's interesting that *Daniel Deronda* is George Eliot's only novel with a contemporary setting) than is any previous George Eliot heroine. I know the author wants Deronda's departure to be a therapeutic scourging of Gwendolyn's ego. But it does seem cruel that he gets to have a "social captaincy,"—such a cleverly equivocal phrase finessing the question of *religious* faith—while she is left with more conscience but little more direction or larger life than when he first met her. *He* gets to discover his proper community, and *she* . . . well, one wonders what will become of her. "Poor Gwendolyn," as Eliot so often refers to her, humbled and stripped of her illusions, is still far from any meaningful self-realization. Yes, she has been saved from real evil, from hatred and self-delusion. Of course, that's important. But what can she go on to do? Lead a less glittering life. Be kind to her mother and sisters? Engage in modest charitable activity? Try a second marriage, maybe to Rex? The options as I have played with them seem plausible but insufficient. Ultimately I do not know how Gwendolyn might become "the best of women, such as make others glad they were born"—or even if that is the destiny one should hope for her.

iv

THE JUDAISM, FROM WHICH Gwendolyn is excluded, might, strangely, have become part of my own self-realization. It turns out that it hasn't, but I believe I understand its appeals as a subject and cause for George Eliot. First of all, it's in keeping with her stress on "those vital elements which bind men together" to be eager to combat prevalent anti-Semitism. As G. H. Lewes writes to Blackwood, "Just as she had formerly contrived to make one love Methodists [see *Adam Bede*], there was no reason why she should not conquer the prejudice against Jews." Then Eliot's friendship with Emmanuel Deutsch in the 1870s familiarized her with the Zionist cause, and the Jewish longing for a homeland attracted her because it grounds our better impulses in a specific community. Eliot believed, as she explains in her tract on Judaism, "The Modern Hep! Hep! Hep!"—a title referring to the modern world's aimless bustle, that "a common humanity is not yet enough to feed the rich blood of various activity which makes a complete man." We have seen how Dorothea and the young Deronda flounder with only a sense of common humanity. They lack "that noble partiality which is man's best strength, the closer fellowship that makes sympathy practical." The Jews, George Eliot feels, offer this. She marvels in "The Modern Hep! Hep! Hep!" that although they are "expatriated, denationalized, used for centuries to live among antipathetic populations," yet somehow they cherish a sense of corporate existence "unique in its intensity," "that sense of belonging which is the root of human virtue both public and private." The fact that the Jews retain this sense even as a scattered people makes their existence relevant to the modern dilemma. Some may reject their heritage. We see Mirah's father, Lapidoth, who has stuck to mocking Jewish custom and Daniel's mother, the Princess, whose assimilation has led her only to lonely desperation. But if these parents have spurned the "kinship of Israel," the children can reclaim it. Twenty years before Hertzl, George Eliot is in tune with the first stirrings of the Zionist movement, making her prophet Mordecai urge: "Revive the organic center: let the unity of Israel which has made the growth of its religion be an outward reality . . . Let the torch of visible community be lit."

Judaism also conforms to the novelist's ideals in that she sees its sense of community, morality, and religion to be one. Speaking of Israel Mordecai asks: "Where else is there a nation of whom it may truly be said that their religion and law and moral life mingled as the stream of blood in the heart and made it one growth?" And the virtuous Jewish characters all evince such self-integration. Mirah's religion is said to be "of one fibre with her affections and had never presented itself to her as a set of propositions." Mordecai has "a mind consciously, energetically moving with the larger march of human destinies, but not the less full of conscience and tender heart for the footsteps that tread near." And even the ordinary Ezra Cohen becomes extraordinary when, as he enters his home after a day of successful moneymaking, religious custom blends with family affection:

> The two children went up to him and clasped his knees:
> then he laid his hands on each in turn and uttered his
> Hebrew benediction; whereupon his wife who had lately
> taken baby from the cradle brought it up to her husband
> and held it under his outstretched hands to be blessed in
> its sleep. For the moment Daniel Deronda thought that
> this pawnbroker proud of his vocation was not utterly
> prosaic.

When worship blends so thoroughly with domestic virtue, and faith with culture, religion need not be feared as mere theology or sect. George Eliot depicts Judaism as a complete and coherent way of life, a faith expressing itself in terms of custom and duty, the valuation of kinship and community, reverence for the past and future. And Daniel Deronda, in a unique resolution in Victorian fiction of the condition of being orphaned (one that also prefigures the artist figure's later self-exile from mundane bourgeois society in the interests of a higher calling), is able to subscribe to it with his whole soul.

But if I grasp how much Judaism comes to mean to George Eliot, I am also struck by how little it has ever come to mean to me. For, as I have said, I, too, like Daniel Deronda, discovered, after believing otherwise, that I was of Jewish origin.

My mother resembled Daniel Deronda both in denying her Jewish heritage and in having ultimately to reveal it to her children. I learned of my mother's early years in an orphanage as well as of her relationship with Scott Fitzgerald only when I was a teenager and she published the first of her books, *Beloved Infidel* (1957), the title that of a poem Fitzgerald had written for her. The movie version, starring Gregory Peck as Fitzgerald and Deborah Kerr as my mother, appeared two years later. Neither the book nor the movie made any mention of my mother's five older siblings or of the fact of her family's being Jewish. She had to tell Robert and me about these siblings and about the Jewishness on a 1959 trip to England because one of her brothers, upset at the family's erasure from her history, revealed the "*real* Sheilah Graham story" to a London tabloid. I was just short of seventeen, about to begin my senior year at Rosemary Hall, where on a daily basis I chanted the responses in the Book of Common Prayer and sang the words of Episcopal belief of the anthems and the hymns. Despite my being an atheist, I was steeped in Christian liturgy, my experience at Rosemary building on Sunday school attendance at All Saints Episcopal Church in Beverly Hills. I had never set foot in a synagogue. In fact, back in Beverly Hills Hawthorne Elementary I had been one of the very few children left in school on Jewish holidays!

When my mother explained about her family in our room at the Dorchester Hotel, I turned to face the mirror behind me and stared hard at my reflection for some sign of difference. As best I could tell, I looked the same as a moment before. "You should have told us," I said. When I got back to school for my senior year, I went around letting people know that I was now "half-Jewish," though some, like my friend Pam, disliked my news. My mother begged me to show discretion (they're going to know this has nothing to do with Trevor Westbrook, she said), but I disregarded her plea. It seemed important to be truthful. I also found my new hybridity enhancing.

My mother's explanation for seeking to escape her Jewishness was similar to the explanation given by the Princess to Daniel. My mother said she had wanted to give us every access and advantage, and being Jewish wasn't one of these. I think for her being Jewish meant, above all, the deprivations of her childhood in the East End of London. My mother's father, Louis, an immigrant tailor to England from the Ukraine, had died on a trip to Berlin when she was an infant, leaving his family quite destitute. She had visited his grave in the 1930s and told us about the German children who came around throwing stones and shouting "Jüden, Jüden." After the father's death, my non-English speaking grandmother, Rebecca, who could get work only cleaning public lavatories, placed her youngest two children in the Jewish orphanage, where my mother's golden hair was shaved to the scalp. We came to know the story. Six years in the orphanage, where Lily Shiel became head girl of "the school," captained the cricket team, and won the Hebrew prize. Her first job as a skivvy in Brighton cleaning a five-story house. Home again to take care of her mother, dying of cancer. An older brother beating her. Escape to her own little flat in the West End. A Pygmalion early marriage. The creation of Sheilah Graham. "Passing,"—blond and blue-eyed (a Cossack twixt the sheets, she surmised)—in the worlds, successively, of the London theatre and English high society, New York journalism, and Hollywood movie making. "I don't want to be in a ghetto," she always said, adding, if challenged, that "all religions are hocus-pocus, mumbo-jumbo." Why should she be bound by one?

My mother told Scott Fitzgerald the truth about herself—not just about the poverty and the orphanage but also her Jewishness. But it's as much a part of the story that Fitzgerald abused her trust as that he had won it. As she put

it in her book *College of One*, during his great drinking binge
of 1939, he screamed "all the secrets of my humble beginnings" to the nurse talking care of him. That same day, my
mother and Fitzgerald grappled over his gun, and she made
the pronouncement of which I think she was rather proud.
"Take it and shoot yourself, you son of a bitch. I didn't
pull myself out of the gutter to waste my life on a drunk
like you." What Fitzgerald had screamed to the nurse, my
mother eventually told me, though she never brought herself to write it in any of her books, was that she was a Jew.

I am pleased that increasingly over the years of her old age
my mother seemed more at peace with her Jewish heritage.
She reestablished contact with her two older sisters, both of
whom lived in Brighton, and was close to them until they
died. She was enormously enthusiastic about Israel, which
she first visited in the 1970s. In London she took me to see
where she had lived in the then still-Jewish neighborhood of
Stepney Green, and together we peered into the windows of
a dismal basement flat. Later in New York we went down to
the Lower East Side one time to eat blintzes, for my mother
truly loved Jewish food. In her eighties she was invited to a
seder though I don't think her hosts knew she was Jewish. I
saw her when she returned from it and—for nothing to do
with the food—she was indignant. "They got the prayers
all wrong," she said. Then with a swell of pride in her good
memory, she proceeded to recite them correctly.

But this is my mother's Jewish heritage, not mine. She
knew those Hebrew prayers; I knew the Nicene Creed. I have
often thought that my mother succeeded in what she set out
to do—in alienating my brother and me from our Jewish
heritage. Not that I can put it all on her. I don't know if my

brother feels this, but I see myself as complicit in remaining an outsider to Judaism. A couple of times I wandered into temples and felt both uneasy with the strange liturgy and a little bored, as always, with religious ritual. I'm just too secular, I told myself, and continued my occasional attendance at Episcopal Christmas and Easter services.

But isn't it possible to imagine another path? I might, like Daniel, have studied Hebrew. I might have moved to Israel. (Wouldn't *that* have been a fine form of daughterly rebellion?) Or, a less extreme option, I might simply have married a Jew. Living in New York in my twenties, I knew and dated many Jewish men. Donald Fairey, however, was lapsed Church of England. Emily, our daughter, sang in the children's choir of the Cathedral of St. John the Divine. Our children's own mates, with whom they have had *their* children, are non-Jews. The genes are thinning out.

Nonetheless, when in 1989, precisely thirty years after learning that my mother was Jewish, I learned right after her death, that she had lied to me about the identity of my father and that my biological father was, in fact, the British philosopher A. J. Ayer, one of my very first thoughts, given that Ayer had a Jewish mother, was that I seemed to be becoming more Jewish. This pleased me, if only for the irony. I also remembered Freddie's well-known atheism. Perhaps the psychological seeds of that intellectual position lay in his experience as a Jew at Eton, just as my own atheism emerged as a form of defiance at Rosemary Hall. Not having had him in my life as my father, I search for parallels in our experience.

I know I have taken pleasure in evading what George Eliot calls "partiality"—commitment to a specific culture and people. Much of my life has been lived in predominantly Jewish milieus, Hollywood and New York, yet I feel a cultural distance between myself and my Jewish friends. But if I'm not Jewish, I'm not non-Jewish either. Despite the Sunday school, I was never baptized nor confirmed, and I would never call myself Episcopalian, though I still enjoy the singing and chanting when I go to church. I still don't pray, though increasingly my determination seems arrogant—a bit like the callow defiance of Stephan Daedalus in *A Portrait of the Artist as a Young Man*—a refusal to bend. I do believe, though, it's important to continue affirming the secular, especially in this age of religious zealotry.

George Eliot came to appreciate the social and moral functions of religion; she is hard on her characters when they turn from their roots. For the rejection of her Jewish heritage Daniel Deronda's mother is emotionally blighted and called to a reckoning.

But George Eliot herself—in a good instance of what feminist critics see as her denying her female characters her own options—never wavered in her essential loss of religious belief. A pronouncement in one of her letters has always appealed to me. As she writes in 1860 to Barbara Bodichon:

> I have faith in the working out of higher possibilities than the Catholic or any other church has presented, and those who have strength to wait and endure, are bound to accept no formula which their whole souls—their intellect as well as their emotions—do not embrace with entire reverence. The highest "calling and election" is to *do without opium* and live through all our pain with conscious clear-eyed endurance.

The last sentence in particular I find rousing. "The highest 'calling and election' is to *do without opium* and live through all our pain with conscious clear-eyed endurance." I often quote this, both to students and to friends or simply intone it to myself. The directive seems both stoic and existential.

V
———

I COME BACK TO the important point of George Eliot's being a moralist. As such she is enshrined in F. R. Leavis's *The Great Tradition*, the work I have alluded to several times that locates the strength of the English novel in its *moral* preoccupation—an urgent and serious interest in how we live. Leavis, as I've said, gives short shift to the Brontës, while Eliot is one of three central figures in his pantheon, the other two being Conrad and James. I don't agree with Leavis about throwing out the whole Jewish half of *Daniel Deronda*. For me, that would leave a less interesting work. But when he assesses George Eliot as "a peculiarly fortifying . . . author, and a suggestive one" for our times, I am led to think of all the ways, both specific and diffuse, that this nineteenth-century novelist has helped to shape my twentieth- and twenty-first-century life.

George Eliot's novels, as I have tried to show, emphasize the importance of roots and of community. "Pity that Offendene was not the home of Miss Harleth's childhood, or endeared to her by family memories!" she begins Chapter 3 of *Daniel Deronda*. "A human life, I think, should be well-rooted in some spot of a native land, where it may get the love of tender kinship for the face of the earth . . . ."

The passage is a long one, stressing the benefit to the soul of attachment even to one's first dogs. I actually had beloved early dogs, I had a cherished home, my childhood home in Beverly Hills. And if my mother declared, following the example of Napoleon, "I am my own ancestor," she was mine, and our home and family milieu provided my first community.

In this home I learned many lessons—how to enter the world, how to be brave, how to make something of myself, how to be both irreverent and honorable, how to have fun, even how to be connected to other people. But spending four years working on the novels of George Eliot shifted my earlier ambitions, which like Gwendolyn's were only in the vaguest kind of way to be "great" while worrying that I was really insufficient. George Eliot teaches the lesson of overcoming excessive ego, of putting community before the self, of making a contribution, of making others glad they were born, if that's not carrying it too far. I'm not saying I consciously assented to this lesson—rather, I sought intellectually to deconstruct it. But I also see that it's a powerful—and beneficial—lesson I am pleased to have at least in part absorbed.

I feel fortunate that I have had the opportunity to be a teacher. The profession is one in which I've been able to develop an ideal of service—subsuming ego, harnessing my Gwendolyn Harleth-like delight in self display to serve literature and, I hope, most of all, to serve the students. It's true that the years at the University of Hawaii were compartmentalized, as I sat on my lanai, only cursorily involved with Hawaiian culture, writing about George Eliot day after day. Yet it was also in Hawaii, now over forty years ago, that I became a full-fledged university teacher, first sharing with students my beloved nineteenth-century novels in the general education courses I was assigned to teach. Of course, the curriculum was Western—no one thought to question this, though students of Japanese, Chinese, Philippine, and Hawaiian origin filled the classroom. One day discussing the setting and metaphor of bad weather in *Wuthering Heights*, I did have a sudden awareness of my students' attire—sleeveless cutoff shirts and shorts. How many of you have ever seen snow? I asked, and we had a good open discussion about cultural differences before returning more strictly to the syllabus.

Teaching in a college setting can give a sense of belonging to what, as I have mentioned, Raymond Williams calls a "knowable community." After my time in Hawaii, I have entered communities at Bowdoin College in Maine, Barnard College in New York, and Hollins College in Virginia. In each of these I participated, richly, but I also moved on, still restless, not quite rooted—still, if it's not too fanciful a conceit, living through my years of wandering in the wilderness. It is at Brooklyn College, where I have now taught for twenty-nine years, that I have at last truly settled in a community and been, in turn, deeply sustained by it. Brooklyn College is an urban and public institution. Its students are the kind of students my mother might have been if she had had the chance to attend a college whose population was greater than "one." I have loved teaching there, I feel connected to the students, and I take pride in the ways I have become a person who contributes to the well-being of others. My contribution is modest, but in my own way I have also been a leader, seeking to create, as the novelist would put it, a "wider life"—wider for others, wider for myself. I have even widened vistas by having students read *Middlemarch* and, on a couple of occasions, *Daniel Deronda*, works they find long but also can appreciate. It's been especially interesting to introduce the large number of Orthodox Jewish students I teach to Eliot's last novel. Their perspectives always enlighten and surprise me, as, for that matter, do those of all my students. In a sense I have my "social captaincy." Yes, George Eliot. Women can be social captains, too!

But there is another way, perhaps more indefinite, that George Eliot is bound up with my life's progress. When Donald went off with that other woman in Hawaii, I suffered a terrible blow. I suspected the affair, then confirmed it by snooping—a love letter in his trousers' pocket urged him to come away into a magic realm. When I confronted him, he said it was best for him to leave. I begged and pleaded with him not to go, but he left anyway. The next day I still had to get the children up and dress and feed them, deliver Emily to her preschool and Sean to his sitter, and go and teach my three courses. I did all this in those three hard months. I also kept writing my dissertation. I hadn't thought I could cope through such a trial, but I did. You might say I learned "to do without opium and live through . . . pain with conscious clear- eyed endurance." I suffered but I learned I could manage. I could carry on despite emotional distress.

I should add that my mother, then almost seventy, near my age now, was a help to me in this time by coming to Hawaii and renting a house about a mile from mine. I would take the children over to her place in the afternoons, and we would sit with them by her pool and talk things over, even laugh. My mother proved quite selfless in a crisis. She came through for me remarkably. George Eliot would have understood this—how most of us can rise above ego when it really matters. My belief in this human capacity helps to make me an abiding optimist.

Isabel Archer and Tess of the d'Urbervilles

The first time I met my father, though I didn't yet know his relation to me, he took me to a London bookstore and bought me *Tess of the d'Urbervilles.* I was eleven years old, on my first trip abroad. My mother had been invited by several Hollywood studios to visit their film locations in London, Paris, and Rome. She chose to have me go with her, while eight-year-old Robert remained at home in California with Bow Wow.

Up to this point, the summer of 1954, I had ventured beyond Southern California's span of ocean and desert, palm trees and eucalyptuses, only in the imagined landscapes of my reading. But as our TWA propeller plane descended over the patchwork fields of "little grey-green England"—Henry James's epithet in *The Portrait of a Lady*—I felt myself, even without quite having words for the experience, on the brink of both an adventure and a homecoming. Little about England surprised me. I was startled that buildings were grimy (dirt seemed not to adhere to the gleaming stucco facades of Southern California) and that horse-drawn carts still delivered the milk. But I took in the sights before me, writing daily in the journal my mother had urged me to keep, a poignantly dutiful record, as I look back on it now, of my observations and activities. Within just a few weeks I also acquired an English accent. "Drop it," advised my mother upon our return to the United States.

In London, my mother's former home, where we began and ended the trip, I saw people from her past, including her two ex-husbands. John Graham Gillam, the first of these—to me "Uncle Johnny"—now old and genteelly impoverished, was assigned to conduct me to Buckingham Palace and the Tower of London. The second, Trevor West-brook, a dour British engineer and the man I thought was my father, used the occasion of my visit to try to get to know me better. We were nearly strangers to one another, as he had always lived in England and had come to California only three or four brief times in my life's eleven years. Now he took me into his homes—a flat in Eton Square and a pseudo-ancestral country house in West Sussex, an imposing brick edifice cobbled together from two laborer's cottages, which he had dignified with the name of Little Brockhurst. I felt ill at ease in these settings, guilty, then and thereafter, at my discomfort in his uncommunicative presence and anxious, every time I was with him, to be back with my mother. Far more appealing than Johnny or Trevor was a trim, wavy-haired man in his early forties, introduced to me as my mother's old friend Freddie Ayer. I knew he was a famous philosopher, though hardly understanding then what philosophy was supposed to be.

That A. J., later Sir Alfred Ayer (who accepted a life peerage despite his ardent socialism), was my real father I would learn only thirty-five years later. My mother's last great secret would emerge six weeks after her death when I was forty-six and Freddie, a few months short of *his* death, was seventy-eight. It was Freddie Ayer, this charming man with a ready smile, who suggested we go to the bookstore.

My mother made the introduction. A standard black London cab deposited us at Freddie's flat in Mayfair. Having since read his autobiography, I know now that the flat was a duplex at 2 Whitehorse Street. I remember a messy room with floor-to-ceiling bookcases and papers strewn about. Freddie, who seemed very buoyant and animated, spoke to me in a direct and friendly manner. I didn't mind when my mother left me with him and he and I then went out from the flat to catch a London double-decker bus—we sat on the top level—to get to the bookstore, which must have been Blackwell's in the Strand. I embraced the adventure—so welcome an alternative to all that riding in limousines and taxis with my mother. Inside the store Freddie stood with me against a long shelf of books, jiggling the watch chain attached to the vest of his dark three-piece suit (I would come to know this as his habitual attire) and discussing our choices for the purchase in his fast-talking, somewhat staccato way. I can't remember how he conducted the process of elimination—surely he must have asked questions about books I had read and liked. At that point I had no experience of Hardy. I left the store with a hard-backed copy of *Tess of the d'Urbervilles*.

The book had a royal blue binding, and I kept it long after it had somehow got waterlogged and warped, even though I had no idea Freddie was my father. I read it back in California, lying with it on my bed in the still, heavy air of late summer. My material inheritance from my father is so slight, and I have so few memories of him, even though we did spend time together, that it seems like the preserving of a precious relic to be able to evoke, over fifty years later, that book's blue binding as well as the typeface of the letters and the map of Wessex, which I have since learned was Hardy's own sketch, that served as frontispiece, showing all the towns and valleys and rivers of an apocryphal southwest English universe. On that map I could trace Tess's sorrowful history in terms of its place markers: the Vale of Blackmore, where as a maiden of sixteen she misses dancing with passerby Angel Clare; Trantridge, where she goes to claim kin with her seeming d'Urbervilles relations and whistles to Mrs. d'Urberville's parakeets; the Chase forest, where, sleeping, she is raped by the roué Alec d'Urberville; Talbothays Dairy in the Valley of the Froms, where she reencounters Angel and they fall in love in the dreamlike fertile landscape; the desolate Chawk Newton, where, abandoned by Angel, she works digging turnips; the fashionable seaside resort of Sandborne, where Alec, to whom she has again succumbed, though only in body, has taken her and where she murders him; and, finally, to primordial Stonehenge, where at the end of the few idyllic days with Angel—at least Tess and the reader are given these—she is apprehended.

Meanwhile, Freddie Ayer wrote me letters in his minuscule script, and I took this as a matter of course. We were both intellectuals, he a famous philosopher and I an eleven-year-old straight-A student. Yet intellect now fails me, or at least fails to suffice, as I wonder about Freddie's selection of *Tess of the d'Urbervilles.* What might my father have been thinking in handing a child of my age, who was, furthermore, his secret daughter, this story of seduction, betrayal, and illegitimate birth? A friend has suggested the motive of linking me more closely to England, since the novel is so deeply rooted in English soil. The theory seems plausible, yet I hesitate to embrace it. Freddie, for all his lucidity as a logician, remains opaque to me. I want his selection to have had meaning for him, but perhaps it didn't.

As for what *Tess* has meant to me, of all Hardy's novels it's the one I am today at once most moved by and find almost unbearable to reread. Tess is not an orphan, but in a sense she is orphaned by the universe. Any place or person to belong to, any happiness, and, ultimately, life are taken from her. She is doomed, moreover, from the moment we first see her at the country dance, the only girl with a pink, not a white ribbon in her hair, a sign of her lush, innocent sexuality, a portent of the red blood later to be spilled. Or perhaps she is doomed even before that, from the opening pages when feckless John Durbeyfield learns of his ancestry. His is a family in decline. Rural England is in decline. God is dead or doubtful, and nothing has yet replaced belief —it is in this novel, not *Jude the Obscure*, that Hardy coins the phrase the "ache of modernism," using it to describe the unsettling effects of Tess's standard sixth-form education. But beyond modernism—Hardy tends to have multiple causes of misery—the universe is inexorable. "We live on a blighted planet," Tess tells her little brother Abraham. Tess will be hounded like the murdered pheasants she sleeps next to in the fields, on her way to join her friend Marian at Chalk Newton. Of course, the family horse dies and she has to claim kin with the false Stokes-d'Urbervilles. Of course, Alec traps her and rapes her while she's sleeping. Inexorably, the note she writes for Angel gets hidden under the carpet, and then Angel lacks sufficient freedom from convention to pardon her "transgression." And of course, the farmer she works for at Chalk Newton is the very man who has a grudge against her, whom Angel has fought with. And when she leaves her dirty boots by the roadside as she musters courage to present herself to Angel's parents, she overhears his brothers mock the boots and this causes her to turn back. And then, retreating from her thwarted mission, she meets the insufficiently "converted" Alec, who relentlessly pursues her and beats her down, Alec, whom the reader dreads as much as Tess does, but who is not even a bad man really, just *l'homme moyen sensuel*.

No interpretation, though, protects me from the anguish of Tess's destiny. I suffer as I turn the pages, appalled yet mesmerized by Tess's pure victimization. I jump ahead to the end to fortify myself with the few pages of respite—Tess's time with Angel—between her killing Alec and her death.

I don't remember such feelings when I first read the novel. Despite the incursion of Bow Wow, I was hardly yet schooled in a tragic vision of experience. Death, disappointment, loss, waste, and even sexuality were largely abstractions in my sheltered and still innocent child's existence. Sometime in the previous year, I had been told about sex, but its power and its consequences remained vague to me. My mother and I had lain next to one another on the floor in her bedroom—she used to stretch out like this to rest—and she had described the sexual act to me, stressing throughout how natural it was, even beautiful. I can see myself next to her, listening, aware of her speaking, pleased to be with her in this almost conspiratorial way. Afterward, back alone in my own room, I marveled at the fact that the man and the woman took off their clothes. That's what I found incredible—that they actually took off their clothes. But as I tried to imagine a naked man and naked woman together in a bed, it certainly wasn't my own self I slipped into this picture. I was ill at ease with my own burgeoning sexuality and, I think, with sex in general, hoping to keep it at bay. In my Beverly Hills public school, the boys in the previous sixth-grade year had started roughhousing with the girls, and I had attended one party where in a game of Spin the Bottle I had to walk across the circle we sat in and bend down to kiss a boy. This moment bewildered and frightened me. But Tess's highly sexualized body, her vulnerability, her impassioned cry to her mother, "Why didn't you tell me there was danger in menfolk?" the terrible price she pays for her initial misstep—I should say mishap—were just parts of a sad and mesmerizing story—the way a child can blithely recount terrible things without express sense of their horror. "And then he ravished her. And then she had a baby and it died. And then she murdered him." That's the story.

In truth, I don't remember much of the experience of reading *Tess of the d'Urbervilles* late that summer when I was back from Europe and waiting to begin seventh grade. I do recollect, far more vividly, rereading *Little Women* in the Illustrated Classics edition, a text I knew almost by heart, and suddenly feeling I wanted to switch from public to private school. I closed the book's pages and went downstairs to try to convince my mother to make this change for me. She proved immediately receptive, and, ever a woman of action, got me admitted to a small private school in Bel Air, where we wore blue and white checked cotton jumper uniforms designed by Lanz. My aspiration was to more refined culture and gentility. It had been stirred in me by the trip to Europe, my disgust with the roughhousing on the playground, and the inspirational story of the March girls, whose fictional lives, except perhaps for that of Beth, who dies, seemed so enviable. Even Beth in a way was enviable—she plays the piano and dies sweetly. Tess, on the other hand, doesn't play the piano, or speak Italian, or paint or write. She is beautiful and truthful, and she suffers. Hardy calls her a "pure woman," defying the social conventions that would brand her otherwise. I hardly knew at eleven what being a pure woman might mean since I didn't understand what it meant to be impure.

Looking back, I think *Tess of the d'Urbervilles* may have been the first book I ever read in which things turn out really badly. The heroine does not find happiness; she is pummeled by men and by the universe, then executed, a sacrifice to society, a "sport," Hardy tells us, for the "President of the Immortals"—his ironic stand-in for God. But I did not, as I have said, possess the frame of reference for registering the impact of such bad fortune—either a personal frame of reference or a literary one. I had not yet even read my first Shakespeare tragedy—that would be *Julius Caesar* in seventh grade. What, in retrospect, I remember best is the book itself—object and fetish—the only present ever picked out for me by my father, except for the silver porringer that I discovered in 1989 he had sent after my birth in 1942. I found it mentioned in my mother's papers after she died in a list she'd kept of presents received for her new baby. The porringer, coming to light so belatedly, hardly counts the way the book does. I fix on that one particular book, even though other books enter into our story. Books, in fact, surrounded our slender history, setting it off almost like bookends.

I knew Freddie Ayer for thirty-five years; of those I knew him as my father for only the last six months. When he died in June 1989, six weeks after I had gone to visit him in London as his acknowledged daughter, I said to my sixteen-year-old son, who was with me when I got the news, that truly I was now an orphan. "No, you're not," he replied. "An orphan is someone who needs parents to take care of her. You've been taking care of yourself and others for years." What my son didn't understand—how could he?—was the sharpness with which I felt cheated and abandoned.

Unsure of my status, ill at ease, I returned to England a month after Freddie's death, to attend a large public memorial for him at University College London. He had been teaching there when I first met him, before his later appointment at New College, Oxford. It was on the second day of my visit that Freddie's widow—an American-born journalist named Dee Wells, now Lady Ayer, who had become Freddie's second wife in 1960, divorced him in 1982, and remarried him just months before his death—broached how Freddie had said to her, "I must do something for Wendy." I held my breath waiting to know what that something could be. When friends in America had asked me whether Freddie had left me any money, I had consistently treated the inquiry as rather crass. "Oh no, I don't think so," I had said. "I didn't expect him to."

"And sooo,"—Dee drew out the word—"he has left you the choice of twelve books of English literature from his library."

The library occupied a floor in the house that Freddie had inherited from his third wife, Vanessa, who had died of cancer. It occurred to me that this was the third London address at which I had known Freddie. I had met him in his flat on Whitehorse Street, frequented the house he had with Dee on Regent's Park Terrace, and then come to "claim kin," as it were, in this house on York Street, once again in Mayfair. Now he was dead, and his library remained—testament in its thousands of tomes of philosophy and history and biography and the literature of different countries, to his breath of knowledge and enthusiasms. Choosing the books of my legacy meant combing through all that to pick out my precisely defined dozen, and it was a hard, even bitter task. A six-volume set of Jane Austen took care of half my bequest and seemed apt. When I had arrived at the York Street house on my earlier visit after Freddie had written me that he was my father, I had found him in the library with his secretary and been subjected to a quiz.

"What is Mr. Darcy's first name?" he had asked, looking up from his work.

"Fitzwilliam," I had said, relieved to know the answer.

"And where in the novel does it occur?" he had pressed.

I hadn't known, and Freddie, delighted to get the better of a PhD in English literature, had informed me it is when Darcy writes to Elizabeth in the wake of her rejection of his first proposal. I tried to laugh off my discomfiture, but the exercise seemed too much at my expense.

Back in that library and forcing myself on in the selection of the books, I chose Oscar Wilde's *Intentions,* which included his essay on "The Decay of Lying," a leather-bound edition of Tennyson's *In Memoriam,* a 1865 leather-bound edition of

Dickens's *A Christmas Carol*, a Hogarth Press first edition of Virginia Woolf's *The Moment and Other Essays*, and an e.e. cummings 95 *poems*, in which the author had scribbled a few words to his friend Freddie.

And there I stopped with eleven books chosen. I looked over others but couldn't decide on a final volume. I kept worrying how much the books would weigh in my suitcase, and though I tried to tell myself this was a silly concern, the books, in truth, felt to me like lead, each chosen one another loadstone to sink my spirits further. I couldn't pick a twelfth and left it at that. Perhaps with a book still to go, any of the multitudinous books of English literature in the library seemed still potentially mine. Or perhaps I simply couldn't bear the dispossessed way choosing these books made me feel. Later Dee wrote to ask me to give back the cummings, saying the whole collection of cummings had been left to her and Freddie's son, Nick, and offering me another choice. I returned the cummings but did not replace it. Twenty-six years after Freddie's death, I have never opened any of the books of my bequest, which sit grouped together on a shelf in my living room bookcase.

When I think of Freddie and English literature, I think of his love of Dickens and I think of *Tess of the d'Urbervilles*. Freddie was Angel Clare for me, a man of quick-paced intellect and bodily lightness of being, a spirit of air like his name, not a creature of gross flesh like the detested Bow Wow. He was a free-thinker, a renowned atheist. But he was also Alec d'Urberville, a roué, a compulsive seducer of women, a sensualist. "What was my mother like?" I had asked him on my daughterly visit. He had smiled and thought for a moment. "I remember her as being rather plump," he said. I expected something else, something more, but that's what he chose to remember.

Both Alec and Angel fail Tess. I could say that Freddie failed me. But that pronouncement seems too blunt—it belies the intricacies of my story. I think I need a different author than Hardy to help me convey its nuances and its treacheries, perhaps someone less fixed on "the President of the Immortals," existent or not, and more on the willful duplicity of human beings. Hardy's characters are too subject to fate and ultimately too fragile for my purposes. I need an author whose personages do more to "choose" the tangles of their lives and then have the stamina to live with what they've chosen.

One of the most cherished books in my library is a tattered Riverside edition of Henry James's *The Portrait of a Lady*, the first work we read in a year-long freshman English course at Bryn Mawr College. Studying *The Portrait of a Lady*, writing papers about its narrative techniques and its use of imagery (I remember tracing window and bird imagery) taught me techniques for approaching modern literature. I learned to appreciate the subtlety of the author's presence, the way, in James's own words, he "get[s] down into the arena" and "rubs shoulders" with the characters, and the emphasis on subjectivity and the drama of consciousness, culminating in the famous Chapter 42, in which his heroine Isabel, eyes closed, ruminates through the night and sees the truth of her situation clearly and deeply—she has married a man who hates her and can do nothing except understand this. "Try to be one of the people on whom nothing is lost!" James writes in "The Art of Fiction." I read that essay three years later in a senior seminar on literary theory. But James's injunction conflates for me with the story of Isabel Archer, on whom so much is initially lost and whose fulfillment, even whose triumph, it can be argued, lies in her painful coming to consciousness. Isabel is yet another nineteenth-century orphan, but she's also something else: a proto-new woman, a modernist heroine of interiority. Because my old college edition of the book is falling apart—it has split in two—I recently obtained a new copy, but I still use my old falling-apart one with all my notes for teaching.

In "The Decay of Lying" Oscar Wilde asserts that life imitates art far more than art imitates life. His serious point, beneath the wit of the epigram, is that art furnishes us with life's plots and its paradigms. We see the sunset a certain way because we know the paintings of Turner. A novel by Balzac shapes our understanding of ambition and betrayal. In my case, life imitates the art of Henry James. My story's themes are adultery and concealment, the question of who knew a sexual secret and who didn't. Its central irony is the blindness of the person who wished to be someone on whom nothing is lost. I am the protagonist kept in the dark, the personage on whom a great deceit was practiced but who finally, only at the very end, too late to do much about it except in terms of awareness, learned the truth. "It's a story by Henry James," I kept telling my friends at the time of its unfolding. "Everyone but me knew that Freddie was my father."

By "everyone," of course, I mean many: my mother, Freddie, Dee, Gully Wells—Dee's daughter by an earlier marriage, my mother's friend Jean Dalrymple, and even my husband, Donald, who took note of the physical resemblance between father and daughter and silently wondered, and who knows who else. But this list did not include Trevor Westbrook. He was the man my mother duped into marriage.

After Scott Fitzgerald had his fatal heart attack in her Hollywood living room a few days before Christmas 1940, my mother kept herself going, among other ways, by returning the following spring to England as a war correspondent. In Hollywood, as she later told me, she had suffered from nightmares that Hitler was personally gunning her down from a plane. In England the nightmares ceased, and she got involved with Trevor. Perhaps it helped on the nightmare front that Trevor was the man Lord Beaverbrook, Minister of War, had put in charge of English wartime aviation production. At any rate, my mother liked his single-minded determination, which was also a kind of narrowness. Trim and dour, his dark hair combed always neatly into place, Trevor used to boast he had never read a book. My mother said she found comfort in the contrast this presented to Fitzgerald.

Back for the 1941 autumn in New York, my mother reconnected with Freddie, whom she had met earlier that year in London. In this new affair she became pregnant— possibly on purpose but if so, her motive, at thirty-seven, was to have a baby, not to entrap Freddie Ayer. He was still married to his first wife, René, and in any case not interested in marrying my mother. I get the sense that she was using sex, probably with a lot of people, to console herself for the terrible loss of Fitzgerald and that Freddie was simply engaged in his habitual philandering. It was not a serious liaison. At this point Trevor Westbrook turned up on a mission to Washington with Lord Beaverbrook. My mother went to see him, told him she was four months pregnant with his child and persuaded him to marry her. Soon afterwards she announced that she had lost the child and soon after that that she was pregnant again. I have pieced together this audacious layer of lies from Freddie and from a Westbrook cousin in whom Trevor confided. He sensed he had been tricked into marriage, but that was the extent of his suspicions.

Trevor died in 1979 without ever knowing I was not his daughter. My mother died in November 1988 without ever telling me the truth. This was her last consequential secret—or at least the last we learned about—coming to light six weeks after her death and thirty years after I had learned she was Jewish. The person who revealed it was Dee Wells, then still divorced from Freddie and living in New York but about to go back to England and remarry him. She had left him for a black American clothes designer, who, in turn, had left her, and, now financially and emotionally rather stranded, she welcomed the return to her former husband. Dee would care for Freddie in his final months, acquire the title of Lady Ayer, and live in the house on York Street for the remaining fifteen years of her not very happy life.

I find it diverting to try to cast this genealogical tale in terms of the characters of *The Portrait of a Lady*. The ones I call into service are the deceived heroine, Isabel Archer, her insidious husband, Gilbert Osmond, Osmond's innocent daughter, Pansy, Pansy's secret mother, the smooth mannered, unscrupulous Madame Merle, and Osmond's "tropical bird-like" sister with her "long-beaked nose" and "shimmering plumage," the Countess Gemini.

Dee is clearly the Countess Gemini, an expatriate American of blunt temperament and sexual indiscretion, someone who had "consoled herself outrageously" for her husband's infidelities. James debated whether it should be Madame Merle or the Countess who tells Isabel about Pansy, and he chose the Countess, regretting, though, "that in that way [he loses] the 'great scene between Madame Merle and Isabel'" Since my story also lacks a great scene between my mother and me—the scene in which *she* might have been the one to tell me who my father was—and the role fell to Dee, her casting as the Countess is perfect.

I had sought out Dee to be a speaker at my mother's memorial and she had then asked me to a dinner party at her daughter Gully's brownstone in Greenwich Village. I gave her a ride in my car after the party to her apartment in the East 30s. She was full of her plans for resuming life with Freddie and invited me to come and see them at their house in the South of France.

"Freddie is very fond of you," she said, as we sat for a moment in the car in front of her building. When I demurred, since her words seemed polite but perfunctory and I was eager to get going, she looked at me in a hard, peculiar manner.

"Has it never occurred to you that Freddie is your father?" she said.

"No," I replied, stunned. I asked Dee if Freddie thought this was a guess or a certainty. Dee said Freddie considered it a certainty. She said that she would get him to write me.

I have my own version of Chapter 42 of *The Portrait of a Lady*. It begins on my drive home to my apartment in Brooklyn after leaving Dee and continues over the ensuing few days. On the drive home I felt I was seeing with Freddie's eyes, smiling his smile, experiencing myself as his daughter from the inside out. Then over the next few days our whole past history rose before me for reevaluation. I remembered how Freddie had befriended me, taking me to lunches and to museums on my frequent trips to England as a teenager and how Donald and I had stayed with him and Dee in London and also in France on the trip we took abroad the first summer of our marriage. It also made sense why Dee had written such a virulent review of *Beloved Infidel* in her days as a journalist for the *Daily Express*. It had a memorably outrageous conclusion. "And I suppose in a way you have to hand it to the ex-East End orphan named Lily Shiel. Just *what* to hand her, I'd be hard put to say. But I do know it's nothing I'd touch with a ten-foot pole. With gloves on."

My mother had walked out of a 1959 lunch with Freddie and me in a London restaurant because he confessed to having seen the review before it went to press and done nothing to stop it. That was before Dee and Freddie married and subsequently had my half-brother Nicholas. Dee then set about befriending my mother. The Ayers were living in Regents Park Terrace, and my mother had bought a little house on Lancelot Place—"a whisper from Harrods and a shout from Hyde Park," as she described it. The visits went back and forth between these residences. "Of course, I can never trust her," my mother would say. But she seemed happy to be invited to tea and to dinner parties, and a mutual if wary respect arose between these scrappy fighters. Finally, it made sense why Dee in 1975, when I, then thirty-two, was living in England with Donald and the children, had invited me for lunch at their house and then, oddly, gone out as soon as I arrived, leaving me with Freddie. He and I had sat on a sofa, both of us stroking a cat. I had thought about his reputation as a womanizer and wondered if he were going to make a pass at me. I think Dee meant for him to tell me then he was my father, but he didn't.

His "I am your father" letter came a few weeks after Dee's return to England. It began:

> Dear Wendy:
> Your asking me to write to you is presumably the outcome of the conversation that you had with Dee after your mother's funeral. You were then feeling your way towards the truth. I am your father . . .

To continue with the casting, I put Freddie, for his part in the concealment, in the role of Gilbert Osmond, though doing so is hardly fair, considering his amiable temperament, intellectual originality, and liberal politics. Freddie resembled Osmond only in his social snobbery and emotional indolence. His letter to me spoke of his regret that Dee's hostile review of *Beloved Infidel* had put an end to my mother's "bringing you to visit me in London but there was nothing I could do about it." It was Dee who took the initiative to make peace with my mother—Freddie's letter marveled that they had later become such good friends— and who took the lead in keeping in touch with me. Freddie was passive. He was not a man of deep emotions. There is a chilling passage in John Osborne's autobiography, describing how Freddie had come to see his ex-girlfriend Jocelyn Richards (then living with Osborne) when he was contemplating marrying Dee:

> He had announced that he was contemplating marriage to an American, but was undecided whether the match fulfilled his standards of wisdom and self-esteem. He

offered his ex-mistress a two-card choice: he was prepared to marry the American unless Jocelyn should feel
impelled to offer herself as an alternative. Anyone less
kindly than Jocelyn [opines Osborne] would have kicked
this pear-shaped Don Giovanni down the stairs and his
cruel presumption. She could find nothing to say except,
"But Freddie, it's too late."

I never noticed that Freddie was pear-shaped (though, indeed,
I am more pear-shaped than was my bosomy, slim-hipped
mother), but without doubt in later years he was physically
inactive. Freddie didn't drive a car. He didn't know how to
fix anything. He did nothing in a house. He read and he
wrote and he talked, and he expected other people to take
care of other matters. I can easily imagine a scene in which he
would be sitting in a drawing room and Dee or my mother
would be standing. In *The Portrait of a Lady* the "impression"
Isabel receives of Osmond sitting and Madame Merle standing is the visual trigger to her discovery of their connection.

There is a way, though, that Freddie was nothing like
Gilbert Osmond. Osmond, ultimately, for all that he allows
Madame Merle to do for him, is the opposite of passive. He
is fierce in his desires and detestations. Freddie wasn't like
that. He was almost always amiable, just sometimes shock-
ingly unfeeling.

My mother becomes Madame Merle, and, again, this
seems an imperfect fit. How can a woman of my mother's
courage and vivacity, someone I've already cast as the zestful
Becky Sharp, also be the smooth and duplicitous Serena
Merle? Isn't sharp the opposite of smooth? James describes
Madame Merle as "not natural" in that "her nature had
been too much overlaid by custom and her angles too

much rubbed away." She is "sympathetic and subtle," "a worshipper of appearances," "a woman of strong impulses kept in admirable order." Serena Merle is all concealment and calculation; my mother, notwithstanding her secrets, *seemed* open, impetuous, and innocent.

But my mother was also someone who assiduously concealed her past and who used people to further her own ends. Madame Merle says, "I don't pretend to know what people are meant for. . . . I only know what I can do with them." That's chilling, but I wonder if it's any less chilling than the way my mother used Trevor Westbrook, a man for whom she had no love; or the way, even, she used the movie stars as fodder for her column. "My paragraphs," I have said she called them. It's interesting to me, however, that when she had the scoop about Ingrid Bergman's running off, pregnant, with Roberto Rossolini, she didn't print it. I like to think this was a show of scruples, that my mother felt compassion for Bergman, perhaps arising from her own experience. I don't think my mother would ever have run off with a Roberto Rossolini and defied the world for love. She did, however, break her engagement with the Marquis of Donagal to take up with the married and debt-ridden Fitzgerald. But my mother also had a healthy respect for convention. If not as zealous as Madame Merle to be "the incarnation of propriety," she detested being referred to as Fitzgerald's mistress and would stress how throughout her three-and-a-half years with him, she had always maintained her own apartment. No less intently than Madame Merle, my mother craved respectability. It bothered her that Fitzgerald had died in her living room, and she made sure the world knew his fatal heart attack had not occurred in her bedroom. Some of her concern for respectability was surely for her children. But then isn't Madame Merle devoted to the advancement of Pansy?

We come to my role in the story. And here I'm torn. I want to be both Pansy and Isabel Archer. I am both the child who doesn't know her parent, the "blank page" who submits to being shaped by others, and I am the "engaging young woman" whose drama of consciousness is the central interest of this tale.

It is tempting to be Pansy, the victim of others' aspirations and conspiracies. A friend to both my mother and me once noted that I was her product. Just as Pansy is sent to the convent to be "finished," I had been sent to Rosemary Hall and Bryn Mawr. The analogy does no justice to Bryn Mawr's fierce secularism and intellectual rigor. But to my mother these schools were the route to occupying a certain place in society. Scottie Fitzgerald had gone to Ethel Walker and to Vassar and had married a Washington lawyer. My mother hoped I would have a similar kind of life, one more privileged and protected than her own.

To hope such things for one's daughter is not criminal. It's just that certain inconvenient truths were suppressed in her plans for me—the Jewish heritage I might have shared with her and the identity of my father. At least, though, I knew my father and I liked him. Pansy doesn't like Madame Merle, but Freddie charmed me from our first encounter. I even told myself I had always loved him, but it was, at best, "post hoc" love that had a kind of backward formation after I knew the truth of his relation to me.

Pansy, though, does not take me far enough. Among the many brilliant metaphors and insights of Chapter 42 of *The Portrait of a Lady*, a passage that has always struck me with special force is the one in which Isabel notes of her feelings for Osmond:

> There were times when she almost pitied him: for if she had not deceived him in intention, she understood how completely she must have done so in fact. She had effaced herself when he first knew her; she had made herself small, pretending there was less of her than there really was.

I, too, understand the notion of making oneself small, when someone one admires seems dazzlingly large. It's an act of mistaken generosity and perhaps a strategy as well for coping with outsized personalities. For me, the first and foremost of outsized personalities has been, of course, my mother. She liked to feel she could do anything but needed others to be lesser than herself. You took a seat in my mother's carriage—James would like that metaphor—and went along for the ride. In one of her books she wrote that her children "had to learn [she] wasn't God." In truth I think God was a role she was loath to relinquish. She enlisted me as her votary, and I performed my obloquies with all due diligence and awe. Often I *felt* like Pansy—small and dependent— but this was a role I had assumed, and I knew that, too.

My more important role, however, is as Isabel Archer. I have wished too fervently to be the hero—or heroine— of my own life to settle for the part of Pansy. I claim the position of the "young woman affronting her destiny," a bit afraid, as Isabel is, to look into "unlighted corners," but nonetheless a seeker of freedom and of understanding.

Henry James knew that freedom consists of understanding, however painful. When, to borrow the words of the novel, I came to know "something that so much concerned [me] and the eclipse of which had made life resemble an attempt to play with an imperfect pack of cards," I doubted, reassessed, and ultimately forgave my deceivers, marveling, though, how others could play so fast and loose with me.

But to have the experience of my discoveries has also stirred new energy. Like Isabel, on the way to the bedside of her dying cousin, Ralph Touchett, in England, I have felt "deep in my soul . . . an "inspiring, almost enlivening" conviction that life will be "[my] business for a long time to come." I felt this when I first learned about Freddie, and I feel it now. As a woman now over seventy, I don't have the span before me that a youthful heroine does. Yet my assent to Isabel's stubborn strain of optimism comes from a part of me untempered by age and undaunted by experience, some fundamental, abidingly innocent core of self that, paradoxically, is all the hardier because it knows the weight of experience. James suggests this possibility when he writes of Isabel:

> To live only to suffer—only to feel the injury of life repeated and enlarged—it seemed to her she was too valuable, too capable for that. Then she wondered if it were vain and stupid to think so well of herself. When had it ever been a guarantee to be valuable? Wasn't all history full of the destruction of precious things? Wasn't it much more probable that if one were fine one would suffer? It involved then perhaps an admission that one had a certain grossness; but Isabel recognized, as it passed before her, the quick vague shadow of a long future. She should never escape; she should last to the end.

That James envisions a long future for his heroine is intriguing in light of the links critics and biographers have made between Isabel and James's beloved cousin, Minny Temple, who died so young. "It is the living ones that die, the writing ones that survive," James wrote famously in a 1870 letter. But in *Portrait*, Ralph dies, not Isabel—Ralph the hands-in-his-pockets observer, a stand in, surely, for one of the writing ones. And Isabel is left with "the vague shadow of a long future."

My general sense is that death intrudes discreetly in the fiction of Henry James. Yes, Daisy Miller succumbs to the bad Roman air, Daniel and Ralph Touchett die in *The Portrait of a Lady,* and Milly Thrale turns her face to the wall in *The Wings of the Dove.* But none of these deaths, however arbitrary, seems the work of a capricious a/Author—small or capital "A." And certainly James would never free his characters from their entrapments the way George Eliot kills off inconvenient husbands. Death serves in his stories as a spur to greater awareness. The living are left to reflect on their shortcomings with merciless clarity.

But sometimes death is important for the way it cuts everything short. And here is a thought that turns me back to Thomas Hardy. In Hardy's last two novels, the deaths of Tess and Jude leave us with a sense of tragic completion— indeed the final section of *Tess* is called "Fulfillment"—but also of incompletion and wasted promise. Tess and Jude suffer and die young. Affected survivors are left not so much to gain new insight as to pick up the pieces of their shattered lives and go on as best they can.

When Freddie Ayer died six weeks after I visited him for the first time as his daughter, I felt that fate had played

a brutal trick on me. It's hard to call his death tragic—
it brought no enlightenment for him or for me—but it
did seem cruel, an example of the sport of the President
of the Immortals. When I try to reconcile myself to it—
and perhaps it's the survivor's "grossness" that propels me
that way—I am thankful I learned who he was before he
died. And also that I went to see him. I knew he was ill
with emphysema but had no idea he would die so soon. My
visit wasn't easy, probably not for anyone involved. Freddie
and I were both very circumspect. No one wanted to make
a "fuss." But he did tell me, one morning, as we breakfasted
together, that he was proud of me. I hold that moment as
precious, if not sacred. It's not on the order of Ralph's dying
exclamation to his cousin, ". . .you've been loved. Ah but,
Isabel, *adored*!" But it is what it is, and it helps to round out
our story. I think it shifts the emphasis from what wasn't
to what was. I marvel at the ways our narratives serve to
console us.

ii

TESS OF THE D'URBERVILLES and *The Portrait of a Lady* have
helped me to think about my father in ways that are harder
to do more directly. The subject numbs me; I falter even in
asking myself why. But through indirection I try to find
direction out. I feel almost as if I have borrowed these books
for that reason, but now it's time to put them back in their
proper section of my library and reading history. If I do this,
it's also a way of keeping Freddie contained, of showing the
life I had without him.

I first studied *The Portrait of a Lady* in that freshman English course in college. I revisited *Tess* in a semester-long graduate seminar on Hardy, in which I made a presentation on his array of vibrant heroines. I didn't know it at the time, of course, but by reading these books, I was becoming the person Freddie would say he was proud of: a person whose outlook, aspirations, and stamina were honed in the study of English literature.

It was the early 1980s, with graduate school a decade behind me and the adventure of discovering a new father still ahead, that Hardy and James came to figure most vitally in my teaching and academic writing. Second-wave feminism was at its crest, and I, in my thirties, could embrace it as my generation's movement. Noting the ways more feminist heroines emerge in late nineteenth- and early twentieth-century English fiction, women who resist, and even reject, marriage and men, I developed a new course to teach that I called "The Heroine's Progress: Studies in the Novel, 1880-1910." James and Hardy were both on the syllabus.

The course examined a group of novels of this period—texts that coincided with the first wave of British and American feminism—in terms of their options for female characters that depart from the traditional plot in which the heroine either marries as a happy culmination of her quest for selfhood or fails to marry and dies. The feminist critic Nancy Miller, my colleague at Barnard College, where I first taught this course, named these the euphoric and dysphoric marriage plot endings in her book *The Heroine's Text*. These trajectories get established in the eighteenth-century novel and extend into the nineteenth. But as the status of women began to shift in the society, with philosophers such as John

Stuart Mill questioning women's "subjugation," laws being passed to protect married women's property, marriage as an institution coming under critical scrutiny, women's colleges being founded (think what George Eliot might have been like if she had gone to Girton!), and the suffrage movement gaining momentum, to name just a few of the heated questions and causes of the day, the established narratives in fiction could hardly remain unchanged. While Jane Eyre can sum up her married life as ten years of unadulterated bliss with the "bone of her bone and flesh of her flesh," George Eliot, even in her earliest stories, dating from 1858, is drawn to exploring marriage as a suffocating trap. Still, she never turns completely from the marriage plot ending. Remember Dorothea gets, if not greatness, at least ordinary happiness in her second chance with Will Ladislaw, and Daniel Deronda weds small-voiced Mirah without a shred of the author's potent irony. But in 1879 when Nora of her own volition leaves the "doll's house" at the end of Ibsen's play to seek some yet undefined fulfillment beyond the scope of marriage, it seemed to me an important step had been taken to expand narrative possibilities for women characters. I thought of this as the heroine's progress.

In my own life I was doing my best to expand possibilities as well. My marriage had stabilized after the turmoil of Donald's affair in Hawaii, at least well enough for us to hold together and go along, and it was also becoming evident that I might build a good career. From 1976 to 1980 we had lived in Maine, where Donald got a job organizing hospital workers and I taught at Bowdoin College. After a year there I was asked also to serve as Dean of Students, and suddenly from lowly assistant professor, I was elevated to one of the college's top administrators, a member of the "President's Council." In 1980 I applied for a position as Associate Dean of Faculty at Barnard back in New York, and I got the job. Donald was able to transfer to his union's New York headquarters. We seemed off and running.

"And how many people applied for your job?" my eight-year-old son would ask as his requested bedtime story.

"Over three hundred."

"And you got it!"

"Yes," I would answer, pleased at his pride in me and happy myself to think about the meaning of this long-shot chance.

My duties were chiefly administrative, but I also had the option each term to teach a course. "The Heroine's Progress," co-listed by Barnard's English department and the new Women's Studies Program, centered on the figure of the "new woman"—that creature of the 1880s and 1890s who was eager to defy convention: Lyndall in Olive Schreiner's *The Story of an African Farm*, who voices an ideal of women's liberation even though she then dies in childbirth; Sue Bridehead in *Jude the Obscure*, who lives and breathes a new kind of equality between the sexes, though she, too, finds the conflicts within her own nature and the tyranny of convention too strong for her; Rhoda in George Gissing's *The Odd Women*, hardier than the others, who turns down marriage to continue running her typing school for women. It went forward as far as Helen and Margaret Schlegel in Forster's *Howards End* (1910), who find different ways of challenging Victorian patrimony. And it began it with *The Portrait of a Lady*. Isabel Archer shares with other of these heroines a dissatisfaction with the idea of marriage as her female destiny and also a certain sexual skittishness that leapt out for me as something I, too, had struggled with. I had been wary, always, when men I had dated pressed me too hard, quick to feel trapped and quick to bolt to regain my freedom of choice. So I appreciated such conflict in Isabel as well as in Eliot's Gwendolyn Harleth and in Hardy's brilliant portrayal of Sue Bridehead. In later renditions of the course I have begun with *Daniel Deronda* and gone forward as far as Virginia Woolf's *To the Lighthouse* (1927).

Isabel Archer seemed to me a bridge figure between nineteenth- and twentieth-century protagonists. She may be an orphan, but she has none of the standard problems of orphanhood such as poverty, loss of status, and social and emotional isolation. (Interestingly, Tess of the d'Urbervilles, who is not an orphan, has these problems.) What Isabel gains by being an orphan is freedom: there are no parents to restrict her; she seems free of obligations to others; she can be swooped up by her aunt and brought to Europe. The legacy Ralph arranges for his father to leave her further frees her to go anywhere she likes and do anything she chooses. But, as James puts it in the preface to the 1908 edition, defining his novel's central dramatic interest, "What will she 'do'?"

James admits that Isabel's external adventures are "mild," but he calls her inner life "exciting." Her friend Henrietta Stackpole works as a journalist, but there is never any consideration of Isabel adopting a profession. Unlike Tess, the poor dairy maid, she doesn't have to support herself. As I think about my course "The Heroine's Progress," I am struck by how minimally the notion of work enters into any of the middle-class heroines' destinies. Rhoda Nunn has her typing school and Lily Briscoe her painting; one assumes that Nora, having left the doll's house, will get a job. But by and large energies are consumed in extricating from old situations rather than in entering new ones.

Isabel's initial goals are vague. She is "fond of her own liberty" and "fond of knowledge," though wary of those "unlighted corners." She wishes to "see" for herself but not "to touch cup of experience. It's a poisoned drink." She is not sure she wishes to marry anyone, and the novel's first startling action is her refusal of Lord Warburton, the closest equivalent in *The Portrait of a Lady* to a Mr. Darcy or Mr. Knightly, on the grounds that she would be escaping her fate to accept the peace, kindness, honor, and security that would come with marrying him.

That, ultimately, there isn't a right suitor is the novel's striking twist on the marriage plot. I don't think we are meant to regret Isabel's refusal of Lord Warburton, the noble but somewhat vitiated English aristocrat, or of her other suitor, Caspar Goodwood, the "hard," "armored," sexually disquieting American capitalist. Marriage is still the only thing the heroine ultimately can "do," but, to begin with, the very idea of marriage fails to meet the requirements of her imagination, and, then, the choice she makes—snared by others and blinded by her own illusions—is a horrific one. In reversal of the formula of fairy tales, the third suitor proves the villain, not the hero.

James leads into Isabel's unhappiness obliquely. Some time has passed, at least a year, since we saw her last on the brink of marriage. We're at a party at the Osmond villa in Rome, an establishment we presume to be sustained by Isabel's money. As Madame Merle talks with Ned Rosier, a young man interested in Pansy, we learn a child, a little boy, has died (thus we infer Isabel has had sex with her husband), and also, as Madame Merle puts it to Rosier, that Isabel would be likely to favor his courtship of Pansy "if her husband doesn't."

"Does she take the opposite line from him?" the scene continues.

"In everything. They think quite differently."

As a reader sympathetic to Isabel I'm relieved to learn husband and wife think differently—this means Isabel is still herself, at least if Madame Merle can be believed.

But as the book continues, with marriage—now the marriage of Pansy—still its preoccupation, we experience the fuller complexity of Isabel's entrapment. Unlike Gwendolyn Harleth, who fears she would have come to hate her husband if he hadn't died, Isabel does not hate Osmond— this is said explicitly—but she knows he hates her. The poisoned cup of experience has clarified her vision. She can name Osmond's egotism, his conventionality, and his hatred of her, his wife, all of which she does, unflinchingly, in the meditative vigil of Chapter 42, which James calls the finest thing in the book. It seems to me important that even before she learns the secret past of Osmond and Madame Merle, she understands her husband's vicious nature and acknowledges her own predicament, even while not seeking to escape it. "They were strangely married, at all events, and it was a horrible life." That terrible statement is exhilarating in its clarity.

My students, most of whom believe in their right to personal happiness, want Isabel at the novel's end to go off with Caspar Goodwood, or at least not go back to Osmond.

The ending is famously ambiguous, and class discussion of it is always intense. What is the effect on Isabel of Goodwood's at once powerfully physical and highly metaphoric kiss? What does it signify that it spreads in her like "white lightening" but that "when darkness returned, she was free?" She knows now "where to turn" and sees "a very straight path." But all that we learn after this—and we learn it indirectly from Henrietta's concluding words to Caspar Goodwood— is that Isabel has "started for Rome." James was aware that he had left his heroine, as he puts it, *"en l'air."* His justification for this open ending was that "the whole of anything is never told; you can only take what groups together."

James may have focused in his conception of the book on what Isabel "will do," but it's what she *sees* that seems to me his more central concern. And hasn't she by the novel's end seen everything she needs to: the malice of Osmond, the roles of Ralph and Madame Merle in her life, even her own abiding strength? As for how her painfully acquired knowledge leads to more doing, the novel does indeed leave us *en l'air*. I believe she will not desert Pansy but don't know what form her abiding loyalty will take. James has not really envisioned a destiny for her beyond the marriage plot—or if you will, the extension of the marriage plot into post-nuptial unhappiness. But that plot is subsumed by the drama of consciousness. The author has taken the consciousness of his young woman seriously. The weight of interest, as he tells us in the preface, is in her being a subject not an object.

For my generation, sensitive to ways women had been objectified and eager to reclaim our power as subjects, *The Portrait of a Lady* could be readily claimed as a feminist text. Including the novel in my women studies course of the 1980s, I did not ask Isabel Archer to be a role model or even to be happy. Rather, I saw the heroine's "progress" in the evolution of her understanding. That reading still seems to me an important one.

I did not teach *Tess of the d'Urbervilles* in "The Heroine's Progress." The Thomas Hardy novel that seemed best suited for the course was *Jude the Obscure,* since "modern," educated, neurotic Sue Bridehead is such an intriguing example of the "new woman" of the 1890s. Tess is also a heroine of the 1890s—the novel was published in 1891, a decade after James's *The Portrait of a Lady*—but despite the "ache of modernism" that Hardy attributes to her sixth-form education, Tess can hardly be called a new woman. In both her d'Urberville lineage and her Durbeyfield ties to the region, she is connected to the land and seems almost its emanation. She digs turnips up from its soil but can't dig herself out of her life, bounded by class, sex, and poverty. Things happen to her; she is not seeking new vistas. She suffers and is sacrificed. It's an old story, though told in the context of late nineteenth-century agrarian and religious upheaval.

Aligning *Tess of the d'Urbervilles* with *The Portrait of a Lady*, as I have done for my own purposes in this chapter, further reinforces the sense of *Tess* as a deeply traditional story. Its setting is rural, not cosmopolitan; scenes occur in English fields and woodlands, not the houses and gardens of urbane expatriates; the ending is classically resolved, not open; Tess, for all Hardy's insistence on her purity, is objectified in traditional ways associated with women and sexuality. When she yawns, Angel Clare sees "the red interior of her mouth as if it had been a snake's." She is also a milkmaid who murders her seducer, a figure one can trace back to tragic maids in old English ballads.

Yet for all this, *Tess* also expresses a progressive, even radical vision. No author of his time more ardently than Hardy fathomed the repressiveness of Victorian morality, the strength of sexual drives in men and women, the unnatural constraints imposed by marriage, and the untruthfulness of novels that ends with "the regulation that 'they married and were happy ever after.'" He wanted to substitute for "the catastrophes" of "this false coloring" the "catastrophes based upon sexual relationship as it is," words from his 1891 essay "Candour in English Fiction." And he anticipated how fiercely the reading public would resist his candor.

For the serial publication of *Tess* in *The Graphic* Hardy was forced to remove the seduction scene and the scene in which Tess baptizes her own baby, both sanitized and published separately as, respectively, "Saturday Night in Arcady" and "The Midnight Baptism: A Study in Christianity." Among other concessions to the magazine's readers, he even altered the scene in which Angel Clare carries the milkmaids across the puddle. "Let me run and get a wheelbarrow . . ." the version in the *Graphic* reads. Hardy was able to restore most of his original text for the book edition, but this greater freedom from censorship did not mean freedom from controversy. Tess as a fallen woman from a lower-class background has fictional predecessors: Little Em'ly in *David Copperfield*, Hetty Sorel in *Adam Bede*, even Hardy's own Fanny Robin in *Far from the Madding Crowd*. All these, however, serve as foils to the pure heroine while Tess, in contrast, *is* that pure heroine, despite her experience and despite what might seem Hardy's own ambivalence towards her (the snake's mouth).

As a contemporary reader I easily assent to Tess's purity, though I find myself eliding that term into others that for me have more meaning: courage, generosity of spirit, or, better still, integrity. Yet Hardy's chosen word is important. Tess is a heroine of her times, but she is also a kind of archetype. She survives violation and neglect, and Hardy's assertion of her purity is his vision of a purity of being that transcends all pressures and accommodations. She suffers "catastrophes based upon sexual relationship as it is" with both Alec and Angel, but she emerges from these uncompromised, even as a murderer, compelling us, as she does Angel at the end, to suspend moral judgment in our awe at her authenticity of feeling. Certainly Hardy idealizes her— James also idealizes Isabel Archer. But idealizing suggests distance. And yet, remarkably, Hardy realizes an exquisite closeness with Tess, a sympathy with her right to live in her sexualized female body. This body is natural and not corrupt. It is attached to a soul.

iii

I COME BACK TO the scene of my mother lying with me on the floor in her bedroom, talking about the naturalness of sex. My mother spoke sincerely, yet she also felt the need to guard her sexual secrets (there must have been others beyond the one about Freddie Ayer) then and for the rest of her life. I have wondered about my mother's secrets, about their influence on our lives. In literature when a secret exists, especially a sexual one, it's bound to be influential, both in its concealment and in its revelation. In *Tess* it's the concealment of her past from Angel and her revelation of it on her wedding night that propel the story towards its tragic end. In *Portrait* the secret past liaison between Madame Merle and Osmond sets in motion the plot to have Osmond marry Isabel, and the revelation of that secret gives Isabel the knowledge she needs to come into her full self, the self that will "last to the end."

The secrets in these novels emerge, but they are so potent as to be almost unprintable. Hardy omits Tess's confession to Angel from his text, while managing to convey its intensity through bodily gesture and the image of the diamond necklace Angel has fastened around her neck.

> She bent forward, at which each diamond gave a sinister wink like a toad's; and pressing her forehead against his temple, she entered on her story of her acquaintance with Alec d'Urberville and its results, murmuring the words without flinching and with her eyelids drooping down.

We cut to a new chapter, which begins: "Her narrative ended; even its reassertions and secondary explanations were done . . ." Tess has told her story, but we haven't heard it. I have read feminist critics who reproach Hardy for denying Tess her own voice in this scene. Yet that's not what I'm thinking as I take in the toad simile (another reptile) or the tenderness of Tess's and Angel's foreheads pressed together. Throughout the novel Hardy is so bold and brilliant in the settings and gestures he finds for his characters—the sleepwalking scene, Tess and Angel among the cows, Tess on the threshing machine at Flint-Ashcomb, Tess sleeping at

Stonehenge. These images remain with me far more than what the characters say. Speech in a Hardy universe seems paltry. There are greater seismic forces at play.

In *The Portrait of a Lady,* on the other hand, whatever the brilliance of James's settings and all his metaphors of houses and windows and birds and gardens, speech matters. Sometimes utterances are passionately direct; often they are enigmatic or elliptical, puzzles that compel our attention. Thus, silences matter, too, the things that aren't said or are hinted at obliquely. In Hardy we see the author creating the ellipses; in James the characters themselves seem to take on this function. I am especially attentive to the words—and words unspoken—that in a series of cautious encounters convey the secret of Pansy's birth. The first is Isabel's wordless shock at the sight of her husband seated and Madame Merle standing, a lingering image she doesn't yet understand; the last is the scene between Isabel and Madame Merle at Pansy's convent in which "Madame Merle had guessed in a second that everything was at an end between them, and in the space of another instant, she had guessed the reason why."

The power of the unearthed secret is then acknowledged in a pointed yet still elliptical exchange:

"I think I should never like to see you again," says Isabel.

And James gives the defeated Madame Merle the last word. "'I shall go to America,' she quietly remarked . . ."

What would have been the conversation, what would have been the "scene" if I had learned my mother's secret before she died? Since these possibilities would have been part of the real world and not literature, I doubt if we would have spoken with Jamesian restraint. In a way I'm glad the scene didn't happen. It may be my abiding reluctance to look into unlighted corners, but I can't help feeling the damage might have been great. As it is, I have been able to confront my mother only in dreams, in which I control both sides of the dialogue. I ask in my dreams, "Why didn't you tell me?" But the dream always ends before she replies.

I hardly ever dream about Freddie. His imprint on my psyche seems faint or is so deeply buried as to be inaccessible to consciousness. Knowing he was my father has changed some fundamental sense I have of myself, but it hasn't done much to change how I live my life or to shift my attachments. Tess learns she is a d'Urberville, and tragic consequences ensue from that discovery. I learned I was the daughter of a philosopher, and the discovery gave me a story. Casting myself as a writer, not a victim, I set to work on a family memoir. Writing the book engaged my best energy and spirits, and its publication, as I've said, helped me gain promotion to the rank of Full Professor. Perhaps I should think of this as Freddie Ayer's fitting last gift to me: the twelfth book of his bequest.

The Odd Women and Howards End

In the fall of 1985, I wasn't thinking about fathers. Trevor Westbrook had died seven years earlier, leaving me with a dreary but soon muted sense of the failure of our connection. The adventure of Freddie lay three years in the future, and I had, in fact, lost touch with this old "family friend" after he and Dee separated and then divorced. I heard he had married someone new, but I never met her. Freddie and I hadn't seen each other since my stay in England a decade earlier nor been in any form of contact.

The only parent in range was my mother, aging and arthritic, who still swayed the lives of those around her as if we were saplings bowing to her strong gusts. "Why don't you just bring in the coffin with the cake and be done with it?" she had grumbled at my plans for an eightieth birthday party. No one except Bow Wow had ever given her a party. She caviled and complained, suspicious of my motives. Then from the first guest's arrival, she was fine. "Thank you for going to so much trouble," she said to me afterwards. "I didn't think I would like a party, but I did." I was very pleased to hear that. As her daughter I seemed always to be ricocheting between despair and elation.

For a long time I had been embarrassed to be a person whose mother figured so powerfully in her life and emotions. I remember a friend's husband, a psychiatrist, saying about me when I was in my twenties and dating one of his friends, "The only thing wrong with Wendy is her mother." His words seared. I was ashamed. Now, though, thanks to second-wave feminism, it had become more acceptable to have a strong mother and more understandable to be enmeshed with her. People even envied me—I had a "role model." Nice cooking-baking, stay-at-home moms were out of fashion. Also in our lives and in our work, we were looking at relations "among women," the title of a 1980 book by Louise Bernikow. Nancy Choderow had written about mothers and daughters. As had Nancy Friday. Mothers and daughters. Sisters. Women as friends. Women as lovers. These were topics feminist writers and scholars and teachers in the classroom were exploring.

So when a delegation of Brooklyn College's women's studies faculty came to meet me, their new dean of undergraduate studies, and asked if I would like to speak on my scholarship at a Women's Studies brown-bag lunch, I was spurred to write an essay that arose from "The Heroine's Progress," the course I had developed as an English and Women's Studies offering at Barnard a few years earlier.

That course had traveled with me in my recent career moves. After leaving Barnard in 1983, I had taught it at Hollins College in Roanoke, Virginia, where I'd spent two years as dean of the college, and now, in the fall of 1985, a newcomer to Brooklyn College, I was planning to introduce it there as well.

My talk drew together George Gissing's minor 1891 classic, *The Odd Women,* and E. M. Forster's *Howards End,* published in 1910. I had been struck by the books' similar endings, noteworthy in the way men have more or less been sidelined, and women, left to raise a child whose father is absent (*The Odd Women*) or dead (*Howards End*), take charge of the future. I titled the talk "Sisters and Progeny" because in both novels the women caring for the baby are sisters and also because "sisterhood" was the rallying call of the 1970s and '80s feminism that was engaging my contemporaries and me, as we joined together to oppose patriarchy and claim equal opportunity for our gender. It was exhilarating to see women escaping the denigrations of Betty Crocker ads, claiming sexual freedoms, enlarging professional vistas, maybe going to medical or law school and not just graduate school in English, or at least having choice, at least not having to stay stuck in bad or avowedly limiting situations. To speak about my work at the brown-bag lunch was a way of presenting myself as a sister feminist to my new community.

But if my theme was the solidarity of women, it was also the enervation of men. I know I was trying to work something out of intense concern to me personally—not just the power and potential of women but also a question about men. Who might they be in the lives of women emancipated from their dominance? In a sense my world was catching up with my own understanding because I had always known women to be powerful. Not just my mother but also the many successful working women of our acquaintance in Hollywood—costume designers, actresses, singers, and writers—gave me models of female efficacy. But what role did men play in such women's lives? I remember "Pops," the husband of couture lingerie designer Juel Park, who often invited us to her beach house. While Juel would gossip with my mother about the stars who frequented her elegant shop on Rodeo Drive, Pops went off to the bedroom to take his naps. That's the image of him that lingers. "Men are children," my mother instructed me. To her they always seemed pitiable, easily manipulated creatures, good for sex, to be sure, but in important matters not to be counted on. From her father who died in her infancy right through Trevor and Bow Wow, men had let her down badly, that was clear. Even F. Scott Fitzgerald, the one man she seemed to have admired as well as loved, had shown his unreliability by dying right in front of her—and doing it just before Christmas! Of course, my experience with men diverged from hers. But in it, too, despite my great longing for an alternate script, lay a fair share of doubts and disappointments. In the books I chose to discuss at the Brooklyn College Women's Studies brown-bag lunch, men are weak or defective. It was not my own history I had in mind, but to have fixed on books in which women are energized and men unreliable cannot have been merely accidental.

My personal situation in the fall of 1985 was a complex one. In the public sphere I was a rising, forty-three-year-old professional, headed, I thought in all likelihood, for the presidency of a small liberal women's college. The job at Hollins represented a step in this direction, and my husband, Donald, never overly invested in his own career, had quit his work as a union organizer in New York to go with the children and me to Virginia. Hollins gave us a big free house that my mother, when she visited, said reminded her of Tara in *Gone with the Wind,* complete with the services of a black maid named Buttercup. Donald was able to find a half-time position at the college assisting the director of adult education, who, it so happened, reported to me. But I lasted as the school's chief academic officer only two years before calling upon my interview skills to help me get back to New York. Going to Brooklyn College constituted what is called a lateral move. The school was much larger and more vibrant than Hollins, but there was no free house, I was one of several deans, and the chain of command had me reporting to the provost, not the president. Still, my mother could retain her bragging rights about "my daughter, the dean." And that person remained someone with a bright future.

Behind this façade of success, however, lay a more troubled story. Forster exhorts his readers in the epigram to *Howards End* to "only connect," but my life at that time was beset by extreme disconnection of its parts. In truth, I had come back to New York for mainly personal reasons and as my mother but not my employers knew, my private life was in shambles. Before leaving Barnard, I had become involved with a woman lover, a philosophy professor nineteen years older than I. For years I had known of my sexual feelings for women but done my best to repress them. Finally, this became impossible. My craving for the experience grew stronger than my fear of it, and I got swept up into an affair. Nothing seemed more urgent to me in those months before leaving New York than to slip out of our apartment on one pretext or another and take the bus down Broadway from where we lived on 113th Street to my lover's place on 97th. I had assumed the affair would end when we left for Virginia, but it didn't. Donald found out about it right at the time of our departure and was enraged. Our children, Emily and Sean, knew because Donald told them. I saw their unhappiness, yet, at once obsessed and guilty, I persisted in my double life, trying to hold onto my family and traveling to New York whenever possible.

In the fall of 1985 our family was still in crisis and in pieces. Donald had moved out from "Tara," and when I left to begin at Brooklyn College, he stayed behind in the house he had bought in Virginia, and thirteen-year-old Sean, for the time being, stayed with him. Donald and I would get back together a year later in Brooklyn before separating for good, more deliberately and amicably, in the spring of 1988. Meanwhile, alone for the first time in sixteen years (the lover and I were winding down), I rented a small apartment in Park Slope, Emily, then fifteen, started as a tenth-grade boarder at Choate-Rosemary Hall in Connecticut, and Sean, clinging to the familiarity of Virginia, was truculent when I visited him there or brought him to New York. In his eyes I'd messed up badly. And I didn't disagree. I felt I'd taken a sledge hammer to my precious family life. My neck was stiff for a year.

How this debacle more or less righted itself to lead to my long, fulfilling career as a professor—no longer a dean—at Brooklyn College as well as to a less fraught personal life for me and greater stability for all of us is a story I will get to. I want, though, to linger in that fall of 1985 when my desires were at such cross-purposes: to be a professional success; to care for a family; to feel accepted by men and stay connected with them, yet at the same time be free to explore deeper relations with women.

Different books engage us at different junctures of our lives. For me, in the mid-1980s, a woman struggling to work out the terms of her adult life and finding conventional paradigms an inadequate fit, it makes sense I should be drawn to the texts of an earlier transitional era—the late nineteenth, early twentieth century—in which heterosexual marriage is questioned and women throw off, or at least loosen, traditional shackles. I was shifting in my fictional allegiance from the Victorian orphan to the turn-of-the-century new woman, and the force of my family background, education, aspirations, era, and sexuality led me on. But while I found quite thrilling every novel's heroine who manages to liberate herself from a tyrannical or inadequate husband or lover, I personally wanted not so much to be freed from marriage as to have it expand its terms. Back in 1974 I had read Nigel Nicholson's *Portrait of a Marriage*, the moving story of his parents' acceptance of each other's homosexuality within the framework of their marriage, and then dared to imagine such accommodations were possible, that loving women did not have to rule out an enduring bond with a man. It took a long time for me to act, but when I did, I still had that ideal in mind. Of course, Vita Sackville West and Harold Nicholson were *both* homosexual, they had Sissinghurst to hold them together, and they belonged to a milieu that tolerated their complex choices. In my own situation I could draw on no such supports, nor reasonably ask such tolerance of my husband. Many years later, when we again were friends, he told me he was sorry to have been so angry and wished he'd acted differently. I'm not sure what either of us could have done differently back then, but the collapse of our fifteen-year marriage, for all its ups and downs, was very painful for us both.

THE Brooklyn College Womens' Studies talk on *The Odd Women* and *Howards End* began with a much clearer delineation of alternatives than I ever faced in my own life. I began by reviewing those final epilogue chapters that provide such comfort in Victorian fiction in which we hear how Jane Eyre and Mr. Rochester have settled down, supremely blessed, and he has regained sufficient sight to see the color of his first-born's eyes. Or how Esther Summerson in *Bleak House* is blissfully happy in her marriage to Allan Woodcourt, he serving as father both to his and Esther's children and to Ada Clare's fatherless one. Or how Dorothea and Celia in *Middlemarch*, reconnected despite their dissimilar marriages, visit back and forth with their husbands tolerating one another and their children forming the close bonds of a new generation. But how might a novel end, I asked, in which marriage no longer serves as any persuasive sort of paradigm for mutual fulfillment and the resolution of problems? What ongoing life, what future possibilities might it point to?

*The Odd Wome*n and *Howards End* preserve a variation of the epilogue Victorian chapter. Strife has been resolved; a peaceful mood prevails; the next generation has been born. But marital relations between men and women have failed, at least in terms of traditional gender roles. Men in these works who have tried to tame and dominate their wives are rendered as tyrants or fools and have failed, moreover, to bring off their exercise in mastery, just as wives have failed, if indeed they ever tried, to be submissive. And marriage itself as a legal and social institution does less to bring unity out of division, realized identity out of fragmentation as to coerce, codify, and kill. Some women really are killed by it; others survive, subvert, or avoid it, but in doing so they part company from lords and masters, actual or potential. *The Odd Women* is more severe in its critique of the institution of marriage than *Howards End*, but in both books the key participants in the epilogues are not marital couples but rather a couple of women, linked in familial and/or cultural sisterhood. A child is in their hands. Men are gone, dead, or debilitated. Women are the custodians of the future.

ii

"'TOMORROW, ALICE,' SAID DR. Madden, as he walked with his eldest daughter on the coast-downs of Clevedon, 'I shall take steps for insuring my life for a thousand pounds.'"

I quote the opening sentence of *The Odd Women* to show its novelistic energy and the way Gissing wastes no time setting up what even the dullest reader can perceive as a prelude to disaster. Nineteen-year-old Alice, "a plain, shy, gentle-mannered girl, short of stature, and in movement something less than graceful"—thus a girl with dim matrimonial prospects—is unaccustomed to her father's confidences. Dr. Madden believes girls should be sheltered from worldly concerns. He reads Tennyson to his six daughters (their mother is dead), and, though it isn't mentioned, he must also be given to quoting Ruskin and Coventry Patmore's "The Angel in the House." By the end of the chapter,

Dr. Madden is dead. Called to attend on a sick farmer, his horse has stumbled on the return drive home and thrown the poetry-loving *pater familias* from his cart. Exit Dr. Madden. The life insurance policy, of course, has not been signed.

I first read *The Odd Women* when looking for texts suitable to include in The Heroine's Progress and within pages saw its potential for my course. After the father's unceremonious elimination, we fast-forward fifteen years to a scenario of two impoverished spinsters, Alice, now thirty-five, loose fleshed and pimply, and her prettier, but equally downtrodden sister, Virginia, second to her in age, sharing dreary lodgings in London and economizing with meals of rice and a little cheese. One has been working as a governess, the other as a companion—traditional occupations for gentlewomen in distress. Their next three sisters are dead, Gertrude "of consumption," Martha "by the overturning of a pleasure boat," and "poor hard-featured Isabel," an overworked Board school teacher, through succumbing to brain fever, then melancholia and drowning in a bathtub. It takes the novelist but a paragraph to dispatch the three of them. That leaves the youngest sister, Monica, whom Alice and Virginia, led by their own disappointments, believe better off in "business" than in "a more strictly genteel position." She is apprenticed to a draper at Weston, but since Monica is pretty (as Virginia *was*), her sisters feel she "must marry." Thus, Gissing covers the traditional options for impoverished gentlewomen and begins his problem novel, in which just about every character and every situation illustrates some aspect of the controversies of the day concerning women and marriage. His title, *The Odd Women*, refers specifically to England's surplus of single women swelling throughout the second half of the nineteenth century—in 1878 the number was estimated at 800,000. I knew this was a book I had to teach.

It appealed to me, too, that Gissing has more subtlety than I may have suggested in recapitulating the book's opening, a characteristic all the more remarkable in the context of a number of similarly themed novels of the times. The most damning diatribe I have ever read against marriage is Tolstoy's intemperate novella *The Kreutzer Sonata*, published in Russia in 1889, in which the jealous husband Pozdnyshev kills his despised wife, whom he suspects of infidelity. The real culprit, though, is marriage, the institution that binds people together in incompatible, soulless unions, in which the corruptions of the flesh—late Tolstoy's special target—pull them down in spirals of mutual hatred. The work was suppressed in Russia, but it circulated in Europe and America. Tolstoy's vitriol shocks me even today. His rage against the flesh, and especially the power of the flesh of women to ensnare men, is terrifying in its extremity. Thomas Hardy's *Jude the Obscure* (1895), another work that shocked its contemporary readers and that also explores the tragic gulf between human passions and marriage's institutional rigidity, is tame in comparison.

Gissing is not as ferocious as late Tolstoy or as relentless as late Hardy. His interest in the psychological nuances of his characters' interactions saves him from the extremes of the polemical. Nonetheless, *The Odd Women* is very dubious about the possibility of marriage bringing happiness. In the situations of even minor characters, women are seen as prostituting themselves to get husbands and then abusing or being abused by them when they've got them. The only conceivably happy couple in Gissing's story, Mr. and Mrs. Micklewaite, lacking the necessary financial resources, have had to wait a mickle twenty years to marry until the lady's cheeks are faded and sallow. *The Odd Women* unequivocally takes its stand against the institution of marriage as it exists in late nineteenth-century England. It is a cry against a situation in which a young woman like Monica "must marry" or suffer the fate of her spinster sisters while suggesting some intriguing new options for women brave and firm enough to choose them. What I have appreciated, though, is that it also promotes sympathy for women and men alike. Gissing himself suffered miserably in two failed marriages, the first to a young prostitute with whom he was infatuated, the second to a woman he had met casually in the London streets and who ultimately proved volatile and unstable. His unhappy life makes one feel for him, and I appreciate the way he feels for his characters. He renders brilliantly and without an iota of condescension the mutual loneliness that men and women can endure in their relationships. If Henry James proclaimed the need to get down into the arena and rub shoulders with his characters, Gissing seems to reside in the arena already, on an authorial level no higher or lower than the fallible yet intelligent men and women he gives life to.

The Odd Women has four entwining stories, two of them focused on women in relation to one another, two on women in relation to men. The relationships between women are more successful than the heterosexual ones, but in each of these stories there is a balance of suffering and relief.

The first story is that of the Madden sisters, Alice and Virginia and their younger sister Monica, the surviving trio of the original family cluster, women constrained by narrowness of conventional opportunity. George Orwell, commenting on the achievement of the novel at a point when it was out of print, praised Gissing for capturing the dreariness of lower-middle-class life and "the form of self-torture that goes by the name of respectability." Certainly the Madden sisters are victims of their clinging to middle-class gentility. Gissing portrays their pinched circumstances, their dreary jobs, their fearful reluctance to spend their small capital, which holds them back from their dream of founding a school, their poignant conventional dreams for Monica, and Virginia's sliding into secret drinking, a strain of the novel that puts Gissing on a par with Emile Zola or Frank Norris in the depiction of dipsomania. Stories of decline have always fascinated me, perhaps because my own family tried so unequivocally to live the counter-narrative to these. My mother told us of her dream in which Karl Marx himself spoke to her and said, "Sheilah, arise, you have nothing to lose but your mediocrity."

But what if one doesn't arise? Poor Alice and Virginia don't give much promise of arising. They decline. Alice has those pimples and her Bible, and Virginia succumbs to her vice. We see her slip from brandy to gin, from the first furtive darts into the railroad station refreshment room to the secret nightly guzzling in her room. At last exposed in all her pathetic drunkenness, Virginia is described as "a feeble, purposeless, hopeless woman, type of a whole class—living to deteriorate."

Yet despite all this, Alice and Virginia Madden still manage to show that sisterhood is powerful. They may not be Jane and Elizabeth Bennet, but the ties between them that Gissing delineates throughout the novel as well as their connection with Monica—their sister who marries so unhappily—are the underpinning for the hope poignantly expressed in the novel's ending. Caring for Monica's baby after its poor mother has died in childbirth, Alice is visited by the novel's other key female protagonist, Rhoda Nunn. Rhoda notes that Alice seems transformed. Her "complexion was losing its muddiness and spottiness; her step had become light and brisk." Alice is awaiting the return of Virginia, who is off drying out but hopes to be back soon. As soon as the baby can walk, the sisters plan to open their school for young children.

I had no sisters, but my mother had two, Iris and Sally, the sisters much older than herself, with whom she reestablished contact when I was a teenager and who led what seemed to me modest, respectable lives. Both had married, but I knew them as widows. Iris owned her own small house in the Sussex seaside resort of Hove and was proud her daughter had married a doctor and could go on continental holidays. Sally, the less prosperous, lived in a council basement flat in Brighton with her son Len, the unemployed barber, and had sent her daughter to the same orphanage my mother had been sent to, but she was unfailingly dignified in speech and demeanor. Unlike Alice and Virginia Madden, Iris and Sally were alienated from one another, but, separately, they doted on my mother and were enormously proud of her success. The sense I had of my family as led by women was reinforced by these aunts, who, in their own right, had persevered in the world. There had also been three sons in the family, but two of them were dead, and the third, Meyer, the brother who had revealed my mother's

Jewish past to a London tabloid, was someone we never saw. Whenever, though, we were in England, my mother would take us—once we knew of their existence—to visit her sisters. We would have lunch with one and tea with the other. My mother loved their good Jewish cooking.

That my mother, the youngest of six children in a struggling immigrant family, found better options than Monica Madden, the youngest of the six daughters in *The Odd Women*, can be attributed to her luck and her spirit, but also to the impact of the first-wave feminists who preceded her. Even less respectable than Monica in origins and early employment (after leaving the orphanage, Lily Shiel worked as a skivvy cleaning a five-story house in Brighton, in a factory where she was fired for dancing in the washroom, and in a department store demonstrating a toothbrush that cleaned only the back of your teeth), she nonetheless could rise to embrace new opportunities. When the toothbrush company, perhaps predictably, went bankrupt, she reviewed the cards left by various men and called upon one whom she remembered as a gentleman. At twenty she married forty-four-year-old John Graham Gillam, a man not so different in age and respectability from Monica's choice of Edmund Widdowson. But Johnny, unlike the miserably jealous and possessive Widdowson, encouraged the woman now renamed Sheilah Graham to enter the world. To improve her accent and her manners, he sent her to the Royal Academy of Dramatic Arts, and she became a chorus girl—a Cochran Young Lady, the British equivalent of the Ziegfield Girls. I have the cup she won as the most beautiful chorus girl of 1927. All this perhaps still fits within familiar paradigms—the stage as a venue for a striking, ambitious young woman. But my mother's next step seems more remarkable. She began to publish newspaper articles about her chorus girl experience, and soon she left the stage completely for journalism. I am not suggesting she was groundbreaking as a woman in this field—far from it. Women wrote for magazines throughout the nineteenth century; my mother in her orphanage loved reading the "penny dreadfuls" of gossip and advice to girls and women, often penned by women writers. But nineteenth-century women writers were predominantly middle class. My mother's path to her career from her disadvantaged beginnings, her sense that nothing was closed to her, needs to be linked to the efforts of a sisterhood. This sisterhood surely includes her own two sisters, who must always have hoped for more for her than they realized for themselves. It also includes her sisters in history and in literature, whose efforts and stories changed woman's lives.

When I try to give a summary description of *The Odd Women* to someone who doesn't know it, I say it's about a heroine who turns down marriage to the hero so that she can continue to run a typing school for women. The wonderfully named Rhoda Nunn, the heroine who engages in an intricate play of passion and sexual politics with her suitor, Everard Barfoot, but ultimately rejects him to continue her work with the typing school, is a quintessential "new woman" of the 1890s. Rhoda strikes me as a kind of gritty poor relation to Isabel Archer. Like Isabel, she values her independence, which in her case she secures by learning shorthand and bookkeeping. (Might not Isabel have been better off to have had such an option?) But Rhoda is distinguished from Isabel in finding a cause beyond the shaping of her personal destiny. By working for the advancement of women, she aligns her life with a great movement. It is no longer enough to say as Jane Eyre does, "I care for myself." Already Dorothea in *Middlemarch* understands the need to link her "ardour"—one of Eliot's favorite words—to something beyond the self, although she can never find what that thing might be. Rhoda has ardor, too. It is outer-directed but at the same time reflects currents of repressed passion in her nature. She makes a cameo appearance in the first chapter as a "thin, eager looking" fifteen-year-old budding bluestocking with a crush on a thirty-five-year-old widower. When she reenters the novel as a rather stern unmarried woman of thirty, working for and with the fortyish Mary Barfoot to run the school, she is in need of some yet-to-be-defined experience to become her best self. But what should that experience be? In her interactions with Mary Barfoot, the center of the second of the novel's stories "between women," Mary is the more conventional figure, a kind-hearted idealist, who combines "benevolence with business" and who would take back into the school one of the girls who has "fallen" by living with a married man. She and Rhoda argue about this, and the strain on their friendship when Rhoda's more puritanical point of view prevails but the girl later kills herself, shows Gissing at his psychologically nuanced best.

Rhoda needs a lover. But here's the odd twist. She needs him to complete herself; she doesn't need to marry him. The experience with Barfoot teaches Rhoda what passion is. It gives her the experience of desiring and being desired. She is sincere in her belief that she has found true love. But ultimately Everard Barfoot is expendable, an important passing chapter in the heroine's progress.

Again, Gissing's rendering of the dance of calculation and desire between Rhoda and Barfoot strikes me as superb in its understanding of human complexity and perversity. The protagonists contend, each seeking the other's "unconditional surrender." He, a freethinker as well as bit of a roué, tries to get her to live with him without marrying; she, in turn, wants to subdue him into an agreement to marry, and she prevails. Brilliantly, the chapter after their engagement begins, "But neither was content." The fact that shortly they fall out in a misunderstanding about Monica and part is almost inconsequential. Both are too stubborn to put love above pride—or above prejudice. And what could marriage be for them? The travel on the Orient Express that he offers her? What would either of them do when the trip was over? Home for Gissing, as seen most compellingly in the terrible claustrophobic marriage of Monica and Widdowson, has essentially no appeal.

To resolve the conflict between Rhoda and Barfoot, Gissing writes a scene in which Monica, depressed, pregnant, and embarrassed, but eager to clarify that she sought involvement not with Barfoot but with his upstairs neighbor, the callow Bevis, comes to Rhoda to tell her story. The scene is so reminiscent of the one in *Middlemarch* in which Rosamond Vincy sets Dorothea straight about Will Ladislaw that one wonders if Gissing had it in mind. The effect on Rhoda, however, is not to throw her back into the arms of her suitor but for her to come into her inspired *feminist* self. "Herself strongly moved, Rhoda had never spoken so impressively, had never given counsel of such earnest significance." She offers encouragement to Monica. "My dear girl, you may live to be one of the most contented and most useful women in England" (echoes of Daniel Deronda exhorting Gwendolyn Harleth?). But Rhoda has a different idea in mind from Deronda's vague vision that Gwendolyn may live to "make others glad they were born" while he himself leaves England to work for Zionism. Rhoda is exhorting Monica to engage with her in a very specific social and political battle to be waged on English soil.

> "We seemed to have lost you, but before long you will be one of us again, I mean you will be one of the women who are fighting in a women's cause. You will prove by your life that we can be responsible human beings— trustworthy, conscious of purpose."

Part of the wonderful balance of *The Odd Women* is that Monica cannot rise to Rhoda's level of impersonal passion. Her heroism is in defying her husband to the extent that she does, understanding that "love needs freedom if it is to remain love in truth," and in deciding to live apart from him. I see her, too, as a descendent of Isabel Archer, valuing freedom and refusing a controlling husband's terms of subjugation, though Widdowson, unlike Gilbert Osmond, seems another victim, not a villain. Gissing's sympathetic portrayal of his pathological jealousy is another of the book's fine achievements. But Monica has been fatally wounded by her experience. The marriage plot having failed her—not just in its aspects of rescue and domesticity, but even in her aborted stab at adultery—she dies in childbirth, while Rhoda carries on. To Rhoda is given the last word of the novel. "Poor little child," she murmurs, holding Monica's motherless daughter in her arms and looking at its dark bright eyes. That she relates to the child feelingly reflects her evolution. One doesn't know, though, if her pity is for the past or for the future.

The scene of Rhoda Nunn seated on a garden bench gazing at the child in her arms somehow softens the death of Monica as well as allowing Rhoda a kind of immaculate conception. But I also find myself wishing that we could see more of Rhoda at her typewriter, for, after all, isn't that her destiny? At one point during their "courtship," Barfoot, curious about her work, asks if it isn't just "copying with a type-machine and teaching others to do the same."

"If it were no more than that," Rhoda counters. She feels she's participating in "the greatest movement of our time—that of emancipating [our] sex." From a contemporary perspective it's easy to make fun of Rhoda's ecstasy about typing. By the time I graduated from college in the mid-1960s, taking a job as a typist or secretary might still be an "entry-level" opportunity to rise in publishing or advertising or some other seemingly glamorous field, but to me it evoked sexually wry New Yorker cartoons as well as T. S. Eliot's "typist home at teatime" who trysts with "the young man carbuncular," and afterwards "smoothes her hair with automatic hand/And puts a record on the gramophone." Yet it's important to remember that typing in the 1890s offered women extraordinary new opportunities to enter public spheres from which they had been previously excluded—spheres such as commerce, publishing, advertising, banking, and law. One of Mary and Rhoda's pupils lands a job in the publishing department of a weekly paper and hopes someday to start a paper of her own. Women's access to office work can be seen as truly revolutionary, radically expanding women's options and also cutting across class lines. Poor girls and even rich girls became secretaries and typists. Might not Jane Eyre have been delighted with such an option? I can imagine her reading the classified ads on a dreary day at Lowood, seeing in them more freedom than servitude, and packing her suitcase for London. Her Mr. Rochester might then have been her office boss.

My brother took a touch-typing course in high school. I purposely didn't, though I'm not sure my lack of skill saved me. As an English major BA, the best job I could find was as an editorial assistant in the textbook division of Harper & Row, where I sat at a desk tapping out form letters with two fingers. "Enclosed you will find your examination copy of the sixth edition of Broom & Selznick. . .," the company's best-selling introductory sociology text. The distinction that I wrote, rather than transcribed, these letters seems hardly worth insisting on. The boss still tried to seduce me. After a year I went back to school to get a PhD.

But perhaps all this is beside the point in thinking about Rhoda Nunn. She lives within Gissing's text, and there the belief she holds in office work as a route to women's liberation gives the chance to reject an Everard Barfoot and still be a fulfilled heroine. It's interesting, though, that if office work offers such great new vistas for women, the very same kind of work, indeed any work at all, seems far less emancipating for Gissing's men. Widdowson has been a clerk, Barfoot an engineer. Yet neither has found satisfaction in his work life. Widdowson confides to Monica the first afternoon they spend together how much he has hated "office work and business of every kind." A clerk's life strikes him as "a hideous fate." Barfoot left Eton to become an engineer, worked hard for ten years, but ultimately found the profession uncongenial.

Nor does he want to do anything else. "I'm not prompted to any business or profession," he tells his cousin. "That's all over for me. I have learned all I care to of the active world." His conclusion is that "to work for ever is to lose half of life."

Barfoot calls himself an "individualist" and sees Mary as standing "at the social point of view." What this means is that Mary has a social purpose; Barfoot doesn't. Mary, Barfoot, and Widdowson all inherit money at around the age of forty. Mary uses hers to start her school. Widdowson and Barfoot give up work but find nothing to engage with beyond their interest in the women they encounter—women more vibrant than themselves. Ironically, they are the "odd" men out. No wonder Mary Barfoot exclaims:

> It's better to be a woman in our day. With us is all the joy of advancing, the glory of conquering. Men have only material progress to think about. But we—we are winning souls, propagating as new religion, purifying the earth!

And no wonder Widdowson and Barfoot can offer Monica and Rhoda so little. Monica's marriage to Widdowson is worse than a mistake; it's a debilitating downward spiral for both wife and husband. As for Rhoda's romance with Barfoot, while Gissing makes it compelling, it suffices as the heroine's detour, not her destiny. How could Rhoda Nunn be satisfied with a man whose only goal is to watch the "spectacle of existence?" Men in *The Odd Women* drift while women stride forward. Widdowson at the novel's end is cut off from the future; he has given the charge of his baby to his dead wife's tattered but still forward-looking sisters.

Barfoot's end is equally bleak, or at least equally ironic. Marrying a lovely upper-class wife, one of the Brissenden sisters, he becomes utterly conventional.

IN the late 1980s the feminist Ti-Grace Atkinson gave a talk at Barnard that I attended. A tall, blond Southern beauty and one of the great radicals of second-wave feminism, she mesmerized an audience of respectful undergraduates with a blistering diatribe against marriage—heterosexual marriage, that is, though we didn't at the time make such distinctions—delivered in a lulling regional drawl. The students were stunned, but one of them gathered her courage at the end of the talk to ask a question. "You're very hard on marriage, Ti-Grace," she said. "I understand all that's wrong with it. But what is the alternative to marriage?"

I recall how Ti-Grace pulled herself to an even more statuesque height and thought for a moment. "What is the alternative to cancer?" she replied.

I repeat this story to my students at Brooklyn College, using it to create a radical perspective on the marriage plot in fiction and, especially in a masters-level course in feminist literary theory, to demonstrate an ideological extreme of second-wave feminism. It surprised me at first but I've come, resignedly, to accept the fact that many of my female students—even in the feminist theory course—want distance from feminism. They see it as radical and uncompromising, as cutting them off from the men they live with or hope to marry or are married to already. They know and care that women face discrimination, but they don't want to lead separatist existences. Many say they find men difficult and exasperating, but they nonetheless want them in their lives. I present myself in this class as someone who lived through second-wave feminism, a movement that made me happy to be a woman in my day. But I also make clear how my feelings about marriage are and always have been very different from Ti-Grace Atkinson's.

Maybe I'm a little like Rhoda Nunn, whose feminism grows more vibrant because she has known love with a man. In my case, to have been married to a man and had children with him may be a very commonplace woman's destiny. But despite the marriage's failure and my ultimate liberation to move on from it, I don't take for granted what it gave me, including important things beyond the children. My husband, oddly, was a lot like Barfoot. He worked because he had to and did not feel truly "prompted to any business or profession." But, while rueful about his own failure to find direction, when it came to *my* professional life, he put himself wholeheartedly behind me. I'm not sure what I might have managed to be or do without him. Our reversal of traditional roles had its strains for us both. Yet I know my debt to him is as great as to any "sisters."

iii

HOWARDS END, WITH THE urging of its famous epigram, "only connect," pairs for me with *The Odd Women* not only because of its similar ending but because Forster, no less acutely than Gissing, understands the trenches of difference between men women, the privileged and the poor, and lays these out in his novel's scheme. *Howards End* ranges from characters that have their choices of fine houses to those forced to settle for a dreary rented basement flat; it shows private affective life in tension with the world of work and establishes the masculine Wilcoxes and feminine Schlegels as not just opposing genders but almost archetypal alternatives. After Helen's initial skirmish with the Wilcoxes, Margaret reflects on the two families:

> "I suppose that ours is a female house," said Margaret, "and one must just accept it. No, Aunt Julie, I don't mean that this house is full of women. I am trying to say something far more clever. I mean that it was irrevocably feminine, even in father's time. Now I'm sure you understand! Well, I'll give you another example. It'll shock you, but I don't care. Suppose Queen Victoria gave a dinner party and that the guests had been Leighton, Millais, Swinburne, Rossetti, Meredith, Fitzgerald, etc. Do you think that the atmosphere of that dinner would have been artistic? Heavens, no! The very chairs on which they sat would have seen to that. So with our house—it must be feminine, and all we can do is to see that it isn't effeminate. Just as another house that I can mention, but won't, sounds irrevocably masculine, and all its inmates can do is to see that it isn't brutal."

Just as Forster's later novel, *A Passage to India*, asks, "Can an Englishman and an Indian be friends?" at the heart of *Howards End* is the question of relations between the two houses: the Schlegel house—cultured, continental, feminine—and the Wilcox house—the masculine world of "newspapers and motor cars and golf clubs." Can their initial collision give way to cooperation? The marriage of Margaret Schlegel, dubbed a heroine by her younger sister Helen because she "means to keep proportion," and Henry

Wilcox, widower and captain of British industry, is Forster's experiment in seeing if the energy of the Wilcoxes and the sensibility of the Schlegels can infuse one another so that the extremes of effeminacy and brutality are avoided.

The suggestion that the two houses need at least a good dose of the other seems tolerant, wise, and appealing. It's also noteworthy, given the fatigue of the marriage plot at this modernist juncture, that Forster chooses marriage— granted a highly symbolic and rather bloodless marriage— as the way to bring them together. He would seem to be more optimistic than Gissing, or at least less cynical, in still looking to the institution of marriage as a way to overcome profound societal divisions and bring harmony out of discord. The best thing Margaret as our heroine can do is not run a typing school, nor even keep attending those afternoon concerts, at which Beethoven"s Fifth stirs her so deeply, but marry Henry. She marries John Bull Henry Wilcox—moreover, is still married to him at novel's end. Marriage still serves here, as the critic Tony Tanner so brilliantly defines it, as bourgeois society's "means to bring into harmonious alignment patterns of passion and patterns of property."

But reading the novel to its end also unsettles this sense of a balanced resolution. Margaret Schlegel is the heroine of *Howards End*, but Henry Wilcox is hardly the hero. Despite a lightly ironic sentence denoting that "our hero and heroine were married," *Howards End*, is, in fact, a novel without a hero, even more completely, I think, than *Vanity Fair*. For Forster cannot restrain himself from emphatically rejecting the masculine as represented by the unfeeling and predatory Wilcoxes. Raised by his mother and aunt in the very "feminine" family house, Rooksend, (shades of the rookery in *David Copperfield?*), and struggling at the time of writing *Howards End* with his own still-repressed homosexuality, he is out of sympathy with their mode of "telegrams and anger," and ultimately pessimistic about their reformation. They remain one-sided human beings, who fail, as much in terms of class as gender, to connect and see connections; they do not avoid brutality.

Forster's lack of real sympathy for the realm of the masculine can be underscored by setting the Wilcoxes alongside Gissing's nuanced portraits of Barfoot and Widdowson in *The Odd Women*. It occurs to me that Gissing's male characters are already so diminished in masculine power through their anomie and inertia that they hardly need to be cut down to size. They are not brisk captains of industry like Henry Wilcox, arrogant eldest sons like Charles, or thoughtless imperialists like Paul. And in ways they would impose themselves on women—Widdowson by means of his jealousy, Barfoot through his freethinking, they are not especially effective. Men in *Howards End*, on the other hand, for all their obtuseness, are still running society and doing their best to retain their male prerogatives and supremacy. At least property-owning privileged men are doing so— not the poor clerk Leonard Bast, an aspirant to culture, not power, who, interestingly, seems to be a victim of both the masculine and feminine strains in the novel. Helen Schlegel seduces him, Henry loses him his job, Charles Wilcox hits him with the flat edge of an ancestral sword, and the Schlegel bookcase falls on him just as his heart gives out (can culture kill?). Possibilities of connection between classes dwindle as Forster's epigram shifts from robust imperative to poignant conditional: if only we could connect!

And what about Forster's grand scheme of connecting the Schlegels and the Wilcoxes, of merging their two houses? When Helen Schlegel, pregnant with the child of Leonard Bast, turns up at Howards End, the country house owned by Henry Wilcox but spiritually the property of his first wife, who wished to bequeath it to Margaret, Henry doesn't want Helen to stop there. Margaret, at this point forced to choose between her husband and her sister, chooses her sister without a flicker of hesitation. "She was fighting," Forster tells us, "for women against men." Henry, a man upholding a sexual double standard, is "criminally muddled." He cannot connect.

Through various ensuing twists of the plot: Leonard's arriving at Howards End in the midst of this crisis; his dying of the heart attack, which the law courts determine is induced by Charles's assault; Charles's having to go to prison for manslaughter, and Henry's collapsing in the midst of all this tragedy, Wilcox masculinity, it is fair to say, is defeated. If it cannot be tempered, it can be tamed.

At the novel's conclusion Henry bequeaths Howards End to Margaret, and the two sisters literally enact their claim to English soil as we encounter them out of doors in the sun-drenched fields along with Helen's baby by Leonard Bast, while a tired shadowy Henry remains indoors with his hay fever. We also learn that Margaret will bequeath Howards End to her nephew.

If we look simply at who is living in the house at the end of the novel, Henry, Margaret and Helen, and the male baby, it would be possible to conclude that the feminine and the masculine, the well-off and the dispossessed, have in some important way come together. But as Lionel Trilling has pointed out, the final connection is forged at the cost of too thorough a "gelding" of the male. Henry Wilcox, according to his wife's diagnosis, is "eternally tired"; he collapsed when he began "to notice things."

Henry reminds me a lot of Mr. Dombey at the end of *Dombey and Son*. Both Dickens and Forster seem to be saying that strong arrogant patriarchs need to be broken in order to be saved. But their gaining of heart doesn't mean they get put back together again. The description of Henry as "eternally tired" is followed two pages later by a view of him as "pitiably tired," just in case we didn't catch the point. Yes, he can still smile, as he manages to do at Helen on the novel's last page. But it is the Schlegel sisters, Margaret and Helen, who are literally left standing in the field, their bond intact and undiluted, beneficiaries of their "love rooted in common things" and their shared sanctification of "the inner life." Glowing with energy and purpose, they have also escaped any taint of effeminacy; ironically, the only effeminate—substitute enervated—character at the novel's close is Henry.

I came late to E. M. Forster, in college introduced only to his *Aspects of the Novel* with its wry, deft voice and wonderful chapters—straightforward yet a touch fey—on plot, story, rhythm, characters. Round characters, he says, are capable of surprising you; flat characters like Mrs. Micawber in *David Copperfield* with her tag phrase, "I will never desert Mr. Micawber!" delight in their energy and sameness. Subsequently I read his novels, in which I recognized the same appealing voice, capable of mustering authority, at times diffident, but unwaveringly humanistic. Forster brings to mind something Lionel Trilling remarked of George Orwell: that he is "not a genius," and that "the virtue of not being a genius "is "of fronting the world with nothing more than one's simple, direct, undeceived intelligence." I don't mean to minimize Forster's imaginative powers, but I can't help responding to an essential modesty in his work, a trait that distinguishes him from many other authors (including even determinedly nonegotistic George Eliot). Forster builds his world out of finely observed encounters, at once simple, subtle, and symbolic: Helen Schlegel's walking off with Leonard Bast's umbrella; Margaret's eating saddle of mutton—and not the fish pie she wanted to order—with the Wilcoxes at Simpson's in the Strand; in Shropshire Margaret's jumping out of the car that has hit what was first thought to be a dog but turns out to be a cat—an animal even less worth stopping for in the eyes of the most unfeline and unfeeling Charles Wilcox. Hinting at our negotiations and accommodations, at stretches of boredom and saving moments of intimacy, at planes of passion and prose, at wells of muddle and mystery, Forster seems so reasonable in what he observes of the world and what he would ask of us. "Only connect," he says. Yet this is exactly what is so hard to do.

Perhaps I also appreciate Forster because he tried to work within heterosexual paradigms as I for so long tried to do. Though his unexpected first kiss startles her and she "nearly screamed," Margaret Schlegel commits herself to Henry Wilcox and does her best to love him. Critics have talked of Forster's inability to portray heterosexual love, but there are many moments, if not of passion then of closeness, that one can sense between them. Margaret does work to be close to Henry. Sometimes this means acting a part as when she pretends to have been silly about the cat that was killed. Sometimes this means gently challenging him. I like the small moment when, after she learns of his past with Jackie, Margaret takes away the newspaper he is hiding behind and asks him to look her in the eyes. She can also, when it is necessary, be fierce—as in her choosing Helen over Henry, choosing to fight for women against men. All sexual connection, Forster recognizes, is not in the bedroom.

Henry Wilcox reminds me of the man who, for forty-six years, I thought was my father. As a self-made engineer, Trevor Westbrook rose during World War II to become head of aviation production for all of England in Lord Beaverbrook's Ministry of War. Working from designs everyone said were completely impractical, he heroically produced the Spitfire, the plane my mother always said saved England in the Battle of Britain. He was persistent and efficient—admirable in the contribution he made to his country. Then after the war he made money, investing in copper mines and other schemes, and took pride in his country house, Little Brockhurst, with its sweeping vistas of the Sussex downs. His emotional life, though, was dismal. Dazzled by glamorous women like my mother, dour, repressed, and hopelessly disconnected from his feelings, he failed, time and time again, to see beyond his own impulses and narrow assumptions. Once he embarrassed me, his sixteen-year-old daughter, by taking me out dancing to the Savoy and resting his hand on my bottom. His life ended sadly in a kind of dystopian version of the conclusion of *Howards End*. Trevor Westbrook fell prey to his venal second ex-wife, Carmel, an Australian gold digger he had married and soon divorced after his equally brief marriage to my mother.

Carmel returned to England to ensconce herself at Little Brockhurst and take advantage of him in his senility. The last time I saw him, on a day I visited with my mother, he was, to use Margaret's words about Henry Wilcox, "pitiably tired." "Wakey, wakey, Trevor," Carmel urged at our pub lunch because he had to be roused to pay the bill. He could hardly walk or talk; palsy seemed to have gripped his whole being. He died soon afterwards.

In my experience with men and marriage, I see parallels between myself and Margaret Schlegel. I have worked to be connected to men, and they have often, though not always, felt very "other" to me. I have liked best men of charm and lightness of being, men who connect easily with women, who have a strong component in them of Forster's "feminine" but without being effeminate. My grandchild Sam, Emily's son now in his teens, in whom I have always delighted, seems one such man in the making—his best friends, interestingly, are girls, indeed, sisters—and any men I've been at all close to, including both Donald and my son Sean, have had a balance of sides. As for dominant men who take charge in the style of Henry Wilcox, choosing the restaurant you eat in and suggesting you order mutton instead of fish pie, my experience with them is slight. I have known a few and shared their company, but never for long.

I hope for a different paradigm for relations between the sexes than that of dominance and subordination, something other than men's bullying women or women's castrating men. And perhaps Forster shows us the way to one in *Howards End*. In the figure of the first Mrs. Wilcox, the older woman who touches other lives through her simplicity of understanding, Forster gives us the image of a woman who prevails, but not through will or willfulness, nor through resistance and opposition. Externally a conventional wife and mother, Mrs. Wilcox reaches out in spirit to pervade rather than impose on others around her. With her ties to the wych-elm and the house of Howards End, she is clearly "connected" to an old agrarian England, which antedates both the motor cars and telegrams of Henry Wilcox's capitalism and the concerts and literary talk of the Schelegels' cosmopolitan culture. I could never be a Mrs. Wilcox—I'm far too combative as well as too reliant on words and wit. But I'm intrigued by the possibility she suggests of a different way to be powerful. Not my mother's way of taking on all comers, of bravery, bullying, self-invention and charm. But a quiet, almost guileless way, in which there is nonetheless full retention of dignity and influence. This is appealing. And perhaps I'm too quick to conclude I could never be a Mrs. Wilcox. Could I not take on some of her attributes, absorb the lesson of her modesty, link to people, men and women alike—in a generosity of spirit free of calculation? Mrs. Wilcox is sustained by her ancestral roots in Howards End, but I have my roots in the soil of English literature. From these I imagine myself rising and spreading, touching generations of my students and my family, a self that is realized through a kind of grace rather than self assertion. I see this figure still as a woman, an avatar of Forster's feminine, but a woman freed by virtue of age and understanding from the divisiveness of gender. She is liberated not by "fighting for woman against men" but by connecting—"only connect" is the mantra—with both in the least defensive, most expansive ways.

To the Lighthouse

I first read *To the Lighthouse* in my Bryn Mawr freshman English course, the same year-long course that introduced me to *The Portrait of a Lady*. Our teacher was Ramona Livingston, a middle-aged plump-cheeked woman, who lived near the college with a husband and daughters and, as a lecturer, taught two or three sections of freshman English. Though I wasn't attuned then to the distinctions of rank in academe, she seemed distinctly less glamorous than some of the English department stars who were teaching friends of mine in other sections, and I envied my friends these more scintillating instructors. Ramona Livingston seemed so average and quotidian, so lacking in any edge of mystery or suffering. Still, the work I did under her direction taught me to read closely, write clearly, and grasp the basic tenets of modernism. In our study of *To the Lighthouse* we looked at the open-ended symbolism of the lighthouse, Woolf's narrative flow in and out of her characters' consciousnesses, and her deft and poignant play with time. It's interesting to me now, though, that we did not consider any issues of gender. This was the early sixties, and though I had chosen to attend a women's college where a female instructor was introducing me to a novel by a woman author that centered on a memorable female protagonist, I failed to have a single conscious thought about any one of them—author, teacher, character, or myself—being a woman.

If there was a theme that most engaged me, it had nothing to do with my gender but rather with conflict between the solitary and the social, the struggle, surely, of my young life then. When it came time to pick a topic for the major paper of the course, I chose to focus on the figure of the artist, a personage at once gifted and stigmatized, in the fiction of Thomas Mann.

I had encountered Mann the previous year in my senior English class at Rosemary Hall under the tutelage of the formidable Miss Fayetta McKown, a much more imposing English teacher than the motherly Ramona Livingston (though I'm trying here, admittedly belatedly, to give Mrs. Livingston the credit I feel is due her). I remember Mrs. Livingston's prescripts, but I remember Miss McKown herself, one of those teachers who live on, magnified and iconic, in the imagination of their students. Revered by many of us as mysterious and intellectual, she sat in class with her chin propped on the back of her long-fingered hand and thrilled us with her musings about literature. One of our texts was an anthology of English and European short stories and novellas. The volume, as I remember it, contained Maupassant's "The Necklace" and "Mademoiselle de Maupin" by Henry James. But the story in the volume I loved best was Mann's "Tonio Kröger," a story about the figure of the artist that seemed to give literary representation to my own alienated yet intense state of being.

"Tonio Kröger" sets forth Mann's concept of the artist—a figure estranged from bourgeois life yet at the same time bound by ties of love and loyalty to the milieu that excludes him. In terms of plot and even character, it is only minimally a full-fledged story—for much of it, the adult Tonio simply reflects on the artist's predicament. But the part I have always remembered, so that it has lingered in my mind as the very heart of the work, is its opening scene. Here the boy Tonio—dreamy, brunette, artistic, half Italian by virtue of his mother, hence his first name—waits expectantly to walk home from school with his blond, thoughtless friend Hans, and Hans treats him carelessly. Poor Tonio Kröger, dark-eyed and different. I understood everything about him: his apartness, his intensity, his efforts to win a friend who prefers more banal pastimes, his failure to be normal, his love for his books, his suffering. Remembering so vividly Tonio's painful and unrequited love for Hans of the blue eyes and Danish sailor suit, I had forgotten, until recently rereading it, the second scene in which Tonio's affections have transferred to blond Ingeborg, with whom he's equally unsuccessful. He humiliates himself at dancing school by mistakenly stepping forward with the girls when the dancing master commands, *"Moulinet des dames,"* and Ingeborg joins in the throng that laughs at him.

There is an androgynous quality to Tonio Kröger, which is part of what makes him an artist and which links him, if I think about it, to other artist figures I've been drawn to. The highly androgynous David Copperfield, after all, becomes a writer, never losing his early "freshness" and "gentleness." And I think, too, about fine-featured F. Scott Fitzgerald, who used to act the girl parts in the Triangle Club revues he wrote at Princeton. My mother in describing him always stressed his charm, his delicacy, his delight in talking to women. As I have touched on in the last chapter, men such as these have always seemed accessible to me in ways that more blatantly masculine men haven't. When I was young, I allied myself with them in a stance of apartness and longing and then imagined the companionship they themselves might bring me.

Miss McKown, who introduced me to Mann's story and through it to Mann as an author, was also a solitary figure, someone who stood apart from the vulgar throng, but in a different manner from Tonio Kröger. Perhaps she was shy, but she seemed aloof, and she had a cutting wit. If the modernist artist is the model for a stance of alienation, I would cast her as a caustic Stephen Daedelus rather than a soulful Tonio. Unlike Stephen, though, and *his* model Lucifer, she was willing to serve. She taught at Rosemary Hall for over forty years, moving with the school when in the 1970s it decamped from Greenwich to Wallingford, Connecticut, and merged with the boys school Choate. I wonder if her effect on coed classes was as strong as it had been on my class of all girls. When in the year 2000 I attended my fortieth Rosemary Hall reunion, Miss McKown had recently retired, but she came to a dinner—grey-haired, heavier, walking haltingly with a cane (she wasn't well and would die a few years later) but still awesome in her benign remoteness. "I enjoyed reading one of your books," she said to me in her measured way. I swelled with pride and at the same time felt embarrassed. The book she referred to, the memoir I'd written about my parents, was then my only published book. Surely Miss McKown, a prodigious reader, must have known that. She hadn't finished her Yale PhD; she had never married; she had lived with her cat and read books. I appreciated her tact in giving me the benefit of the doubt, in suggesting the row of scholarly tomes that I, a nearly sixty-year-old college professor, must have produced.

When I won the English prize my senior year at Rosemary Hall, the prize was a copy, inscribed by Miss McKown, of Thomas Mann's *Dr. Faustus*, a further exploration of the artist's gift and linked curse of apartness. By then I had also read *Buddenbrooks* and *The Magic Mountain*. I loved Mann's characters for their loneliness and eloquence, their ruminations and their impotence. Somehow I had endless patience for their paragraphs and pages on end of talk. But since writing my paper on Mann at Bryn Mawr, I have not returned to any of his novels. I think of Susan Sontag reading *The Magic Mountain* at fourteen and loving it so much that when she came to the last page she immediately started over on page one. Perhaps Mann, for all his weightiness, is an author well-suited to young readers—or at least young would-be intellectuals. Occasionally I eye the group of books on my shelves. I think of rereading them—after all, they were books I once loved—but they seem too long, too ponderous.

To the Lighthouse is another story. It was the subject of my MA thesis and I have taught it often. My original hardback copy from freshman English is in tatters from overuse.

Curious about that old thesis, I recently dug it out, a rumpled carbon copy, from where it lay in my closet amid other school papers and old tax returns, and I read the first few lines:

The novels of Virginia Woolf reveal her preoccupation with a unity that transcends the egotistical self. Her characters must identify and merge with the life around them in order to fulfill the potential of their existence. Similarly, the novelist must escape from the narrow chambers of her own mind in order to create a fictional world that is "round, whole, and entire."

The phrase that jumped out at me is the one about transcending "the egotistical self." I knew I had focused on egotism as the theme of George Eliot but didn't remember it in connection with Woolf. I have to question my persistent concern. Surely, the need to overcome a solipsistic inclination, the imperative to make common cause with others, was my own. I remember how arrogant I was at Rosemary Hall—believing myself the best student in the school, defiantly unpopular despite a small circle of friends. At that fortieth reunion, one of my classmates told me how proud of me the class had been. I felt deeply humbled by this revelation. It had never occurred to me that my achievement could connect me to the girls in my class rather than distance me from them. But it was only at the fiftieth reunion, which I also attended—still hoping for what: continuity with the past, shared marking of a milestone, renewed connections, I'm not quite sure—that I felt more poignantly how much I'd missed. I sat at breakfast talking to a classmate who'd been one of the "smokers," the girls who laughed and gossiped on the steps outside the library while I, so dismissive of them, sat inside at a long wooden table and studied. She seemed very nice, this woman also in her late sixties, as we gave the outline of our lives. Soon, others joined in. The conversation turned to reminiscing about old high jinks in the dorm, and I could remember nothing. I could name so many of the books assigned but had taken in so little else. The books had been wonderful, to be sure, but I'd chosen them over living people.

College was better. Others seemed more like me: bright and awkward, a collection, perhaps, of Tonio Krögers and Stephen Daedaluses—or the American female version of these. Many were indeed artists: dancers, poets, painters. But we saw ourselves reflected in one another and yielded to a spirit of community. Twenty years after graduation from Bryn Mawr, as a candidate to be its dean, I was asked to say what made Bryn Mawr different from other colleges. Someone asked this—I think it was a trustee—as I sat in a roomful of faculty, trustees, and students being put through my interview paces. As if confronted with a Delphic riddle, I felt myself tunneling into depths of buried knowledge for the answer. It couldn't be that Bryn Mawr was unrivaled in being an elite women's college. After all, it was one of seven sisters. Nor, I thought, was it unique in being small or Quaker-affiliated, or highly intellectual. I kept excavating and at last felt my response taking shape. "The girls who choose Bryn Mawr," I said, "have often been outcasts and misfits. When they come to Bryn Mawr, they're transformed." And I set forth my theory of our empowerment in our collective oddity. The answer the person was looking for was that Bryn Mawr enrolled more international students than other colleges did. What I had said still seems to me a deeper truth. But I wasn't offered the deanship.

After college, I spent a year away from school. My summer job, arranged for me by my mother, was in Rome, writing

movie publicity for the American producer Joseph E. Levine—
his company was making a film starring Marcello Mastroianni
and Sophia Loren. A couple of times I went out to Cinecittà and
once glimpsed the director Vittorio DiSica talking to his stars
on the far side from me of the set, but mostly I was clocking
time in a little office off the Via Venito, pounding out copy on
my typewriter in which I took little pride of authorship. Then
I was back in New York in the textbook department at Harper
& Row. For the first time since I'd started kindergarten, I felt
free in these jobs of all the pressures of academic achievement.
I did what I was asked to but didn't need to try to be the best,
didn't have to hole up in a library or worry about tests and
term papers and grades. That year I made it my goal to be
easier and more gregarious, someone who had fun and lots of
friends, a person with and within a social circle, the express
opposite of a Stephen Daedalus choosing "exile, silence, and
cunning," and even of a Tonio Kröger with his apartness and
his longing for Hans and Ingeborg. You might say I wanted
to *be* Hans or Ingeborg, not long for them.

At New Year my mother urged my friend Helen and me
to give a party as a way to improve our social lives. "Girls,
give a party," she pronounced, as if that would set all good
things in motion, and offered her apartment on East 65th
Street as the venue. Helen's mother sent a Virginia ham up
from Middleburg, Virginia, where she lived, and we made
up our guest list. Donald Fairey, my future husband, came
to that party, the date of a Bryn Mawr classmate. I remember
thinking he was handsome and can still see him silhouetted
against the living room window, looking down and cupping
his hands to light a cigarette. Donald had no memory of the
party when I met him again three years later.

The success of the party pleased me—I hadn't thought I was someone who could bring people together like that. Virginia Woolf's catalytic hostesses Mrs. Dalloway and Mrs. Ramsay weren't particularly in my thoughts then, but I had a sense of our party as endowed with the kind of glow Woolf might have accorded it in one of her novels. The guests, the food, and the setting were the party's components, but then something spontaneous seemed to happen—something that emanated from Helen and me, or rather from us in conjunction with everything and everyone else, to create a sense of wholeness. When the next year I was back at school, my master's thesis topic became "The Quest for Unity in *To the Lighthouse*," a study of the overcoming of the feeling of apartness as Woolf's thematic and formal concern.

My own sense of apartness had also dissolved in a love affair that began my summer in Rome and continued, on and off, over the next few years. I met Ezio Tarantelli in the Villa Borghese, when, sitting on an adjoining bench, he plucked a laurel leaf from a tree, crumpled it and asked me to smell its fragrance. I was twenty-one and Ezio twenty-two. He was a student in economics at the University of Rome—the best student in the university, he boasted, and that impressed me. In the summers he supported himself by working as a tour guide since he spoke English, French, and some Spanish as well as his native Italian, and soon I was riding along in the buses as Ezio conducted tours of *Roma di notte*.

At first I had resisted him in my usual skittish way, and then I didn't. The relationship was sexually exciting, in fact my first fulfilling sexual experience, and it was playful in a way that minimized the differences between us. We were playmates, comrades, co-conspirators in exuberance, he a male Italian economist and I a female American student of literature, but we seemed the same—each drawn from a separate and potentially lonely gender into some miraculous commonality. I think of Virginia Woolf's man and woman getting into a taxi in *A Room of One's Own* and from the sight of these converging figures, her building a notion of the androgynous mind that is "naturally creative, incandescent and undivided." Ezio and I together seemed "creative, incandescent and undivided." He would pick me up in his little Fiat at midday from my office, and we would make our way to the public swimming pool or to one of the barges on the Tiber, where the whores, off-duty, sunned themselves. Together we swam and ate a simple lunch of bread and fruit. On weekends we drove out to the nearby beaches, usually Ostia, talking and often singing. Ezio taught me the words to "Bella Ciao," which I now understand to be a very commonplace song, but it didn't seem so then. "*Una mattina mi son svegliato. O bella ciao, bella ciao, bella ciao, ciao, ciao . . .*" Then he took me to meet his mother, maiden aunt and younger sister, the three women he lived with in a small apartment in a modest residential neighborhood. I remember the address—Via Tripolitania 115—from all the letters we wrote after that summer. His father, decades older than his mother, had run off for ten years to America but then had come back, an old man needing to be taken care of. The father had been an opera singer but now also was a tour guide. Ezio revered his mother for keeping the family together, and the women of his family, in turn, worshipped him and expected the world of him.

At the end of our summer, Ezio did not ask me to stay in Rome, and I didn't volunteer to. Vague though it loomed, some undefined destiny seemed to await me in New York, and I was eager to encounter it even though this meant leaving him. On the day I left, we kept taking pictures of each other with my camera, then asked a taxi driver at the airport to take more of us together. Back in New York, I would lie on my bed and stare at these as if trying to reanimate that day. I looked back at myself, dark-haired and tanned in my yellow sleeveless linen dress, exuding happiness though about to leave for New York, and at Ezio, a blond Italian with his domed forehead and lovely smile, dressed in the rumpled blue summer jacket he wore to do the tours for *Roma di notte*, both of us young and joyful and about to part. In one of the photos Ezio is hugging a palm tree; in another we have our arms draped on each other's shoulders, for he was only a little bit taller than I am. I sent him a set of the pictures, and we wrote back and forth about them. They were precious, these pictures, capturing something both tangible and ineffable. Yet I had left him to board my plane, and he had driven home in his Fiat to his mother, maiden aunt, and younger sister and his elderly prodigal father. And surely a day came—who knows how soon thereafter—when he sat again in the Villa Borghese and plucked a laurel leaf for some other girl.

Given all odds, the relationship should have ended as a summer romance. Apart, we kept writing letters—weekly at first and then less frequently. After a while I started dating other men in New York, gave my party with Helen, and ultimately started an affair with a man who visited occasionally from Boston, while Ezio, in Rome, fell into a number of casual involvements. When I went back to Europe the next summer, I based myself in Paris and went to Rome only briefly. Seeing Ezio wasn't the same, and I returned home with no expectation of a shared future. But then—I can't quite say why, perhaps just because nothing else was happening and I found it hard to form another meaningful relationship with a man—I invited him to New York for Christmas, and we started up again. By that point I had begun graduate school at Columbia, and he was headed to England to spend the spring semester at Cambridge. In May, when I was done with my classes and needed only to prepare for the MA exams I would take in August, I joined him abroad. We lived in an old house outside of Cambridge, where you had to put shillings in the meter to keep the heat going and we were always running out of change in the chilliest hours. Then going back with him to Rome, I rented an apartment with spare furniture and marble floors, and he drove his little car back and forth between his family and me. We weren't thinking of marriage yet were trying to be together as much as our respective commitments allowed. In Rome, as in Cambridge, I found libraries with all the books of English literature I needed.

Our last stretch together was a semester that ensuing fall of 1967 in Cambridge, Massachusetts. Ezio by then was working for the Bank of Italy, which sent him to study with a prominent M.I.T. economist. I rented an apartment for us in Cambridge, a few blocks from the Harvard campus, and then commuted each week by bus to New York to attend my classes, crowded into two days, at Columbia. Neither of us felt we were where we belonged. Ezio would meet my bus when I returned from New York, and I remember taking the Boston subway in the cold fall evenings back to our apartment on Trowbridge Street, where Ezio in my absence had never washed a single dish. For Christmas my mother wanted me to come to California, but she wasn't prepared to pay his ticket as well. "If you go, don't come back," he said to me. I was standing and he was sitting on a sofa as he said this. Shades of Gilbert Osmond and Madame Merle. I went to California to spend that Christmas with my mother. The pull of her orbit was simply too strong. Two and a half years later, after a few short involvements with other men and my first tentative sexual encounter with a woman, I married Donald Fairey. I didn't see Ezio Tarantelli again for seventeen years.

I had got the idea for my master's thesis on *To the Lighthouse* almost a year before the end of my relationship with Ezio, when he and I had just got back together. Seeing him off after his holiday visit to New York, the thesis sprung, fully shaped in my mind, on the bus back from the airport to the city. I would have a Part I focused on Mrs. Ramsay and her two experiences of merging: her contemplation of the lighthouse in her moment of solitude and then her blending with the assembled family and guests at dinner; Part II would look at the experience of the artist Lily Briscoe and the impulses that allow her to complete her painting; and, finally, a Part III would focus on Woolf's aesthetic as a novelist and the attempted wholeness of *To the Lighthouse*. I wrote of my academic epiphany in a letter to Ezio, and he was pleased to have his visit to me end so productively. You could say that I, too, had my vision and that somehow it linked with loving another person. Beyond this, though, a tie between Ezio Tarantelli and Virginia Woolf seems tenuous. While someone like him might make an appearance in a novel by E. M. Forster—Forster would extol his physical grace and, notwithstanding his ambition and discipline, his freedom from Protestant shame, Virginia Woolf doesn't seem especially interested in her fiction in foreigners. There's the Swiss maid in *To the Lighthouse,* lying in bed at night and homesick for her father and beautiful mountains, and Lucrezia, the Italian wife of Septimus Warren Smith in *Mrs. Dalloway*, who, back home, sewed hats with her sisters. But these characters fail to introduce any ethos into the novels that competes with Englishness. Woolf doesn't look outside English society or landscape for any of her values.

In the end I couldn't as well. I didn't want to leave my language and my culture for more than an extended excursion. When I married, it was to an Englishman who had emigrated to the United States in adolescence and resided as long as I had in New York. Ezio Tarantelli, in an ironic twist, married an American with a PhD from Tufts in English literature and a BA from Wellesley, who did indeed go to live with him in Italy. She and I would have been classmates if I'd chosen Wellesley, which I also applied to, and not Bryn Mawr. Ezio met her the winter he stayed on in Boston, something I learned only seventeen years later when I saw him again in Rome.

In the summer of 1984, during the period I lived in Virginia, the Barnard philosopher I was still involved with rented a villa close to Florence, and I was able to join her there for a few weeks. Immersed in early Renaissance art—churches, frescos, sculpture, and painting, Donatello, Massacio, Fra Angelico—she and I and a couple more visiting friends took side trips to Siena, Pisa, and other towns, and a plan formed for a short excursion to Rome. Whom do I know in Rome? I wondered in momentary amnesia.

Remembering, I dialed Rome phone information and got numbers for three Ezio Tarantellis. The first I tried was the right one. *"Ti ricordi* Wendy?" I asked. "You've got to be kidding," he answered in English.

I arranged to meet him for lunch, and he picked me up at my hotel in a much nicer car than his old Fiat. We were now in our forties. I had worried I might find him bald or fat or dull, but he wasn't any of these things. He looked and seemed the same, and without effort or strain we fell into our old familiarity. Though I didn't divulge my affair with a woman, I spoke of my marriage being in trouble, and he urged me to try to work it out. At the same time, however much he valued family stability, he confessed to being habitually unfaithful to his wife. He had tried to change for her, he said, but just couldn't do it, and I was grateful not to be in her position. I'm sure if we'd had a bit more time, he would have proposed driving out to Ostia for a tryst, and I might very well have gone and then regretted it. Instead, we talked on about our children—he had one son, my son's age—each other's friends and family, and our careers. He had realized most all of the ambitions he'd harbored when I knew him and was proud now to be the youngest full professor at the University of Rome as well as an economics advisor to a major trade union. He'd done well, he said, since I'd abandoned him in the cold Boston winter. "Poor boy," he said, miming grief. The pain was remembered playfully. "You'll always have a friend in Rome," he assured me, as we walked to his car with our arms around each other's shoulders.

In November, when I was back at work at Hollins, he phoned me from Toronto, where he was attending a conference. I felt very happy to hear from him. We chatted on a bit about our lives, and he still expressed concern that I work to save my marriage. In March 1985 I received a call from my always up-to-date-with-the-news mother. "Isn't it terrible about Ezio?" she said. "What?" I asked. I hadn't heard. After delivering a lecture at the University of Rome, Ezio Tarantelli had been gunned down in a parking lot by two members of the Red Brigade. They killed him because of his opposition to the *scala mobile*, automatic wage increases to adjust for inflation. All that ebullience and aspiration and talent, and dead at forty-three! He died one year younger, it now occurs to me, than F. Scott Fitzgerald was when he suffered his fatal heart attack in my mother's living room in Hollywood. Feeling terribly cut off from other mourners, I wrote a letter of condolence to Ezio's wife, who did not write back to me.

I am moved to revise my thinking about Ezio Tarantelli and Virginia Woolf. For I see ways they do connect, after all. It's not so much that Ezio could be a character in one of her novels—he resists that still. But Virginia Woolf helps me better to understand how, growing older, one looks back to the loves of youth. Clarissa Dalloway and Peter Walsh remembering each other young. Classira remembering Sally Seton. Mrs. Ramsay remembering Mr. Ramsay handing her into a boat. Lily Briscoe seeing again the dead Mrs. Ramsay seated on a rock. And I remembering Ezio Tarantelli, who similar to Mrs. Ramsay, persists *only* in memory, his future comprised exclusively of the memories others have of him. I defy time with these memories—at least in those moments I muster sufficient heart and stamina to yield to their full power. That's Virginia Woolf's insight along with her concomitant sense of each moment's terrible fragility. Being and annihilation, retrospection and anticipation, loss and recovery, remembrance and also forgetting—these are the conditions of mortality that enter the very rhythms of her sentences.

It is now thirty years since Ezio Tarantelli's death and fifty since I fell in love with him in Rome during the summer of 1964. I can see him in the Villa Borghese, proffering the crumpled laurel leaf for me to smell. I am with him on a boat returning from a half-day excursion to the island of Iscia, the two of us lying side by side on the deck with our legs stretched out and the afternoon sun in our faces. We had been sea-sick on the trip to the island, but coming back we had taken Dramamine and were sleepy. I sit next to him in the Fiat, which he drives with locked elbows—the safest way to drive, he tells me—and he talks about the beauty of the colors of landscape when the sky is overcast. I remember his smile and his opinions, his way of sleeping and sitting and walking and making love. For years after we separated, I would be behind some man on the street who had broad shoulders and a lopey walk, and my heart would quicken at the chance it might be he.

Virginia Woolf understands how you might love one person a great deal and yet have good reasons for choosing to be with someone else. I am not sorry that Ezio and I parted. I have no doubt at all about that. But he was someone, like her heroine Mrs. Ramsay, who could make of shared moments "the thing . . . that endures." Or perhaps we did that together. Of course, his horrendous death, a kind of bracket of violence in the flow of time's more commonplace erosions, intensifies my sense of an idyll at once lost and reclaimed.

ii

THE EMOTIONAL CORE OF *To the Lighthouse* has always for me been Mrs. Ramsay, the character who dominates the first section of the novel, dies within square brackets and in a subordinate clause in the second, and suffuses the memories of survivors in the last, a character of intense inner and outer beauty. (These sections are respectively "The Window," "Time Passes," and "The Lighthouse.") "Mrs. Ramsay, Mrs. Ramsay!" Lily Briscoe cries, and I cry with her, drawn into her consuming desire. I cry for the mother of those eight fictional children, for the life Mrs. Ramsay creates for her family and that motley assortment of guests at the prewar summer house in the Hebrides, all dining on *Boeuf en Daube* and merging into a magical unity when the candles are lit, a creative wholeness, the ineffable achievement of Mrs. Ramsay, in which the moment at hand seems enough. And I cry for the mother I myself had and didn't have. By virtue of class alone, my mother couldn't be a Mrs. Ramsay. She was too busy, all her life, running from the grim poverty of her childhood. There was no time to be a gracious lady who visits poor cottages and knits scarves for the lighthouse keeper's son. But my mother did knit for her children. I take from my closet—the same closet in which I've stashed my master's thesis on Woolf—a fragment of green scarf she was knitting for me when she died, all knit and no purl, because her eyesight had grown too bad to do both stitches. Though it's hardly more than a rag, I can't bear to throw it away. My mother, too, created moments of which I might say: "The thing is made that endures." She led a very different life from Mrs. Ramsay and was a very different mother, but she, too, had a mesmerizing—and maternal—beauty.

My students write almost as many papers about Mrs. Ramsay as they do about Jane Eyre. Last year I directed a master's thesis on "Silence in *To the Lighthouse* and Murk Amand's *Untouchable*," written by a young woman of Bengali descent who grew up in New Jersey. The student was interested in silence as a mark of women's oppression but also silence as a form of resistance and inviolability. She brought together Mrs. Ramsay with Sohini, the untouchable sister of the untouchable hero of Amand's novel. My student saw Mrs. Ramsay both as a victim of patriarchy and as a survivor who escapes, through silence, her husband's excessive demands. When she handed in the finished manuscript, she told me of two developments in her own life: she'd got engaged to another Indian American, a medical student at Columbia, and had landed a promising new job in publishing. As a twenty-first-century young woman, she enjoys far wider opportunities than Mrs. Ramsay. Yet she is tied still to traditions of culture and gender that draw her to the subject of women's silence.

In class discussions of *To the Lighthouse* strong opinions get expressed. Students champion Mrs. Ramsay over Mr. Ramsay, whom they tend to see as arid and egotistical, and many deem the Ramsay marriage a failure. They point to its conflicts and tensions and find unpersuasive the final line of "The Window" section: "She had not said it; yet he knew," Woolf's assertion that Mrs. Ramsay has "triumphed" in an

indirect expression of love for her husband. To some *Mrs.*
Ramsay seems smug and controlling—though perhaps this
is not surprising since even Lily Briscoe, so mesmerized
within the novel by Mrs. Ramsay and so "in love with them
all," acknowledges "there must have been people who disliked her very much," who found her "too sure, too drastic."
Students seeking to be more analytic write papers about
Mrs. Ramsay's role as a participant in the Freudian triangle.
Or cast her as a Jungian archetype of the great mother. Or
see the yearning of the other characters for her, and their
failure to possess her, as an expression of Lacanian desire that
must always remain unfulfilled. And so it goes.

My own young take on Mrs. Ramsay was to see her as
the creative center of the novel, almost a kind of artist—not
one who is separate like Stephen or Tonio but rather one
who dispels separateness in those extraordinary transcendent moments.

I was fascinated by the moment when Mrs. Ramsay
contemplates an inanimate object—the lighthouse—and
essentially merges with it. In the novel's third-person indirect discourse, the narrator tells us that

> often she [Mrs. Ramsay] found herself sitting and looking,
> sitting and looking with her work in her hands until she
> became the thing she looked at—that light, for example
> . . . . It was odd, she thought, how if one was alone, one
> leaned to inanimate things; trees, streams, flowers; felt
> they expressed one; felt they became one; felt they knew
> one, in a sense were one; felt an irrational tenderness thus
> (she looked at that long steady light) as for oneself.

Mrs. Ramsay merges so completely with the lighthouse
beam that looking at it, "it seemed to her like her own eyes

meeting her eyes," and the character feels, "It is enough! It is enough!" Throughout the novel, individuals search anxiously for meaning and coherence in their fleeting lives. Here the searcher is rewarded. Life—if only for a moment (Mrs. Ramsay relinquishes her out-of-body state to return to her web of human attachments; we next see her engaged in random chatter with her husband as they stroll across the lawn)—is enough.

I have never felt myself to be one with a thing. Perhaps the closest I've come is at the ocean, where I truly lose the sense of time as I succumb to the water's vastness and rhythms. Virginia Woolf knows the dangers of such identification. If Mrs. Ramsay is not to be "blown forever outside the loop of time," like Rhoda in *The Waves*, or lapse into insanity like Septimus Warren Smith in *Mrs. Dalloway* when he confuses himself with a tree, she must be able to move from intense to surface levels of existence, from the life that denies the individual body to the life that is lived in it. Mrs. Ramsay breaks her bond with the lighthouse by seeing it "with some irony." She realizes that it is "so much her, yet so little," and she calls out to her husband who has been waiting for her to emerge from her reverie.

I love the way Virginia Woolf passes from one consciousness to another, the way she shows the shifts and shoals in human intercourse. She sees that we are opaque to one another, that we use others to bolster our own egotism. And yet communication occurs. I am one of those readers who see the Ramsays' marriage in a favorable light. But I also think its successes are largely Mrs. Ramsay's doing.

Mrs. Ramsay has seemed to me the heroine of *To the Lighthouse* not only because everyone in the book, from

her husband to her children to Lily and even disagreeable
Charles Tansley, her husband's disciple, is in love with her
but also because more than any of the other characters, she
rejects "inventing differences" and strives to bring people
together in the face of powerful forces that keep them apart.
I find it interesting to compare Woolf's sense of the factors
that impede connection with E. M. Forster's. As does he,
she understands differences of class and gender and all the
slights and wounds and miscommunications they can cause.
But added to these is something else, something more basic.
Morally condemning egotistical individuality, she nonetheless sees that human beings must maintain their "screens,"
as she puts it in a diary entry, to preserve their sanity. "If we
had not this device for shutting people off from our sympathies," she writes, "we might dissolve utterly; separation
would be impossible. But the screens are in excess; not the
sympathy."

At the dinner gathering, which is the culmination of the
novel's opening section, the screens, because of Mrs. Ramsay,
not so much let down as become transparent. Woolf builds
the scene for twenty pages in a fascinating crescendo. The
gong sounds, bringing to a common table the people who
have come and gone throughout the day. But when Mrs.
Ramsay takes her place at its head, she feels that "nothing
seemed to have merged. They all sat separate." She is over-
whelmed by the barrenness of her life, the shabbiness of the
room, and even the depressing length of the table.

If the general gloom is to be alleviated, Mrs. Ramsay
knows she must exercise her special feminine qualities of
sympathy and tact and take upon herself "the whole effort of
merging and flowing and creating." Woolf shows how hard

this effort is, how recalcitrant are the individuals around the table. But finally, almost magically, the movement towards harmony begins. Mrs. Ramsay and the poet Mr. Carmichael look simultaneously at the fruit arrangement, and it occurs to Mrs. Ramsay that "looking together united them." Then the candles are lit, and William Bankes, the old botanist friend of Mr. Ramsay, pronounces the *Boeuf en Daube* "a triumph." At last, looking at husband, children, and friends, Mrs. Ramsay feels they are safely held together in an "element of joy" and observes:

> Nothing need be said; nothing could be said. There it was, all around them. It partook, she felt, carefully helping Mr. Bankes to an especially tender piece of eternity; as she had already felt about something different once before that afternoon; there is a coherence in things, a stability; something, she meant, is immune from change . . . so that again tonight she had the feeling she had had once today, already, of peace, of rest. Of such moments, she thought, the thing is made that endures.

There's the phrase that had such an impact on me—"the thing is made that endures." Because Mrs. Ramsay "makes" such moments, I have called her an artist. But, of course, if an artist is ultimately someone who creates artwork, that she is not—this woman whom marriage and motherhood have absorbed so entirely that it's hard even to imagine what she might have been or done, had she not become *Mrs.* Ramsay. The actual working artist of the novel is Lily Briscoe struggling to complete her painting, a character completely without glamour and to me perhaps most interesting for that reason.

Like Tonio Kröger, like Stephen Daedalus, Lily Briscoe is more onlooker than participant in life's feast. She compares the act of painting to "walking . . . out and out, . . . further and further, until at last one seemed to be on a narrow plank, perfectly alone over the sea." This image reminds me of Stephen in *Portrait*, walking out of the city and seeing the wading girl on the beach, whom he takes as his muse and inspiration when he decides to devote himself to art and beauty. To paint, whether she paints well or badly, Lily must remain apart.

But Lily Briscoe is not just an artist; she's also a woman, and an "odd" one at that—the spinster with her Chinese eyes and puckered-up face, "keeping house for her father off the Brompton Road." Mrs. Ramsay views her with some pity and thinks she should marry the widowed William Bankes. We as readers know she probably shouldn't since her friendship with him is described as "without any sexual feeling." Yet Lily doesn't escape the marriage plot for anything grand. We don't see her opting for "silence, exile, and cunning" or pronouncing herself the great artificer of her race. Rather, as she catches sight of the salt cellar on the patterned table cloth at dinner, she thinks, "at any rate . . . she need not marry, thank Heaven: she need not undergo that degradation. She was saved from that dilution. She would move the tree [in her painting] rather more to the middle."

Both as a woman and as an artist Lily's ambitions appear modest. She returns to the Ramsay summer house after the war, ten years older and seeming, to Mr. Ramsay, "to have shriveled slightly." She is terrified of the demands the bereft widower will make of her as the only adult woman at hand,

and she is uncertain, as well, about the enduring value of her art—"it would be hung in attics, she thought." But she is still the frail vessel chosen by Virginia Woolf to penetrate to the heart of things and have a "vision."

I ask why Virginia Woolf didn't choose a grander figure for this task. Perhaps she needed to contain Lily Briscoe in order to keep Mrs. Ramsay at the heart of the novel. No one looks longingly at Lily Briscoe; no one is mesmerized by her presence. Lily serves not to rival Mrs. Ramsay but to see, love, and paint her. Or rather, in keeping with the tenets of Woolf's art critic friend Roger Fry, to paint a "significant form" created by a relation of parts, one of which is the figure of Mrs. Ramsay. And why not make her a bolder artist? I think Lily dramatizes the difficulty and uncertainty of being any artist at all and especially of being a woman artist. Her painting, she feels "would never be seen, never be hung even, and there was Mr. Tansley whispering in her ear, 'Women can't paint, women can't write.'" Lily struggles against great odds to hold her ground—figuratively and even literally—as men bear down upon her.

It's hard for me, raised by a mother who had little time for doubts, or whose reflex in the face of them was always to charge full steam ahead, to yield myself as a reader to Lily's lacks and insecurities. In a way I'm back to the kind of choice I set up between Becky Sharp and Jane Eyre, between defying constrictions and feeling their pain. And Lily is constricted not just as a spinster and a woman artist unsupported by the culture, but also as a woman silently in love with another woman. Though "in love with them all, in love with this world," her especial object of desire is Mrs. Ramsay.

Could loving, as people called it, make her and Mrs. Ramsay one? For it was not knowledge but unity that she desired, not inscription on tablets, nothing that could be written in any language known to men, but intimacy itself, which is knowledge she had thought, leaning her head on Mrs. Ramsay's knee.

It's not surprising that critics and writers of the last twenty or so years have reclaimed Lily Briscoe as a lesbian, part of the interest in seeing Woolf as one and exploring the extent to which her Sapphic life imbues her fiction. I think this is important work, especially given the powerful resistance it has met with and continues to encounter. If I find myself at all holding back, it may be because I've not found labels of much use to me personally in sorting out questions of reality. Should I link to Jewish or Episcopal traditions? Am I a Californian or a New Yorker? Did I have Trevor Westbrook or Freddie Ayer as my father? Each choice seems only a partial truth. I'd now not hesitate to say I am or Lily Briscoe is gay, but that label, as do others, seems to flatten rather than illuminate identity. Whether Lily seeks intimacy as a daughter or lover, whether she wants Mrs. Ramsay or her world, I don't want to have to choose. "Mrs. Ramsay, Mrs. Ramsay," Lily cries. I can't help wondering if sexual consummation with Mrs. Ramsay would have assuaged her yearning. Maybe a little. Probably not for long. I think ultimately Woolf identifies Lily's longings less as specifically homoerotic desire than a general human condition, our isolation from one another in our separate bodies, the insufficiency of language to connect us, the body's feelings of "emptiness." Lily looks at the empty drawing room steps and feels unpleasant "physical sensations."

To want and not to have, sent all up her body a hard-
ness, a hollowness, a strain. And then to want and not
to have—to want and want—how that wrung the heart,
and wrung it again! Oh, Mrs. Ramsay! She called out
silently to that essence which sat by the boat, that
abstract one made of her, that woman in grey, as if to
abuse her for having gone, and then having gone, come
back again. . . .Suddenly the empty drawing-room steps,
the frill of the chair inside, the puppy tumbling on the
terrace, the whole wave and whisper of the garden became
like curves and arabesques flourishing round a center of
complete emptiness.

That Lily, experiencing all this pain, can persevere and
make art out of her yearning is really quite extraordinary. It
brings me back to the importance in my own life of push-
ing on with work but also to the way that work can relieve
pain when it carries you out of yourself to receive the gift
of inspiration. One thing, interestingly, that helps Lily in
this process is the way her concentration relieves her of the
shackles of gender. There's a telling moment in Part I when
she allows William Bankes to look at her unfinished painting and Woolf describes how

> she took up once more her old painting position with the
> dim eyes and the absent-minded manner, subduing all
> her impressions as a woman to something more general;
> becoming once more under the power of that vision
> which she had seen clearly once and must now grope for
> among hedges and houses and mothers and children—
> her picture.

So many words intervene between "becoming" and "her
picture" that the reader might easily miss the astonishing

assertion that Lily becomes her picture. Yes, Lily becomes her picture, and to do this she goes beyond gender, just as Mrs. Ramsay does in merging with the lighthouse beam.

I think I understand this state of being. Intense concentration has never seemed gendered to me. I never think I'm female when, say, writing a thesis or playing a match of tennis. Even loving people, though expressed through a gendered body, seems to me to dissolve gender's bounds. If Lily Briscoe is less magnetic than Mrs. Ramsay, it's because there is nothing alluring about her as a woman. But Lily's androgynous sensibility grows more interesting the closer attention one pays to it. When she returns to her painting in "The Lighthouse," again she loses consciousness of "outer things, and her name and her personality and her appearance, and whether Mr. Carmichael, the poet sleeping on the lawn, was there or not" as her mind from its depths throws up images and memories "like a fountain spurting over that glaring, hideously difficult white space while she modeled it with greens and blues." Yes, Mrs. Ramsay seems crushingly gone. But then she imagines what Mr. Carmichael might say: "How 'you' and 'I' and 'she' pass and vanish; nothing stays; all changes, but not words, not paint." And if the painting itself—"this scrawl," Lily calls it—might "be hung in attics," it's "what it attempted" that "remain[s] forever." To paint, though, she must leave all vestiges of safety behind. It's not enough to be metaphorically on a plank overlooking the sea. She must "step off her strip of board into the waters of annihilation" or "leap from the pinnacle of a tower." And she must also incorporate both genders into her psyche. Imagining what the impenetrable Mr. Carmichael would say about art is as if he and she are making a joint statement.

Then connecting with Mr. Ramsay must happen, too. She is able to finish the painting not merely because someone inside the house throws "an added shaped triangular shadow over the steps" that brings the composition back to more of its original mood in which a triangle represented Mrs. Ramsay reading to James; it's also necessary to achieve a "razor edge of balance" between the picture and *Mr*. Ramsay, whom she imagines arriving in his boat with James and Cam at the lighthouse and opens her heart to him. Only then can she turn back to the painting and draw the final line in its center. She completes the painting only when she has drawn both Mrs. Ramsay and Mr. Ramsay into herself—male and female, mother and father, the man and the woman getting into the cab of the self.

I admire Lily's achievement all the more because of how hard it has been for me to keep always in sight that Mr. Ramsay goes with Mrs. Ramsay. I never had a father who went with a mother, and I have spent my adult life ricocheting between men and women in my attachments, struggling to achieve a "razor edge of balance" between gendered forces but deeply craving a vision in which these seeming opposites can be reconciled. Lily Briscoe, modest artist, achieves this vision. The great novel *To the Lighthouse*, in which Virginia Woolf made art of the intense memories of her parents, does the same. But I, too, as modestly, surely, as Lily, have turned to art to have my vision. I wrote the family memoir that my old English teacher Miss McKown read and praised. It pulled my mother and my father from their separate spheres, retrieving them through the power of memory and language and bringing them together. It was myself I wrote into a kind of wholeness. And perhaps that freed me at last to follow my gendered heart.

IF I find myself growing more appreciative of Lily Briscoe, I also draw closer to Mrs. Ramsay, in whom my interest has shifted over the years. These days I'm focused on her standing as an older woman. Her fatigue at having to worry about the cost of fixing the greenhouse roof, her astonishment that the lives of the Mannings have gone on for twenty-five years without her having once thought about them, her looking across the length of the dinner table at her husband and having the double vision of him now and as a young man helping her out of a boat, her pleasure in the beauty of her daughter Prue, and generally, the depth in her life of time past and passing that Woolf conveys so brilliantly—these are details and aspects of the character and story that hold new resonance for me. When Mrs. Ramsay thinks of the future, she thinks of others' futures—that her son Andrew will get a scholarship and Prue will be happier than other people's daughters. She is excited that Paul and Minta are engaged and determined that Lily and William Bankes must marry. Certainly some older women, in and out of fiction, can still have personal adventures: they can work, travel, love, suffer, and possibly, even, themselves decide to marry (an opposite-sex or same-sex partner). But Mrs. Ramsay's bright hopes are for others, not herself—a function of her stage of life as well as character.

Mrs. Ramsay links for me with three other memorable older women in modern British fiction: Forster's Mrs. Wilcox from *Howards End* and Mrs. Moore from *A Passage to India* and, another Woolf heroine, the eponymous Mrs. Dalloway. Of these, Mrs. Moore and Mrs. Ramsay don't even have first names. And although Mrs. Wilcox and Mrs. Dalloway do—Ruth and Clarissa—they're not Janes or

Beckys or Isabels or Rhodas, young women whose stories we read to watch their destinies unfold, to see what husbands' surnames they will succeed or fail to acquire. Mrs. Wilcox, Mrs. Ramsay, and Mrs. Dalloway have longstanding husbands and with these a settled social position; Mrs. Moore is a widow. All four are devoted mothers, women who at least in conventional terms have ceded the place of narrative adventure to the next generation. Yet they draw us into their stories. We care who they are and wish for their happiness. The question is not what they will do for themselves—their moods change but not their place in the world—but how they will exert maturely formed selves. Our concern is with their being rather than their becoming, and the palpable mystery of that being seeps like air into others around them. No matter that three, including Mrs. Ramsay, die well before the end of the works in which they appear and death figures prominently in the thoughts of Mrs. Dalloway, the only one still alive on her story's final page. They are potent figures, lingering in the minds and hearts of those they have touched. You might say they are as potent in death as in life. Potent and creative.

Whereas I used to think of Mrs. Ramsay as the mesmerizing living character of "The Window," now I pay more attention to her haunting presence in "The Lighthouse." The future for her that is realized in the novel's final section—when so many of her hopes for others have proved so poignant (Andrew dies in the war and Prue in childbirth; the Rayley marriage turns out badly; Lily and William Bankes don't marry)—is as a memory in others' lives. I think about this kind of future, too, how my children and grandchildren might remember me, and I hope their memories of what I was or said or did, perhaps some remembered moment of fun or counsel, might somehow linger, as if out of time, to comfort and inspire them, to help them to greater happiness. There's a way of being older that seems to make you more detached and impersonal, less invested in self. Mrs. Ramsay has this quality. I like it in her and aspire to it in myself.

This being said, I know I'm not ready yet to become a permanent "wedge of darkness," Mrs. Ramsay's metaphor for her escape from self. I hope still to experience an abundance of moments when life coalesces into wholeness and those inevitably succeeding moments when these become "already the past." This is our life in time, as Virginia Woolf so beautifully captures its poignant rhythms in her fiction. "So you're still at it," my son remarked when I told him some time back of a new important relationship in my life. Yes I am. I have formed a partnership with a wonderful woman who brings to my life new hope for the future, a new chance to mitigate separateness, at least as much as two people can. Her name is Mary Edith Mardis, and she's an artist—a photographer. She also reminds me a bit of Hans and Ingeborg in Thomas Mann's story, not only in being blond and blue-eyed but also in seeming more readily sociable than I am. She has a great laugh and an easy manner. And the great thing is that she has chosen me as well as I her. Yet part of me, I know, still remains a Tonio Kröger—or perhaps I should say a Lily Briscoe—buried within myself, always marked as a little apart, caught up with the phantoms, living, dead, and even fictional, "wound about" in my heart, as Mrs. Ramsay is wound in the hearts of those who loved her. I'm in their grip. There's no safety from their ambushes and surprises.

A stray sight or sound stirs a memory of my mother that brings me to the point of tears. It swells and fades. Next I'm talking or making dinner or lost again in thought, perhaps another memory, perhaps the working out of sentences for a piece of writing. And all this, too, is being "still at it." "Could it be," Lily marvels, "even for elderly people, that this was life?—startling unexpected, unknown?"

A Passage to India and Beyond

In 1992 a friend invited me to travel with her to India. We would be there for the month of August, after the monsoon season but still at a very hot time. India is the most foreign place you can visit, she said, that will be accessible to you through English. I was just short of fifty and had never ventured beyond a narrow circle of Western European countries. To have gone many times to England, France, Italy, and Switzerland and dipped into Germany, Ireland, and Spain, to know good French, fair Italian and German, and a smattering of Spanish had seemed broad enough to confer cosmopolitan credentials. But I also knew my experience was limited—the word we were beginning to use was "Eurocentric." There was the whole rest of the world to reckon with, and my friend, who taught Asian Studies at a nearby college, seemed a good person with whom to begin this reckoning. She had lived in Delhi and Calcutta and done field work in Bengali villages; she knew India well and would be an astute guide.

I had no way of knowing I was on the brink of a phase of experience that would extend over the next twenty years and lead me to unexpected new places both through travel and in my reading and teaching. If I think of my life in stages, I can see that just as my attachment to the struggles of the orphan once gave way to fascination with the freedoms of the new woman and the scope of the artist, so now like the immigrants I would soon be teaching about in my courses, I was about to exchange roots for "routes"—the title of anthropologist James Clifford's 1997 work as he explores "traveling in dwelling, dwelling in traveling," no longer opposing concepts in a world on the move. Through friendships and accidents of family (my son married a Frenchwoman), I would travel twice to India as well as a number of other non-Western countries, teach a semester at a university in Paris, and embrace in my reading and teaching the postcolonial broadening of the field of English literature.

In 1992 all of this lay ahead. I was excited at the prospect of going to India, but I was also afraid, and not just because this distant and unknown land would most likely prove too hot, too poor, too polluted, too upsetting to my somewhat delicate stomach to make traveling there an easy trip. For all the places I had been to, I was not someone who easily encountered the unfamiliar. It's not that I considered staying home. My mother's daughter, I had been taught to say yes to opportunity. "Step into the tennis ball; don't back away from it," my mother had repeatedly exhorted. When someone asks you to do something, say yes, and then figure out how to do it. And at all costs, keep your doubts to yourself.

It's not a bad way to live. I had said yes, for example, when offered the teaching job in 1971 at the University of Hawaii, even though it was so far from my life and friends in New York. And however hard my time there, those three years in Hawaii, in which I taught students from many different Asian countries, opened my world a little more. I had said yes again when offered the job of Dean of Students at Bowdoin, even though I hadn't the slightest notion of what it meant to be a college administrator. The prospect of the job gave me nightmares, but I took it anyway. Over twelve years I had a succession of dean's positions, enjoying the challenges of the work though without ever feeling this was quite my true vocation. Still, always I went forward, always dismissing reservations, trying to step into the tennis ball.

But if Hawaii had seemed far away from my New York vantage point, India seemed even farther. Anticipating our trip, I had the sensation of a kind of freefall. It was similar to the way I had felt as I child when I was afraid that the road ahead, as we wound along the curves of the Pacific Coast Highway, wouldn't be there if I couldn't see it. I had loved plunging into the winding streets of European cities, but always with a sense of how I could get back to the main artery: the Seine or the Tiber, the Ramblas or the Brompton Road; always knowing where the subway stops were and where I was in relation to some home base. Going to India seemed like venturing beyond where I could see the road ahead; it seemed like going behind the length of any lifeline. On the level of a very primal fear, I worried how I could go so far away and still make it home again.

To give myself courage and prepare for the trip, I started a program of reading. Books would show me where I was going and make it more palpable to me that I would get there and back. I read histories of India, ancient and modern, books on Hinduism and Islam, travel books—one wonderful one, *Arrow of the Blue Skinned God*, recounts a modern traveler's journey tracing the route of Rama in the ancient epic the *Ramayana*—and soon I settled into the novel, in this instance novels by Indians who wrote in English. The first were by authors of an earlier generation. R.K. Narayan's *The Guide*, the story of a con artist who fakes being a holy man and perhaps becomes one, engaged me with its wryness and its subtle understanding of human nature. *Nectar in a Sieve* by Kamala Markandaya, the story of poor rice farmers whose village and traditional lifestyle is despoiled by a tannery but whose heroine, Rukmani, clings to hope throughout the most dire hardships, evoked my childhood reading of Pearl Buck's *The Good Earth*, a familiar story in which the valiant peasant suffers and endures.

Kanthapura by Raja Rao was more perplexing. The villagers who were its characters had strange, similar-sounding names such as Akkamma and Waterfall Venkamma and Rangamma and Subbayya and Chandrayya, and its prose tumbled breathlessly along as the author explicitly set himself the task of conveying "in a language that is not one's own the spirit that is one's own." The book has a memorable scene in which a Brahman, a follower of Gandhi who returns to his South Indian village of Kanthapura, forces himself to eat in the house of an untouchable. That gave me insight into the viscerally felt prohibitions of the caste system. I also could follow the buildup of fervor for Swaraj, Gandhi's concept of home rule, climaxing when the villagers march on a British-run coffee plantation and their leaders are arrested. Overall, though, *Kanthapura* didn't seem to have much of a plotline or characters you could get deeply involved with. Characters and plot aren't so important, my friend explained. What is, she said, in Indian literature, is mood; the overall tone and feeling. Okay, I said to myself. Think about mood in poetry and music.

By the time of the trip I had a roadmap in my mind of the Aryan wheat-eating North of India and Dravidian rice-eating South as well as rudimentary knowledge of such concepts as caste, karma, dharma and rasa, and the achievements of the great Mogul emperors. I had also started reading more recent fiction: works by Salman Rushdie, Anita Desai, Amitav Ghosh, and Bharati Mukherjee, among others, writers with the exception of Rushdie I'd previously not even heard of. It's amazing, given all the postcolonial literature I've read since, to think that in 1992 the only works I knew by authors living in non-Western countries were *The Story of an African Farm* by Olive Schreiner, a novel I'd discovered in the 1980s as part of my interest in late nineteenth-century feminism, a few works by Nadine Gordimer, and *Things Fall Apart* by Chinua Achebe, my choice—and the choice of most of my English department colleagues—for the mandatory single non-Western text we were asked to include in the core curriculum Great Books literature course at Brooklyn College.

I did fall sick in India. A spicy meal in a palace hotel in Jaipur led to a bad stretch on an eighteen-hour train ride from Delhi to Calcutta. Then in Calcutta the fume-filled acrid air seemed literally to take me by the throat and infect me. Dr. Chatterjee, a sympathetic young Bengali doctor, came to our hotel and was impressed that we had books with us—serious novels and tomes of theory. He warned us against the danger in India of succumbing to lassitude. Lassitude, as its syllables hovered in the air, seemed such a poignant word and seductive concept that we felt ourselves half in love with its invoker, our own Dr. Aziz. I must say, though, that neither my friend, the seasoned Indophile, nor I, the neophyte, succumbed to lassitude. Being sick didn't matter. I got better. The heat didn't matter. We took shelter from it when we could and otherwise pushed through it. And in all the places we visited—Delhi, Agra, Jaipur, Calcutta, Madras; through transportation adventures that included long rides in careening buses, days and nights in second-class AC trains with their shared compartments (I had a Muslim gentleman praying through the night in the berth above me on the thirty-six hour ride from Calcutta to Madras), travel by rented cars with hired drivers, and rides in rickshaws pedaled through the heat by bicycle wallahs; through the visits to imposing mosques and exquisitely carved temples, a session watching a class of Bharatnatyam dancers in Tamil Nadu, shopping expeditions to bazaars and government emporiums, meals of Tandoori lamb and chicken, grilled cheese sandwiches, and Chinese food (easier on my poor stomach) and drinks of fresh lime soda—through all this and more, I had a surprising sense of ease.

In *A Passage to India*, E. M. Forster expresses the fear I had before I went there, of India as dangerous—or at least dangerous to the Westerner. You could say it is India that kills his Mrs. Moore. Dr. Aziz impetuously befriends her as an "Oriental" when they first meet in the mosque, but I'd argue it's her distinctly Christian charity that she relies on to guide and sustain her. With the echo in the Marabar cave reducing all sound to sameness, "poor little talkative Christianity" becomes only "boum," and Mrs. Moore spirals into her strange and permanent withdrawal—not gentle lassitude but numb disengagement. The vastness of India, or least the sense of that vastness, annihilates order, individuality, and purpose. Even as sturdy a character as the Englishman Cyril Fielding welcomes the relief he feels upon reaching Venice in being able to recognize its "beauty of form" and "Mediterranean harmony." In contrast, the "idol temples and lumpy hills" of India, remain for him always a little menacing and confusing.

I, too, had a kind of Mrs. Moore moment on a visit to the temple of Kanchipuram south of Madras. After getting beyond the beggars and the pigeons outside it, and lingering over the erotic carvings of the playful gods on the exterior walls, I passed through the temple portal (my equivalent of the entrance to Forster's cave) into a dark interior courtyard, redolent with incense and the heavy smell of jasmine garlands. A rush of sound made me look up to see bats swooping and screeching over my head. Terrified, I spun around and hastened towards the entrance. My friend, alarmed at the stir I was causing, called out that I needed to keep to the right around the image of the deity in the womb of the temple—that's a tenet of Hinduism, to do *pradakshina*, or circumambulation, always keeping the sacred object to the right. But I didn't care. I needed to get out of there.

As I describe my hasty retreat, it seems closer to Adela Quested's bolt down the hill from the cave than to Mrs. Moore's quietly borne claustrophobia. But it's really not accurate to compare myself to either. The bats unnerved me for a moment; then I continued on my travels. India, as my friend had foretold, was indeed the most "foreign" place I had ever been to. The mix of faiths, the heat, the crowds, the languages for which I didn't know words or grammar or even scripts, the cows and elephants and monkeys seen along the roads: all this was unprecedented in my experience. But that being said, it did not seem remote or difficult. Cyril Fielding's experience to the contrary, Indian temples seemed no more idolatrous and Indian hills no lumpier than did the features of culture and landscape I'd encountered traveling in Italy. In fact, India seemed to me to have much in common with Italy. So much vibrant life in both these parts of the world is visibly lived in the streets rather than hidden behind the stolid fronts of houses as in England. India seemed exuberant, and I felt exuberant being there. Someone puts up a corrugated roof and calls it a barbershop. People talk readily to you, and you can talk to them. Of course, I was a tourist—being catered to as a tourist, nothing more. I don't lose sight of that. But the way I felt, especially after so much pre-trip apprehension, was wonderful. Though I took in strange sights, I did not feel a stranger. The world seemed safe to me. I was someone, it turned out, that felt more at home in it than I would have ever imagined.

WHEN I returned home, the reading project continued. More Rushdie, more R. K. Narayan, more Anita Desai, the discovery of such authors as the Parsee novelists Rohinton Mistry and Bapsi Sidhwa, the worldly Pakistani Sara Suleri, who was then writing both memoir and criticism, the Sri Lankan novelist and poet Michael Ondaatje, Vikram Seth, who in *A Suitable Boy* had relocated and rewritten *Pride and Prejudice*. Indian authors were beginning to be more generally read and written about, so I found myself at once on the cusp of things and in the stream of literary fashion. By

1995 I felt I had read enough and perhaps knew just barely enough about Indian culture to propose teaching a course at Brooklyn College on Indian English fiction. A Comp Lit course on Literature of India had been offered in the past by Professor Rahman, but he had recently retired and no one in the department had more background than I did. Still, I felt trepidation. How could I, someone who had spent only a month in India, knew no Indian languages, and had read only a few books on Indian history and religion and perhaps two dozen novels by Indian English authors, dare to profess knowledge of this field? And to do so, moreover, at a time when identity politics made it problematic to be a white person in any way presuming the ability to speak for people of color?

My first syllabus was a cautious one, frontloaded with English authors already incontestably within my purview. I had taught Kipling, Forster, and Orwell in other courses, but now the focus became their relation to India, their engagement with its culture, their inevitable British, one might say Orientalist, perspective. When Kipling turns his enervated Anglophile Muslim, Wali Dad, in the short story "On the City Wall" into a fanatic, frothing at the mouth and beating his breast raw during Mohurrum, is this not saying scratch a Muslim and find an atavistic beast? When Forster mystifies the experience of Mrs. Moore and Adela Quested in the Marabar caves, leaving vague the causes of their breakdowns, is he not contributing to the image of India as overwhelming and indefinable? And even though the British characters in Orwell's *Burmese Days* are detestable, his lisping Indian character Veraswammi is craven. But postcolonial critics such as Rushdie and Suleri explore these issues, and we read them as well.

From the British writers, I moved to Indian ones, though still with a foothold—theirs and mine—in familiar literary terrain. R. K. Narayan's early novel *The English Teacher*, in which, among other themes, a young teacher in an English-language Indian secondary school wrestles with his relation to English literature, offered a chance to explore the cultural legacy of colonialism. There's a wonderful scene in which the protagonist is just trying to get through the class hour—what teacher doesn't know that feeling?—and starts to read *King Lear* aloud to kill time. The language soon draws him in and so engages his imagination and emotions that he loses consciousness of everything but its beauty and power. At the end of the book the protagonist leaves the English school to teach in a Hindi school for young children, but the novel has made its complex statement about the abiding imprint of his English education. I also taught for the first time Rushdie's extraordinary *Midnight's Children*, a novel that for all the ways it plays with Hindu mythology, Mogul emperors, and Bombay cinema, among the myriad influences in its epic sweep, has a deep interplay with English literature. The protagonist Saleem Sinai is oedipal Hamlet and impotent Tristram Shandy as well as resilient Ganesh and the enigmatic Buddha.

I'm sure one strong reason I was drawn to Indian writers was because they loved books with connections to a faraway England much the way I had as a girl in Southern California. I had read *David Copperfield* and imagined an inviting land of rooks and village greens. R. K. Narayan writes about the primer he had as a child. "A is for apple pie," it begins. "B bit it, C cut it." He could understand B and C but had no idea, nor had his teacher, what an apple pie was, or, indeed, an apple. Perhaps, they speculated, an apple pie was like an idli, an Indian rice cake. Narayan came to love England and its apples through his reading.

And he himself, writing in his lucid English prose about his Indian sweet vendors, taxidermists, English teachers, bharatanatyam dancers, and guides, became someone difficult to categorize. The Indian Chekov, early critics called him, because of his nuanced portrayal of ordinary lives. I think of Thomas Babington Macaulay's arrogant assertion in his 1835 "Minute on Indian Education" (a document that argues for the adoption of English as the language of instruction in the Indian school system) that "a single shelf of a good European library [is] worth the whole native literature of India and Arabia," and I wonder to what shelf he would have relegated Narayan. Or Rushdie. Or any of the Indian novelists writing in English that I was reading and teaching. Notwithstanding Macaulay's aim to "form a class of persons, Indian in blood and colour, but English in taste, in opinions, in morals, and in intellect," English-educated Indians (never so docile as hoped for) had always been refused admittance to the British "club."

For "club" substitute "canon," and you come to the major cultural and curricular debate of the 1980s and '90s. By the time I began teaching my course on Indian English fiction, the work of postcolonial critics, challenging exclusive notions of Britishness, was recasting authors not just from India but from all parts of the former British Empire, where the language remained though the colonizers had departed, as just as legitimately part of English literature as, say, John Milton or James Joyce. "Commonwealth Literature does not exist," Salman Rushdie had asserted as the title of a 1980 essay. His position in the essay is that he does not want to be ghettoized. Writing in English, he not only claims his place as an English author but also contends that English literature written by Indians and other Common-wealth writers is the English literature of the moment. "It's our turn now," he radically proclaims. Not to be the Indian Chekhov. Or Indian Dickens. But to contribute works of great originality and gusto. "The Empire Writes Back," the title of one critical survey, became a rallying cry. And Indian authors were at the forefront of the charge.

I still have my copy of the June 1997 fiction issue of *The New Yorker*, which was entirely given over the Indian authors. The cover shows two khaki-clad white explorers, a man and a woman, coming upon a temple statue of a portly Ganesh, who sits peering down his elephant trunk at a book held between his hoofs against his round belly. The issue's table of contents, a mix of generations and of genres, fea-tures essays, fiction and poems by Rushdie, Kirin Desai, Amitav Ghosh, Amit Chauduri, G.V. Desani, Max Vadu-kul, Mihir Bose, Vijay Seshadri, Ruth Prawer Jhabvala, AK Ramanujan, Chitra Banerjee Divakauni, Jayanta Mahapa-tra, and Shamin Azad. And this list, of course, merely sug-gests the depth of field. "These days," says Rushdie in his essay within the volume, "new Indian writers seem to be emerging every week. Their work is as polymorphous as the place." He further contends, "Indo-Anglian literature rep-resents perhaps the most valuable contribution India has yet made to the world of books. The true Indian literature of the first colonial half-century has been made in the language the British left behind."

THAT I have taught a course on Indian English literature nine times over the last sixteen years, which is far more often than I have taught my supposed specialty of Victorian fiction, seems to me really quite remarkable. In addition to offering the course several times at Brooklyn College, I taught it five years in a row at NYU (1996-2001) as part of a Brooklyn College-NYU faculty exchange program. The NYU undergraduate curriculum included courses with a general focus on post-colonialism, but no one else had at that point developed a concentration on India.

Both at Brooklyn College and at NYU my classes invariably had a few Indian or Indian-American students, many from families living in Queens, some of whom knew a lot about Indian culture and some very little, all motivated to know more about the literature. The irony of my being their instructor did not escape me—or perhaps them, but with each successive round of teaching, I felt more flexible and adept in my approaches to the material. I grouped Rushdie's *Midnight's Children,* Bapsi Sidhwa's *Cracking India,* and Anita Desai's *Clear Light of Day* as novels structured by metaphors of breaking and crumbling in their treatment of India's 1947 Partition and then added Arundhati's Roy's *The God of Small Things*, another book with images of fragmentation, as soon as it appeared in 1997. I taught Vikram Chandra's sweeping epic *Red Earth and Pouring Rain*, narrated by the monkey god Hanuman, and Manil Suri's The *Death of Vishnu*, a novel focused on intersecting lives in a Bombay apartment building, among them that of Vishnu, the sweeper who lies dying on the building's landing while ascending in his dreams of immortality to the realm of his namesake. Seeking to end the course with a work that encompassed the Indian diaspora, I taught in successive years Bharati Mukherji's *Jasmine*, in which the heroine, propelled by global violence from her Punjabi village to Florida, New York, and Iowa, plays out the roles of both Kali and Jane Eyre; Anita Desai's *Fasting Feasting*, two novellas focused on the constriction of women's lives, one set in Benares, the other in Boston; and Jhumpa Lahiri's *Interpreter of Maladies*, the collection of stories, some with Indian, some with diasporic protagonists, that won the 1999 Pulizer Prize. As new works engaged me, I juggled my syllabus to make room for them, excited about the additions though always a little rueful about having to set works aside.

And just as Shakespeare's history plays had once taught me about the War of the Roses and *Vanity Fair* been my guide to the Battle of Waterloo, so now I understood more about the Amritsar Massacre, the genocide of Partition, and the war between West and East Pakistan from Rushdie's *Midnight's Children* or about Syrian Christianity and Kathakali dance from Roy's *The God of Small Things*. I learned, too, about Indian cities—Lahore in the Punjab, the setting for Sidhwa's *Cracking India*, Bombay, Rushdie's beloved city in *Midnight's Children*, and from all the books I learned about the gods and the myths and the foods and the customs and the words: namaste; chapatti; dhoti, mol. And I learned what it's like to weave so many cultural traditions together in works that are increasingly, in Rushdie's words, "de-centered, transnational, inter-lingual, cross-cultural."

I found myself on the kind of steep learning curve I hadn't experienced since college and began to consider writing a book about Indian English fiction. A grant from the

City University Research Foundation funded a return visit to India in January 2000. I wanted to travel in the South, the part of the country least explored on my earlier trip and interesting to me in being both more heavily Hindu and more Christian than the North. I especially needed to learn more about Hinduism. However cross-cultural the texts I was teaching, the great Hindu religious stories still seemed to infuse almost all of them, and I was aware how little I really understood these.

Thus, with the grant funding a car and driver and another friend agreeing to come along, I spent a month on the road between Madras (Chennai) and Bombay (Mumbai), never quite sure which name to use, old or new, as I read the passing Tamil/English, Kannada/English, Malayalam/English, and Gujarati/English road signs. We stopped in temples in Chidambaram and Madurai, ascended to the old colonial hill station of Ootacamund or Ooty, visited a game preserve and a coffee plantation in Karnataka, spent a night on a houseboat in Kerala, and watched Kathakali dancers in Cochin put on their makeup and perform for visitors. If this sounds like standard tourism, to a large extent it was, though we also met with Indian academics on their campuses and with relatives of my students back in the States, who took us into their homes and shared meals with us along with their hopes for their lives and insights about their country.

All in all, I fulfilled the goal of the trip, which was to gain a better understanding of India's geography, peoples, history, and cultures. As for my specific hope to deepen my grasp of religion, my knowledge grew exponentially of temples and gods and the ancient sagas performed in song and dance. I also understood better the cross-fertilization of India's diverse traditions by one another to create what Rushdie celebrates as its "impurity." Above the altar of an Anglican church in Madras hung a blue-skinned Christ figure standing on a lotus petal. That's the image that lingers for me as a vibrant representation of India's ingenious accommodations.

By the end of that trip, though, I had reached what felt like a conclusion. For all the fascination of India's richly intersecting strands, a month on its bad roads left me eager to get safely home and not at all sure about coming back. The book project hung in the balance, and I decided I would not pursue it. Like Cyril Fielding after all, I recognized the limits of my flexibility and understanding. I had gone a certain distance but did not have the stamina or desire to go further. I did not want to stay on in India, literally or metaphorically, beyond my tourist's visa. To do so would not be right for me—I knew that clearly. I could travel with verve and enthusiasm, but to become a true expert on Indian culture would entail a greater commitment than I had it in me to make. So I would remain someone passing through, culling impressions, zealous to learn everything possible, to know where I had been, but with an end date to the trip, an end to the syllabus.

I have continued to teach Indian English literature, both regularly at Brooklyn College and once in Spring 2007 at the University of Paris VIII. The students at Brooklyn College—Jews, Christians and Muslims—are of Caribbean, Russian, German, Italian, Lebanese and African-American descent as well as South Asian; those in Paris were mostly

Eastern European and North African. All have been curious about Indian culture, respectful of its layered richness, and at the same time inclined to sift the readings through their own experiences of colonization and immigration.

That I came to be teaching at Paris VIII, a cluster of run-down buildings in St. Denis in the northern part of the city with a predominantly immigrant student population, is one of my own life's latter-day adventures—a different kind of adventure from going to India but in its own way as eye-opening. I had been a regular visitor to France for many years because my son had lived there since his 1994 graduation from college. He had married a Frenchwoman, and now with three children, they had settled in the Ardèche, my daughter-in-law teaching elementary school and my son restoring old houses. People often remarked how lucky I was to have an excuse to visit France, but in truth it was hard to have my son and his family so far away. When the opportunity arose for me to spend a semester in Paris as part of a Paris VIII-Brooklyn College faculty exchange, this seemed a welcome way, thanks to the *vitesse* of the TGV from Paris to the South, to see them more easily and more often. I was unattached at the time (meeting Mary Edith lay two years in the future) and mindful as well that I'd soon be sixty-five and unlikely to have many more chances to teach in a foreign country. So, despite a tug of reluctance to leave home for so long, off I went for the semester to be part of the *département de la littérature anglaise et anglophone* at Paris VIII, while the professor from France, a specialist in postcolonial theory, took my place at Brooklyn College. The Paris department head seemed especially pleased to have me offer my course on Indian English fiction.

Soon I found myself installed in a rented apartment in Montmartre, spare in its furnishings but crammed with books (French and English) in floor-to-ceiling shelves that lined a long corridor. There was an upright piano in the small front room, which inspired me to revive a few short Bach and Chopin pieces I had learned in childhood. I wandered about Paris a lot on my own, lonely at times but also enjoying the freedom of anonymity as I observed the life around me. And twice a week I took the metro to St. Denis to teach my two courses.

Paris VIII had been founded in the 1970s by Hélène Cixous and other French intellectuals as an experimental, more democratic option within a hierarchal university system. But by 2007 it was in serious difficulties—underfunded, chaotically administered, and beset by internal feuds than absorbed much of the energy of my colleagues. My own six-person department of English and Anglophone literature was in danger of a takeover by the larger department of English language and engaged in ongoing efforts to ward this off. I was surprised to learn that our department was not permitted to teach American literature—that was the purview of the language department. This seemed silly to me (what turf wars don't?), but I devised my syllabi accordingly, content to remain a marginal figure, lunching sometimes with two of my colleagues (one from *littérature* the other from *langue*—our own mini *détente*) at the neighborhood kebab place and otherwise going my own way. I also found myself drawing closer to my students.

My undergraduate course on Memoir and Autobiographical Fiction had only six of them: a young man from Senagal, a young woman from Poland, three young women who were French, and another woman, a Berber from Algeria, who as a graduate student was auditing the class for the help it might be to her English writing. I assigned the students some exercises in creative writing and was surprised at how constrained they were, especially at first, by a certain French *pudeur* about revealing anything personal. We need to know more, I would respond to the hint of some childhood mishap or disappointment. *Oh non, Madame, c'est trop personel*, came the answer. I realized that in English we say "I" without shame, but the first person in French is habitually buried beneath the impersonal *"on." On est allé*, not I. By the end of the semester, though, the class did some wonderful work, and the student from Senegal had us all on our feet teaching us "dance kuku."

In the MA-level class in Indian English fiction, the major challenge was getting students the texts they needed for the course. You can get anything copied, I was told, but warned at the same time that asking the students to buy books was problematic. English books were hard to find; the students didn't have the money to buy them; and, in any case, you couldn't expect them to read more than one book or two since English was for many of them a third language. With these warnings in mind, I tried to steer an intermediate course. I had the students buy *A Passage to India* and *Midnight's Children*, readily available at W. H. Smith and other English-language bookstores. But for R. K. Narayan's *The Guide*, I just stepped into the department Xerox room, made a master copy of its 219 pages, and delivered this to Reproduction Services. No questions asked.

I taught in English, taking pains to speak clearly and slowly, beset by a heightened awareness of the nuanced vocabulary, syntax and contexts of our English-language texts. *Midnight's Children* posed the most extreme challenge. I assigned only the book's first section with the hope that at least some of the students would be motivated to read on after the semester. Rushdie's tumbling, eclectic language and layers of allusion made this book daunting for most of them, but I could feel how much its energy and iconoclasm engaged the class.

I have said that no one in the class was Indian or had ever been to India, but coming as many of them did from former French colonies in North Africa, they understood the colonial experience in an acutely personal way. Unlike the immigrant students I taught in New York, who by and large had come to the United States as children as part of their families' search for a better life, the Paris students had left families behind in Algeria or Tunisia or Morocco. I was surprised to learn that in France they had to submit letters from their professors every semester to the prefecture of police saying they were students in good standing in order to have their student visas renewed, and, ultimately, most of them would have to leave and go back to their poor countries. They encountered reserve, suspicion, and even contempt from the French, of whom they, in turn, were highly critical. Yet above all else, they wanted to stay in the country that, despite its drawbacks, offered them far greater opportunity. They responded to Rushdie's arrogance and bravado and hoped to make it their own. It's our turn now. The empire writes back.

I, too, was a foreigner in Paris, and despite all the times I'd been there, despite the ties to my son and his family, I got at least some small sense of what it can mean to uproot from your own country and be plunged into a foreign system with its own rules and cultural signs that are not always easy for the outsider to decipher. No one was sending me off to the police or threatening to deport me, but many small differences from the procedures at the university to my not knowing the French have only chocolate eggs at Easter, not hard-boiled ones, kept catching me unawares and making me feel my American identity more keenly. I also found myself accentuating this identity. When the grades I gave turned out to be too high—French professors, so my students informed me, don't give 18 or 19 *sur vingt* the way in America we give "A's—I considered correcting my "mistake" but decided not to. Since I was an American, I would give American grades—that is, as long as the students honored their part of the bargain and did the work.

My nationality also came into play when I discovered that two of our weekly meetings fell on French national holidays and I scheduled a make-up session of the Indian Lit class at my apartment combined with a potluck supper. One of the colleagues I lunched with was highly disapproving. "We are workers, and these are our holidays," she told me. "You are introducing dangerous capitalist ideas." But I persisted with the make-up idea, and the students seemed grateful to participate. They had never been invited into a professor's home before. A Polish young woman brought pizza; a French young woman a casserole. We sat together for hours over some bottles of red wine, while Hussein from Morocco told us what it was like driving a cab around the city. I was especially fond of Leila, the Berber from Algeria who was also auditing the memoir class, and her friend Kossaila, a soft-spoken young man from a small Algerian village who was probably my most sophisticated student of English literature. These two went together to the Paris *Salon du livre*, which that year featured Indian authors, and came back to class full of their excitement at having heard Vikram Seth. When I left to return to the States, Kossaila, who was also an artist, presented me with an oil painting he had done of a brightly plumed parrot. "Flaubert's Parrot, Madame," he said as he handed me the canvas. He hoped to go to England. I wonder where he is now.

Kossaila's painting now hangs in my house in East Hampton, New York, a reminder of this gentle talented person and of my four months teaching in Paris. Soon enough it came time to say goodbye to the bookcases and piano in the Montmartre apartment, turn in my perhaps overly generous grades at Paris VIII, make a final trip south to my family in the Ardèche, and then fly home to New York City and to Brooklyn College. I felt sad to be again on the other side of an ocean from my son but relieved, nonetheless, to be back with the friends and known routines of home. Paris, strangely more than India, had made me aware of cultural differences. I can't say to what extent this was my own state of mind, to what extent the maddening arrogance of the French. But I know that experiencing myself often as the outsider, I had drawn closer to my immigrant students and understood, in ways I hadn't done at home, their struggles to advance their lives in a foreign culture. My sympathies were unequivocally with them. I hoped it really could be their turn now.

ii

THERE WERE MOMENTS ON that first trip to India when, looking about me at all that was strange and wonderful, I worried it would fade from memory, that I wouldn't properly retain what I had seen and understood. I'd never been much of a photographer, but I fretted that I should have been taking more pictures as an aid to retention. "Can't you just let it pass through you?" asked my friend. Her words acted on me as a kind of release. Yes, I could do that, I thought— let the experience pass through me in a way that would keep me free and clear and open to whatever came next, which, in turn, would pass through as well. I have always thought of myself as a staunchly secular person. But that being said, there is a way in which I see India as encouraging an aspect of self I might venture to call spiritual. I was encouraged to relax caution and control, be less tied to the fixed and the familiar, more willing to follow the path of surprising transmutations and transfigurations, feel safer in a state of flux. The Indian gods are shape shifters. There are ten incarnations of Vishnu. All seem different yet are essentially one. If this is a core reality, then the wanderer will never lose her way. At least that seemed an appealing philosophy.

This leads to my saying that my course on Indian English Literature was shape-shifting as well, and eventually it shifted into something quite different from its original incarnation. Somewhere I read Arundhati Roy's rather acerbic comment that she was the only writer of current Indian English fiction who actually lived in India (in Delhi). I thought about this and made a list. There was Michael Ondaatje in Toronto, Bapsi Sidhwa in Houston, Vikram Seth in London, and Salman Rushdie in New York. Manil Suri taught at George Mason in Virginia, Bharati Mukherjee at Berkeley. And so on. And in addition to the Indian writers who had started life in India before moving abroad, there were those born abroad in diasporic families: Jhumpa Lahiri in the US, Hanif Kureishi, Monica Ali, and Hari Kunzru in England, among others. Some of these writers turned back to India in their work, as Rushdie did reclaiming his "imaginary homeland" in *Midnight's Children*. Others wrote of the diasporic experience, the straddling of two or more cultures. This is when I first thought about the immigrant as the representative figure of the late twentieth-century and decided to develop a new course in which the Indian transnational narratives that by this point I knew well would mix with ones from other heritages.

My new course, "Transnational Narratives and Theory," looked at the stories that get told when people leave one home for another and may no longer know to which nation they belong. Among postcolonial critics terms such as globalism, diaspora, displacement, borders, multinationalism, transnationalism, migrancy, nomadry, refugeeism, and hybridity were gaining currency—umbrella words under which to group writers of wide-ranging cultural experience. Crossing all sorts of national boundaries, I could bring together Rushdie, Roy, Lahiri, Hari Kunzru, and Kiran Desai (Indians with links to Britain or America), Talik Sali (Sudanese with a sojourn in England), Sandra Cisneros and Gloria Anzaldua (Latinas), Ariel Dorfman (North and South American), Chang-rae Lee (Korean-American), Eva Hoffman (Polish immigrant to Canada, now resident of London), and Junot Diaz (Dominican-American), among others. I had not been to many of the countries these authors wrote about. Often my students had, but even when they hadn't, together we could try to make sense of a world in motion.

I have become a bolder traveler, especially in books, someone much freer to go where I haven't been before.

Because my reading for the India and transnational courses led me to books that were very contemporary, in 2008 I had an idea for yet another new course that I called "The Shape of Twenty-First-Century Literature." The title, of course, begs the question. I'm not sure twenty-first-century English literature can as yet be said to have a shape, though 9/11 might serve as a date that sets a before and after. Global terrorism, the Internet explosion, climate change—these were some of the new century's markers I used to organize the course. I imported Lahiri, Kunzru, and Diaz from my other syllabi and also read a spate of new authors—Jennifer Egan, Kate Walbert, Cormac McCarthy, Rick Moody, among others—another steep learning curve. Again, as in teaching about India, I wondered about my qualifications. Surely someone my age (now nearing seventy), never especially avant-garde, and with a primary attachment still to Victorian fiction, might not be the likeliest person to take on literature of the twenty-first century. But why should such qualms stop me now?

THERE is no single work of fiction, or pair of works, I have read in the last twenty years that I can confidently choose as pivotal to this chapter of my story—no *David Copperfield* or *To the Lighthouse* that I knew I had to write about, no Jane contending with Becky, or Isabel in dialogue with Tess. The books of this chapter sparkle for me in their accumulation and abundance. They might be said to resemble the plethora of gods on the walls of a Hindu temple, so many of them, embodying principles of fecundity and generation, each pointing the way to another on a journey that seems unbounded. But just as Hindu worshippers choose allegiance to a particular diety—Vishnu or Shiva, Ganesh or Lakshmi—as their path to a divine essence, so I, too, have my particular devotions, books I praise and recommend to others and need to keep where I can find them on my shelves. Among these, I have chosen three to round out this saga of a reading life or at least to bring these pages to a close.

Cracking India by Bapsi Sidhwa (1991), *The God of Small Things* by Arundhati Roy (1997), and *Brick Lane* by Monica Ali (2003) are works that range in their settings and the cultural traditions they derive from, though all fall within the rubric of Indian English fiction that has reached an international readership. *Cracking India*, set in Lahore in the Punjab at the time of Partition, has a Parsee child as its narrator, a young girl with a limp, who witnesses the sectarian changes that "crack" the world around her; Arundhati Roy, moving between 1969 and the 1990s, tells the story of a Syrian Christian family in Kerala rent by issues of class and caste; and Monica Ali, born in Dacca to a Bangladeshi father and an English mother, raised in London and educated at Cambridge, writes of the struggles of present-day Muslim Bangladeshi garment workers both in India and in the East End of London. Before reading these books, I knew little or nothing about Parsees, Syrian Christians, or Bangladeshi Muslims. At the same time there are aspects of these novels that reverberate as deeply familiar.

All three books, as in much Indian English fiction, draw the reader into the intimacies of family life—what it feels like, for example, to be a young child dependent on parents who both protect and fail to protect that child, or a young mother with secret yearnings for herself that conflict with commitments to a husband or children. In many respects Indian

English fiction, for all the ways that it introduces Western readers to foreign cultures, continues in the great bourgeois tradition of the novel in which individuals are important but so are families and customs, and the struggle between the individual's impulse towards freedom and self expression and the pressures to keep him or her within castes and classes and patriarchal strictures play out what for readers of Western fiction are very recognizable themes. Such struggles occur, in one way or another, in the books I have cited here.

But these books have also surprised me in touching some of the most sensitive recesses of my personal history, and I am led again to reflect on the ways we bring ourselves and our own stories to everything we read. Lenny's limp in *Cracking India* comes from her having had polio. On a symbolic level the polio is the wound of colonialization. "If anyone's to blame, blame the British," says Colonel Bharucha, the doctor who operates on Lenny. 'There was no polio in India till they brought it here." But if Lenny's lack of eagerness to be cured says something about India's internalized dependency on its colonizer, it also reflects conflict within a young girl's psyche. The polio and the limp it leaves her with make Lenny feel special in many ways—for one thing, she gains her access to her parents' bed.

For me Lenny's polio brought back my conflicted feelings when my younger brother had a bout of what his doctors thought was polio when he was two. He spent a few months with his leg in a cast and got a lot of attention. What I remember most from that time—a stretch of summer—is that other children at the beach were told not to play with me, and I felt quite dreary and lonely. I don't know if this links to my fantasy a few years later—I must have been six or seven—that I was a wounded soldier in the jungle. The wound was to my leg, and I would get down on the floor in my bedroom and crawl around dragging it behind me. My object was to get to the nursing station—this involved hoisting myself onto my bed—where I would be taken care of.

I had always been ashamed of this fantasy—it seemed so perverse and peculiar. But once I mentioned it to a friend, who said that she, too, as a child had pretended to have a crippled leg and used to limp around for hours at a time. We marveled at this coincidence, but perhaps it's not so amazing. Special and wounded—isn't this the sense so many of us have of ourselves?

Cracking India also brilliantly conveys how a child can feel both protected and at risk. Lenny's world is presented at the outset of the novel as "compressed." She lives with her mother, father, and younger brother in their well-to-do Parsee household sustained by Hindu and Muslim servants; her aunt and godmother live nearby, and she ventures no further than the neighborhood park where she watches her Ayah, a beautiful young Hindu woman of eighteen, flirt with her suitors—Sikh, Muslim, Pathan, Chinese—and somehow keeps the peace among them.

This is the small realm of Lenny's childhood—seemingly safe, though with its undercurrents of sexuality that the child does and doesn't understand. Her male cousin lures her into sexual games; one of Ayah's Muslim suitors, the character called Ice-Candy-Man, whose name was the novel's original British title, tries to wiggle his toes under the nubile young woman's sari. But all this is on the level, if not of innocence, then at least of contained sexual play. Lenny's world comes dramatically unraveled with the intruding violence of partition, as the Punjab cracks in two and Ayah, abducted, raped, and turned into a prostitute by Ice-Candy-Man, becomes the body on which sectarian violence is written. In the course of the novel Lenny's mother and Godmother rescue Ayah and return her to her family in Amritsar. What struck me so forcibly in reading and teaching this book is the simultaneous strength and vulnerability of women, the disruptive force of sexuality, and the inevitable end of the idyll of childhood.

My own parallel "compressed world"—one lived on orderly streets within a household sustained by people doing their jobs—included our beloved housekeeper Stella, who walked me to school, my mother's secretary Adele typing the column in our bookcase-lined den, and the Japanese gardener working shirtless out of doors. To me this world was circumscribed and sheltering, though the potential for disruption was, of course, always there. I could sense it in my mother on the phone scrambling to get material for her columns or in small things that happened: a man, for example, who was staying with us at the beach, getting his penis caught in his zipper and having to be rushed to the hospital, though I didn't question what he was doing with us in the first place. I think that was the same summer, when I was nine, that I can remember sitting on the sand in the shade of a wooden chair and listening to my mother and her friends talk about Joseph R. McCarthy and their fear of his politics. We were Democrats, but my mother was afraid to put an Adlai Stevenson sticker on our car. None of this touched me, though, until the intrusion of Bow Wow abruptly made the world unsafe.

Of course, I'm not equating my personal trauma of Bow Wow with the tragedy of a whole region torn by sectarian violence. I'm only saying that Bow Wow taught me the destructive power of a sexual predator, so that when Lenny has an epiphany about such power, I understand it well. In one of the book's most striking and dramatic scenes, Lenny's Godmother excoriates Ice-Candy-Man for what he has done to Ayah as the child looks on, and Lenny in her role as narrator reflects on the significance of this moment:

> The innocence that my parents' vigilance, the servants care and Godmother's love sheltered in me, that neither Cousin's carnal cravings, nor the stories of the violence of the mobs, could quite destroy, was laid waste that evening by the emotional storm that raged round me. The confrontation between Ice-Candy-Man and Godmother opened my eyes to the wisdom of righteous indignation over compassion. To the demands of gratification—and the unscrupulous nature of desire.
>
> To the pitiless face of love.

In the ensuing chapter Lenny goes with her Godmother to visit Ayah in the brothel district where Ice-Candy-Man has been keeping her. Ayah comes into the room teetering on high heels, draped, bejeweled, and bereft of all her former "radiance" and "animation." Her eyes are vacant. Even her voice has changed to a gruff rasp "as if someone has mutilated her vocal chords."

This for me is the novel's most terrible moment, the moment of greatest loss for Lenny—when someone you love has been crushed beyond recognition or recovery. Although Ayah is subsequently rescued, brought to the fallen women's compound and then repatriated with her family, she cannot be restored to her former self. A beloved person has been cracked and broken.

There is a similar jolt of loss in *The God of Small Things*, another novel that uses the fragility of the body as both physical reality and cultural metaphor. Among the many sharp moments of loss in this tragic text, there is one I find especially poignant. It's when Ammu, the twins' mother and lover of Velutha, a woman whose beauty has so beguiled her children, comes back to the family home in Ayemenem after an interval of a few years, sick and swollen with cortisone and is "not the slender mother Rahel knew." As the adult Rahel remembers the change, Ammu's hair has lost its sheen, she coughs up vile-smelling phlegm and speaks "in a deep unnatural voice."

In Roy's non-chronological organization of the novel, the description of Ammu's decline is placed for maximum impact. Coming in a chapter midway through the novel, it digresses from the book's two main strands of narrative: that of the present in which the adult twins, Rahel and Estha, have returned to Ayemenem and the account of the 1969 "Terror," occurring when the twins were seven, in which their cousin, the half-English Sophie Mol, drowned and Ammu's lover, the untouchable carpenter Velutha, was brutally killed. In the present-time narrative, Rahel finds some childhood exercise books that trigger her memory of her altered mother. In the next chapter we return to the earlier events of 1969. But now, when we reencounter Ammu's beauty, a beauty Roy, with her acute eye for corporeal details, makes so tangible, it is shadowed by our knowledge of its brevity. We also experience fully what it means for Ammu's life to end at the "viable, die-able age" of thirty-one. The chapter "Wisdom Exercise

Notebooks" ends with Rahel's memory of Ammu's beautiful body being "fed" piece by piece to the crematorium when Rahel was eleven.

> Her hair, her skin, her smile. Her voice. The way she used Kipling to love her children before putting them to bed. *We be of one blood, thou and I.* Her goodnight kiss. The way she held their faces steady with one hand (squashed-cheeked, fish-mouthed) while she parted and combed their hair with the other. The way she held knickers out for Rahel to climb into. *Left leg, right leg.* All this was fed to the beast, and it was satisfied.

As a reader of the novel I wept at the death of Ammu and shuddered at the specificities of loss that stirred my own memories. It's not that my mother died young; she lived to be eighty-four. But I, too, remember a child's perception of a beautiful mother's hair and skin and smile, the stories she read from *The Jungle Book* (we didn't think of colonial implications), her goodnight kiss and the songs she sang to me at bedtime. My brother has said that as a little boy just sitting next to her was thrilling for him. Both of us huddled in the aura of her "radiance" and "animation," wanting, I think, to stay there forever. We still speak to each other, sixty years later, of how we used to love getting into her bed in the morning—as Rahel and Estha love to be in bed with Ammu—to plan all those fun things to do. That was our haven, our world at its most compressed and most expansive.

And, of course, as all children do, we lost this paradise. Bow Wow intruded. My mother, as I've said, was never the same after him. She gained weight and seemed more volatile and unhappy. Or maybe much of this was just the passage of time. She grew older and I did, too. I saw things I hadn't seen before.

When I read The *God of Small Things* for the first time, I couldn't bear for my immersion in the book to end, and, as the young Susan Sontag did with *The Magic Mountain*, I immediately turned back from the last page to the first and started reading through it again. There are many reasons I love this book: its language that is at once lyrical and playful; its brilliant non-linear form, in which the whole story is cryptically compressed at the outset but only fully felt and understood by the end; its deft juggling of multiple layers of time; its rendition of the lush landscape of Kerala; its radical defense of the natural against the social, the oppressed—children, women and untouchables—against their oppressors; its insightful postcolonial critique; its earnest yet witty engagement with other literature from *Hamlet* and *Heart of Darkness* to *Midnight's Children*; its visceral depiction of the body along with compassion for the body's yearnings and weaknesses. But I think what most transfixes me is the story of Ammu and her twins, theirs an even more compelling tale, if that's possible, than that of the untouchable Velutha—carpenter, lover, river God and Christ figure—who is betrayed and sacrificed and whose beautiful body, though not his soul, we also see destroyed. I can feel what it's like to be in the position of Ammu and the twins, to be part of a truncated family unit that feels both less and more than other families. My mother used to say, as Ammu does to reassure her children, that she had to be for us both mother and father. She seemed all we had, and, in the same compensatory way that Ammu tries to love Rahel and Estha, I believe our mother did everything she could to love us "double." There are also ways in which she failed us out of her own great, unmet needs stemming from that childhood in the orphanage. So we felt the cuts of her careless comments, the uncertainties of her labile moods, the limits of her capacity to protect and sustain herself, let alone emotionally shelter two young children. Roy's novel evokes both the magic circle of my own childhood and the shattering of the magic, both the gift of our beautiful mother's love for us and the wound of it.

BRICK *Lane* by Monica Ali, the last novel I will introduce into these pages, differs from *Cracking India* and *The God of Small Things* in that the family at the heart of the book is working, not middle class. *Brick Lane* moves between two major settings: the eponymous London ghetto, into which Nasneen, one of two sisters, has come from her Bangladeshi village to enter into an arranged marriage with an older man, and Bangladesh, where the other sister, Hasnia, has remained. The novel begins in 1967 East Pakistan (not yet Bangladesh), briefly recounting the birth and girlhood of Nasneen before shifting to London (1985–2002) as the book settles into its close third-person presentation of Nasneen's experience of her immigrant neighborhood. The main narrative is spatially confined, with few scenes occurring beyond the Brick Lane council flats, though this is punctuated throughout by letters received from Hasnia (written by Ali in poor English, to reflect Hasnia's limited literacy in Bengali) that convey that sister's ongoing life in Bangladesh.

Ali met with strong protests from London's actual Brick Lane Bangladeshis over what they deemed an unflattering portrait of their community. She was attacked as a person of privilege, someone with neither the right nor the credentials to speak for garment workers and other poor Bangladeshis. As an outsider to the culture, it's hard for me to judge these concerns. Hasnia's poor English does seem something of a contrivance. But from my vantage point, one of the greatest strengths of *Brick Lane* is the author's compassion for her characters as they struggle to find their bearings in diaspora.

The stricter meaning of diaspora is the experience of a people who have been dispersed and who desire to return to the homeland. Nasneen's husband, Chanu, who for all his degrees can find steady work only as a limousine driver, holds to the notion of return in the face of his own failures and the assimilation of his daughters into British culture and actually does return to Dhaka at the end of the novel. Karim, the middleman in the garment business who brings Nasneen piecework and becomes her lover, turns for self-respect to Islam. And he, too, though born in England, chooses return to his "imaginary homeland." Whether going back to Bangladesh will bring the restoration of dignity these men seek is left at the end of the novel up in the air. But I like Ali's respect for their struggles. *Brick Lane* is a solidly feminist book, yet never unkind to men.

Diaspora has also come to signify, more broadly, all aspects of cultures of displacement, and *Brick Lane* explores the diasporic experience in these more general terms as well. Hasnia in Bangladesh is equally alien and equally resilient as her sister is in England. Both their lives are rooted in place yet at the same time reflect the routes of globalization. In Hasnia's life there are many vicissitudes as she moves from runaway, then battered bride to worker in a garment factory to prostitute to exploited nanny for a nouveau-riche family that has made its money in global plastics. Finally, not giving up, she runs away with the cook!

Nasneen leads a seemingly more settled life in England, although in a sense nothing can be settled as her husband and lover struggle to find their dignity in a global economy that offers them such constricted choices. Still, we see her evolve from a woman passively accepting her fate to one taking charge of it, and the novel ends with a satisfying scene. Having for the sake of her daughters decided not to accompany Chanu to Dhaka, Nasneen has entered with two friends into their own fusion-style dress making business. At the end of the novel her friends and daughters give her a surprise. Since her arrival in England she has been fascinated by ice skating, and they take her to a rink. As her daughter hands her a pair of boots, the text reads:

> Nasneen turned around. To get on the ice physically—it hardly seemed to matter. In her mind she was already there.
>
> She said, "But you can't skate in a sari."
>
> Razia [her friend] was already lacing her boots. "This is England," she said. "You can do whatever you like."

The metaphor of ice skating with its suggestion of the sweep of movement within a confined space seems well chosen for this slowly unfolding yet powerfully moving novel, and I come now to my personal relation to the book. It lies, first of all, in my admiration for Ali's characters. Nasneen and the others find power within themselves, despite their dislocations, in their tolerant ties of affection that strengthen family and community. The ties occur in specific places— indeed the book takes its name from place. But more than place, more than Bangladesh or England, *Brick Lane*, it seems to me, celebrates a kind of sweep of spirit—spirit that adapts and resists and even flourishes in whatever cramped inhospitable settings it may be asked to dwell.

This achievement is all the more moving for me because the Brick Lane neighborhood of London, now inhabited by Pakistanis and Bangladeshis, was home a century ago to an earlier immigrant group of Russian and Ukranian Jews. Stepney Green, where my mother lived with her mother and two of her brothers in their two-room basement flat, is adjacent to Brick Lane. I see the two place names a half inch apart on the map I have pulled up on my computer, and I feel a surge of excitement that Ali's novel is set in the same part of London where my mother experienced her early poverty.

Then I'm led to ponder the differences between my mother and Ali's heroine. My mother couldn't wait to leave the East End of London. Nasneen takes root there. My mother believed that only through a herculean act of self-reinvention could she find and seize adequate opportunity. Nasneen lives within her family, an ordinary woman but also a heroic one as she slowly and steadily evolves. Nasneen, Chanu, Karim—these are good, ordinary people. They aren't physically beautiful. Chanu is called "froglike," Nasneen's eyes are too close together. But the novel shows the beauty of their loyalty and decency and persistence. It teaches the important lesson that it isn't necessary to be mythic to have a good life. There is dignity in the ordinary. The ordinary is extraordinary. I'm not sure my mother knew this. I think that I do.

Given who she was, growing older for my mother was especially hard. She faced old age with courage and without complaining but at the same time missed her former status and influence and the effect she had had simply walking into a room. An incident I consider poignant brought this home to me—occurring in the early 1980s. My children and I were on a train with her going from New York City to Darien, Connecticut, where my mother had arranged for us to spend a weekend at a Holiday Inn—pale reprise of our old getaway weekends in California. I sat in a row of seats with the children, while my mother sat in the row in front of us. At one point she seemed to be whispering to the woman beside her, and I couldn't help overhearing. "I don't want my daughter behind us to hear me," she said, "but do you know who I am?"

I wish I could tell her about the Illinois junior high school girls who recently got in touch with me. They were doing research for their National History Fair project, a play about the "Unholy Trio" of Hollywood gossip columnists: Louella Parsons, Hedda Hopper, and Sheilah Graham. Why the Unholy Trio? I asked when we had our conference call. They explained that the project needed a link to Illinois, and it had this in Louella's being from that state. I hadn't known about Louella Parsons's Illinois connection, and it amused me to imagine my mother's tough old rival as a girl in the Midwest. The present-day Illinois girls had already garnered a prize for their play at the state level, and it was headed now to "the nationals." They sought details for their portrayal of my mother and questioned me about her clothes and her gestures, her way of speaking and her opinions. I told them what I could. It was nice to enter into the spirit of their project and to sense their young energy. The girl who had the part of Sheilah Graham was named Anjalika Mohanty.

When I got off the phone, I thought how wonderfully apt it was that Sheilah Graham, born into a family of immigrants and spending her childhood years in a London orphanage, should converge with an Indian-American girl who came from the same Midwestern state as Louella Parsons! So much of my life seemed to come together in that moment: Hollywood, my mother, my interest in the Indian diaspora, the reading trajectory that had carried me from orphan to immigrant, my dedication to helping young people. Anjalika on the phone sounded very self-possessed for an eighth grader. I found myself wondering afterwards if she was a reader.

POSTSCRIPTS

April, 2011

I sit tonight at the dinner table with my fourteen-year-old granddaughter Zoé, who is visiting from France with her cousin Salomé, also fourteen, for a two-week stay with me in New York. They are bright, competent girls who have persuaded their parents to let them come by themselves on this adventure. I've been impressed by their ease in getting about on foot and by subway. (And we discuss that in English you say ON foot and BY subway.) By themselves they have gone to the top of the Empire State Building and ridden the Staten Island Ferry in order to take pictures of the Statue of Liberty. They've shown an interest in art as well with both MOMA and the Metropolitan Museum on their must-do list, though they also spend a lot of time on the computer—my partner Mary Edith's Mac that she graciously has let them use—giggling together as they post on their Facebook walls and watch videos. This evening Mary Edith has gone out—we've been living together since

I sold my Upper West Side apartment the previous year and moved downtown into hers on the Lower East Side—and I'm alone with the girls.

"Do you girls like to read?" I ask them, as we sit at dinner over the precooked chicken I picked up at the supermarket around the corner. Yes, they say. I learn that Zoé has read Jane Austen's *Emma* in English, and Salomé, even more of a reader than her cousin but with less advanced English, has read *Jane Eyre*, *Pride and Prejudice*, *Sense and Sensibility*, and *Wuthering Heights* in translation. "Eeetcliff," she says. "Ah yes, Heathcliff," I respond. In French the novel is called *Les Hauts de Hurlevent*. Hearing this alliterative foreign title gives me pleasure. It suggests at once the same and a different meaning from the title I know, the way that the book itself is the same and different for any two readers. I draw closer, though, to Salomé than I've felt before in that each of us has been intimate with the same novel. She, too, has paused in the world of the Heights and the Grange, Heathcliff and the two Cathys. Lockwood and Nellie. And she's just the age I was when I first read the books she's reading.

So it all begins again! Zoé and Salomé are readers. I imagine their lives of reading, of making the connections that reading encourages in us. It's possible we will like more of the same books. That would please me. But I'm also excited to think of our different trajectories, for surely they will discover books ignored by me, books I've never heard of, and—stretching through the many decades I hope they will survive me—books not yet written, the literature of the future. For now, I cherish the moment as we touch and pass, generations crossing.

June 2014

Reader, I married her—my partner Mary Edith Mardis. The ceremony took place in East Hampton, New York, on September 23, 2011. We had a quiet wedding. Mary Edith and I, the female judge who performed the service, and two of our friends as witnesses alone were present. We alerted only the members of our families and a few close friends and promised to have a party at a later time.

I have now been married for almost three years and hold myself supremely blessed to have this late-in-life chance at happiness. We do a lot of little things together: shop for groceries, cook, watch movies, play golf, and think about small home improvements. As a photographer, Mary Edith is much more visual than I and is always helping me to see better the world around me. We both like to read and, her interest whetted by my enthusiasm, she is currently half way through *David Copperfield*.

When we sent out the word about our altered status, the congratulations soon poured in. I was touched by a message from my brother Robert, who lives in New Mexico, happily married to his second wife. Though we're only intermittently in touch, he's the person who has known me longer than anyone else alive. After I had phoned him with my news, he emailed me the following message:

> Dear Wendy,
>
> You caught me by surprise with your news that you and Mary Edith have gotten married, so I'm not sure I managed to offer my congratulations and true best wishes.
>
> How incredible that you should be married again! It must be very nice for you . . . for both of you. My

feeling is that Marriage #2 is usually a huge improve-
ment on Marriage #1—in my case, certainly, and I hope
in yours—something you embark upon with much more
wisdom and with your eyes open.

So good luck and all happiness to you both.

It's the marriage plot ending, after all! Thank you, Robert,
for your heartfelt good wishes. I imagine our mother being
pleased about us both and confiding to a sidekick ghost she
has charmed, "You see, I hoped they would be happy in
their marriages." Thank you, *Jane Eyre*, for accompanying
me to the last paragraphs of this journey. And thank you,
Mary Edith, for our life together that goes so far beyond the
bounds of fiction.

READING GROUP QUESTIONS AND TOPICS FOR DISCUSSION

1. What does reading mean to Wendy Fairey? What does it mean to you?

2. *Bookmarked* explores the works of fiction that have most deeply affected one reader and marked the stages of her life. If you were to draw up a comparable list for yourself, what titles would it include?

3. What personal experience would you bring to your reading of one or more of the books discussed in *Bookmarked*? How would your relation to these books be similar to or different from the author's?

4. Do you like to reread old favorites? If so, take one example and describe that rereading experience?

5. Wendy Fairey's mother, Sheilah Graham, is a central figure in her book. What do you think of her as she's portrayed in *Bookmarked*? Do you have someone equally important in your own life?

6. The author explores the way that socially marginal figures such as the orphan, the new woman, the artist, and the immigrant became central in the English novel. Do these protagonists have an abiding appeal to contemporary readers? If so, how and why? If not, why not?

7. Can you name the literary character that you identify with most closely? Explain the basis for your choice.

8. In this age of rapid and abbreviated communication (Facebook, Twitter, blogging, ten-second sound bites), what place remains for the classic works of English fiction, some of them indeed "loose baggy monsters?" Do you have patience for long books? What is your experience of reading them?

9. Wendy Fairey explores the persistence and permutations of the marriage plot in life and in fiction. Is this a theme that engages you? Why/why not?

10. The final chapter of *Bookmarked* focuses on Indian English fiction of the last twenty years. To what extent are you familiar with this work or with other Anglophone fiction? What might be its interest and appeal?

11. Is there any novel discussed in *Bookmarked* you hadn't previously read but would now like to? And if so, why?

12. Do you like/not like the mix in *Bookmarked* of personal reflection and literary analysis?

ACKNOWLEDGEMENTS

Thanks begin with loving remembrance of my mother, Sheilah Graham, who set me on the path of reading and loving English novels, and of all the English teachers who inspired and encouraged me.

In the years I have spent writing this book, there are many people who have helped me, both with insights about particular novels they, too, feel marked by and with critiques of my work. I thank Roni Natov, Rachel Brownstein, Ellen Belton, and, above all, the indefatigable Ellen Tremper, all colleagues at Brooklyn College, not only for reading my chapters but also for sharing their very personal responses to the books we teach in common. And I thank my students, who have helped keep literature alive for me.

I am also deeply grateful to Jeanne Betancourt, John Major, Lee Quinby, and Sandra Robinson—other friends who gave so generously of their time in reading and commenting on drafts of my manuscript. I thank them for consistently challenging my language and formulations and supporting my project from its start to finish. And I thank, too, the participants in our nonfiction writers' group, who, mostly as non-academics, critiqued my drafts and helped me be mindful, always, of the common reader: Mindy Lewis, the late Susan Ribner, Joanna Torrey, Ingrid Hughes, Christine Wade, and Patricia Laurence.

My agent Charlotte Sheedy, whose own abiding love of English novels infused her support of my project, also deserves great thanks. Not only did she take on representing the book, but both she and her daughter Ally Sheedy also offered extraordinarily insightful readings of its earlier drafts that helped me bring the project to conclusion. I also wish to thank Jeannette Seaver of Arcade Press for her faith in this book as well as her astute input and editing, Maxim Brown of Skyhorse Publishing for his care and competence in guiding the manuscript through production, and other staff of both the Charlotte Sheedy Literary Agency and Arcade/Skyhorse Publishing.

Finally, thanks to Mary Edith Mardis, a support to me both as reader and life partner, to whom *Bookmarked* is dedicated.